Some Recent Reactions to Working with Michal

'For so many successful and well to do professionals something appears to be missing from their lives. Michal Levin has provided me with the insights and tools to fill this emptiness with meaning, joy and a zest for all that life has to offer.'
Ruth Nisson-Ladner, former general manager of a business risk consultancy, and corporate investigator

'I am enormously grateful for the help I have received from Michal, both personally and in my professional work. I have found she cuts straight through to the heart of an issue with incisive clarity, wisdom and compassion rooted in the practical realities of the everyday. She uses her gifts with great skill, always respectful of the other's insights, and without being prescriptive – yet in one session she can facilitate a depth of self-understanding that would take years to develop by other means, for example the two disciplines I have many years experience of, psychoanalytic therapy and Tibetan Buddhism. Her modesty and low-key approach belie her truly outstanding abilities.'
Ruthie Smith, psychoanalytic psychotherapist

'Michal uses her wisdom to challenge us to be wiser in the way in which we deal with ourselves, our relationships, work and community life. Her approach enables us to learn more about our unique contribution to the world and our connections to each other.'
Gill Avery and Mike Vernon, business consultants

'Michal Levin is an extraordinary woman. Her seminars work at a deep level and are life-changing.'
Dr Ruth Whittaker

'Michal Levin's teachings have enriched every aspect of my life. What a joy to discover and explore deeper ways of seeing and being, a process that goes on and on. I was asleep. Michal, with generosity, kindness and humility, has woken me up to an expanded awareness, and my own understanding of spirituality.'
Rosalynd Ward, radio producer

'Michal has an extraordinary capacity to be very closely in touch with the core of my energetic being. I have met with her for over seven years and have experienced her presence as a beacon of light for my spiritual journey of discovery.'
M. J. R., Jungian analyst

'As a scientist I find the direction and content of Michal's work interesting, stimulating and very helpful. The direction of scientific progress at the current time resonates strongly with her work, and I find exposure to Michal's approach most relevant to my own work and life.'
Mike Thompson, senior lecturer in environmental studies

'To work with Michal has offered the opportunity to embrace the highest ideals of truth, integrity and, dare I say, "love" I know, while remaining completely down to earth and "normal". My gratitude is unbounding.'
Kolinka Zinovieff, an aromatherapist, who runs a business selling organic aromatherapy products, and a member of the Inner Council of British Complementary Medicine Association

'Working with Michal has given me insight and clarity into situations in daily life from a spiritual perspective. Operating from the heart and from an awareness of our inter-connectedness as human beings, it acknowledges that there is more to life than just the accumulation of material possessions'
Nicky Bell, website designer

'I was drawn to Michal Levin's work by the words that she chose. She described ideas, that often seemed new or unusual, in language that was neither obscure nor over-simplified. And she never asked me to take what she said on trust; only to try it out for myself. I was intrigued; it was like coming home.'
Kim Flitcroft, film maker

'In a world where spiritual awareness is growing by the day Michal Levin, unlike many others, successfully manages to convey to anyone who is prepared to listen with an open mind, the essential elements of her many years of insights and experiences in this complicated and sensitive subject. From my own experience the revelations and knowledge acquired from her seminars and books will enable people to find a more healthy balance in all aspects of their home, business and emotional life as a result of which their contribution to our society will be greatly enhanced.'
David Lewis, director of a private investment company

'Working with Michal has been a gradual awakening and an acknowledgement of my truest self. It feels like a strengthening of being and relating to others that I know will deepen as time goes on.'
Tina B., local council officer

'To say that Michal offers "a journey into the heart" is one thing. To begin to know in your heart what that might mean is another. And when you do begin to know, in a way that is impossible for me to articulate, everything

– relationships, work, family, shopping at the supermarket – starts to change, even as it may very well stay the same. It is an unfolding journey into true clarity, and I am profoundly grateful for it.'
Victoria Trow, film editor

'Working with Michal is about remembering. I listen to her, and as time goes by her voice is not her voice any more, nor is it outside. It is within, deep inside, and is my voice, or rather our voice.'
Marta Niccolai, language teacher

'Through Michal's work I have learnt how my spiritual journey can be an integral part of everyday life and transform it completely – from within.'
C. A., interior designer

'Michal has a rare gift for turning uncommon wisdom into common sense, being soaringly inspirational whilst down to earth, and putting accessing your intuition right up there with boiling an egg! I feel fortunate and grateful to study with her.'
Michael Wardle, company director

'Michal's teachings cut through time-worn dogma and new age fancy to reveal the pure light of spirit. Their clarity and resonance are extraordinary.'
Neil Spencer, writer and astrologer

'I found Michal's meditation a profound and transforming process. It gives great insights, yet its true working is at a deeper level than any insights.'
Dr Meena Krishnamurthy

'Michal Levin is a "seer" who clearly percives the various subtle energetic systems that constitute the individual and his/her relationship to others and the universe. From her own direct experience of different levels of reality she has discovered principles and a new language of "energy" of immense and timely practical usefulness for individual and collective progress and development.'
Tom Aisbitt, trader

'To work with Michal Levin is to work with Love and transformation, it is a blessing which brings inspiration, insight, and information, all deeply relevant to Medicine, Science and Healing.'
Professor Kim Jobst, Visiting Professor of Healthcare and Integrated Medicine, Oxford Brookes University

Also by Michal Levin

The Pool of Memory: the autobiography
of an unwilling intuitive

SPIRITUAL INTELLIGENCE

Awakening the Power of Your
Spirituality and Intuition

By Michal Levin

Hodder and Stoughton

Copyright © 2000 by Michal Levin

First published in Great Britain in 2000 by Hodder and Stoughton
A division of Hodder Headline

The right of Michal Levin to be identified as the Author of the Work has been asserted by her in accordance with the Copyright, Designs and Patents Act 1988.

10 9 8 7 6 5 4 3 2 1

British Library Cataloguing in Publication Data
Levin, Michal
Spiritual Intelligence: awakening the power
of your spirituality and intuition
1. Spirituality 2. Intuition
I. Title
133.9

ISBN 0 340 76846 0

Typeset by Palimpsest Book Production Limited
Polmont, Stirlingshire
Printed and bound in Great Britain by
Mackays of Chatham plc, Chatham, Kent

Hodder and Stoughton
A division of Hodder Headline
338 Euston Road
London NW1 3BH

I dedicate this book to those who may be silent but know the truth in what I am saying, even if they might have chosen different words with which to say it. To those who feel the ache and wonder what to do. To those who are the future and know, instinctively, the reality I am outlining. To those who care. To those who put their caring into action. To those who would know joy. To the inevitable majority.

Acknowledgements

To the finer vibrations first. My special love and thanks. May I continue to grow in understanding, and the ability to act on that understanding.

As ever there are too many others to name. A few of the many who have helped me on my journey, in all their different ways, are Susan Arnold, Tom Aisbitt, Mana and Michael Brearley, Nicky Bell, Dr Alan Costall, Kim Flitcroft, Judy Fraser, Jill Furmanovsky, Margi and John Graham, Paul Halloran, Vicki McIver, Nick Segal, William Shawcross, Ruthie Smith, Beverly Sommer, Neil Spencer, Victoria Trow, Rosalynd Ward, Dr Alan Watkins, who shared some of his medical knowledge, Kolinka Zinovieff, Rowena Webb and all the splendid Hodder team.

And of course my family, who share and support my endeavour so closely – it would not be possible without them. Especially Tom and Ellie. Lastly, my heartfelt thanks to Chris Fallon.

Contents

PREFACE

No man is an Island, entire of it self; every man is a piece of the Continent, a part of the main; if a clod be washed away by the sea, Europe is the less, as well as if a promontory were, as well as if a manor of thy friends, or of thine own were; any man's death diminishes me, because I am involved in Mankind; and therefore never send to know for whom the bell tolls; it tolls for thee.

John Donne, 'Meditation XVII'

This book is for those who don't have much appetite for the contemporary taste for magic and mediums – rightly or wrongly – though they may sense that there is an aspect of the movement covered by the all-embracing term 'spirituality' that is relevant to them. Equally, conventional religion may not seem to answer their need. Perplexed as to the nature of the problem – or unsure whether there is a problem – they may wonder about jobs, relationships, partners or lack of partners, money, or even our environment, in a disconnected, increasingly uncomfortable way. It is like sensing an ache that disappears at moments, only to re-emerge with renewed strength just when you thought you had eradicated the cause. If you recognise an element – or several elements – of your experience here, then it is time to understand the concept of spiritual intelligence.

Spirituality is not like the sky. Or water. Or even happiness. Essential though they all are. Neither is it a creed, or set of rules. It's very different from religion which lays down the law for believers. It's not an academic subject – though it's sometimes treated as one. It's not best learnt in institutions. It's not dependent on book learning.

Spirituality is a perspective. It is your heart's perspective. It is a vision that belongs to love, in the widest sense. But the words may mean little. The heart and love have been consigned to the realm of chocolates and champagne, a long way from their true meaning. To penetrate the perspective of spirituality is to begin to learn the real lessons of love – the gift of your heart.

Spiritual intelligence is the combination of that essence with the power of your mental faculties. Intelligence is a measure of your intellectual skill – or mental brightness, along with your faculty for reason. It plays a crucial role in enabling you to understand and evaluate the world around you, your own circumstances and change in general. It is especially important at the moment because the changes we all face are so momentous and are happening so quickly.

A crucial aspect of those changes is being driven by technology. In recent memory the telephone, with elaborate land lines and human operators, was a new invention. Today we hold tiny instruments in our hands that can not only connect us to another individual almost anywhere in the world, but to the myriad services of the internet, are able to offer information about our location, and soon may provide even wider services – know our buying patterns and predict our needs from them, for example. All by passing invisible pulses through the atmosphere.

We have never been in such close, technological communication with the rest of mankind. At the same time, we in the West may have never been so far from communicating with our fellow humans, face to face. And all the while our communications network purports to show us – and often does – deeper and deeper levels of the working of the world around us. We see famine, wars, mass murders, unimaginable brutality. We also see our leaders in a way hardly thought of by earlier generations. For example, our parents or grandparents never saw images of President Roosevelt in a wheelchair. Instead they saw him as a strong, resolute leader, sitting, for example, with Stalin and Churchill at Yalta.

Today we know details not simply of our leaders' physical health, but their private lives and much else too. Whether what we know, or are told, is the truth is another matter. But it's no wonder that we sometimes feel our personal frameworks are crumbling. We don't understand. Or we understand too well.

Increasingly we struggle both to exert and protect ourselves in a world where human standards can seem capricious and pressures ever escalating. Social misery abounds. Social structures are under huge pressure. Many of our relationships, or our lack of them, seem to pose huge pressures. All of which can move us towards cynicism, sometimes even a despair that shows in our attitudes towards our own lives, and those of others. Or simply an undefinable ache.

So we look for answers and ways to order both our inner and outer worlds in our institutions, laws and traditions. We may be conscious of a lack where once religion played a part in keeping our society's order, but it doesn't draw us to a church. Instead a number of alternatives have presented themselves, particularly in recent years. The New Age, the so-called Age of Aquarius, has thrown up all sorts of potential beliefs, remedies for our situation and would-be spiritual solutions or leaders.

But, spirituality does not equate with superstition. Crystals, incense, chants, gurus, tarot cards, even alternative therapies may all be offered up as new forms of spirituality. Some may play no useful role other than increasing our superstition quotient, and making us vulnerable to those who wield power by playing with the forces of fear. Some may bring us closer to the deeper mysteries which perhaps an inner instinctual or even intuitive sense suggests. But at the same time they may affront our intelligence, or do little to build our sense of well-being in and for the world. The ache is persistent, but what we are aching for is still not clear.

The marriage of spirituality and intelligence offers a new perspective on the problem. It offers a way to bring together the spiritual and the material, using the language and concepts of our time to formulate its vision, which is in fact a new reality. One which addresses our ache, and much else. Inevitably, with the passage of time and events, its perspective is wider than many – wider, perhaps than any – before. Of course, it sees what has always been there to be seen. But it expresses itself in modern concepts, with the benefits of our experience.

Spiritual maturity, which is the product of spiritual intelligence, is not concerned with holding power over others, or amassing personal wealth, or even benefiting one particular clique (your 'friends'). But rather with the well-being of the universe and all who live there. At the same time, it recognises wider perceptual powers than the five senses that we have paid allegiance to in recent times. And hurries to learn what it can from contact with a greater reality, and a new way of seeing.

Of course, our age and idiom play a crucial part in how we see this reality. What we take to be 'the truth' is only our age's interpretation of the forces of the universe – the way we understand them. It is only 'the truth' for a moment in time. Both our perspective, and what we call true, change over time. Understanding this fact – the role of history – has clear consequences. Ultimately it has led me to a deeper understanding of the role and meaning of love, as the true foundation for spirituality, and it has helped me to know the development of what I am calling spiritual intelligence.

I am not going to give you 'the rules' for develop-ing spiritual intelligence. Or 'getting the knack' of intuition. Widening your perception, which leads towards that end, is rather different. It depends on the development of your independent vision. Laying down prescriptions would only undermine that effort, or even achieve exactly the opposite effect.

What I can do is tell you how my experience, particularly as an intuitive, suggests a new metaphor – a new way of seeing and understanding – at this time in history. I will try to offer ways to help you achieve this vision and understanding, which is spiritual intelligence, for yourself, from within. Ultimately it is the result of experience, the opening of your heart and deepening of your understanding, not a creed.

What follows once you embark on this path will depend on you. The ache will disappear. Joy, perhaps in a new form or forms, will make itself known as you take up the power inspired by your spirituality, and respond to the challenge to use it wisely. It is a path that invites you to find and know 'the truth' for yourself. Not by repeating, mantra-like, someone else's sayings, but by taking the tools I'm offering and working with them yourself. Answer the questions I am asking. Consider the answers and experiences I am putting forward. Then, if you choose, you may use them to widen, deepen and enrich your reality, in a way that will both significantly empower you and multiply your connections to our world.

Part I

First Steps

Chapter One

The Ache

Jamie was the first to arrive. He prowled the room. He prowled most places. Usually to great effect. You didn't become a freelance writer whose work appeared in a major newspaper every Sunday by luck alone, he reckoned. He had looked to use every circumstance he met. If he was honest, that probably meant people too. Or at least that was one way of putting it. He'd never forced anyone to do anything they didn't really want to, and he'd never broken the law on anything significant (everyone jumped red lights from time to time).

But it, something, life, hadn't come together. Or hadn't come together enough. He had the great bachelor pad. Women weren't a problem – or rather that was the problem. It was easy enough not to go to bed alone, but there never seemed any reason, or he never had the desire, to make it much more than that. He liked his work – true, there was a certain element of boredom creeping in now that the big four-oh loomed, but he didn't seem unique in that. So, what was the problem? Was there a problem? He didn't know for sure. But recently the pressure had got much worse and a friend suggested this woman, so he was just checking it out. He didn't intend to go easy on her in this seminar, as it was called, he saw no reason to fall for this sort of stuff.

Rosie and Maria arrived together, a minute or two after Jamie. Psychotherapists, they were looking forward to the day. Maria had studied spirituality for several years. More recently she had discovered Michal's work and was hugely excited by it. It had transformed not only her personal life, but her dealings with her clients as well. Intellectually, too, it fascinated her. Rosie had taken rather longer. At around fifty she was ten years older than Maria. Professionally, more senior. She had investigated orthodox religion first, when it became clear that it was a spiritual dimension she was seeking. But that hadn't satisfied her needs. Now, this was the third occasion she'd come to listen to this woman, and she felt there was something here she wanted to consider very carefully. She had some questions.

A group of others all entered together and the room settled to a quiet anticipatory hum. Twelve present. Two to come. Rod opened the door. He looked around. Three grey heads. They seemed quite old, older than him anyway. But there were also one or two who looked as if they were in their twenties. He had just fancied coming along. He hadn't thought about it too much. He'd been to a few Mind, Body, Spirit events, picked up quite a few ideas. He didn't know why, but it felt really important. More important than anything else. He was just on time. They were about to begin.

An hour later, we pause. The faces of the group around me bear a familiar stamp. A financial analyst, a great city success, not yet thirty-eight, grey face, grey hair. Two psychotherapists, kind and knowledgeable but with a question mark in their eyes. A slim young man who works in information technology leans forward, determined. A woman who runs a pottery workshop, a home and two small children weeps softly, and openly. A teacher, a journalist, another computer buff, a writer, a martial arts expert, a psychologist, a doctor. I sit with my back to the window, which is like a base or plinth for the circle. The early summer light is soft. It's no match for the intensity we create in the room. Each face, some wide-eyed, some more cautious, or caught in a stronger grip, burns from within. There are two common denominators.

Intelligence is the first. This is no group of gullible New Agers. Even the fiercest sceptic couldn't tarnish them as a bunch of freaks, or cast some similar (usually altogether unwarranted) aspersion. This is a group of achievers. What distinguishes them is their intelligent, questioning approach.

The other common feature is the question. All ask the same question. Only the words are different. How to deal with the ache that has so many different names? Or no name. The ache that cannot be defined in a simple sentence. That money, success, education, fame even, does not wash away.

And how to make sense of the glimmers that come

at unexpected moments, like the flickering of leaves, never quite still, shimmering in a faint movement of the air. Because a dream of some elusive joy haunts the group who have come to work with me, just as surely as the pain, which intensifies from time to time, stalks them.

The salve I offer is simple. The only one I know. I try to teach those who come to me how to embrace their spirituality – how to extend into the realm of spirit – to develop their spiritual intelligence. Because that is the solution to the deepest cause of their pain. Many other factors may contribute to it. But the root, the very core, is the pain of missing. Not missing someone or something, but missing a part of oneself. A crucial dimension of your own existence. Your spiritual reality. The other half of the whole which is you. Your wider, greater, further self – and its connection to the whole of the universe.

To find it is the journey of spiritual evolution; to claim spiritual intelligence. And it is a journey that will simultaneously develop your intuition and teach you love. Intuition because it is part of the process. Love because that is the goal – but it is not the love of chocolates and champagne. It is a different understanding of love, one that comes from a wider, deeper perspective. Love for yourself. Love for your fellows. Love for living, and for the spirit that infuses all living. Eventually, for our world to survive, we will all have to tread that path. Some have started sooner than others.

But let's be clear, I don't promise to help those who

see me to make more money, increase their intelligence, influence others, or get a better job. Though often dramatic changes follow. Integrity and authenticity will take on a new reality for you. But my chief aim is to name the ache. And in naming it, to reveal the way towards what it so hungers, even craves, for.

The journey that I will help the group I am working with to take, or further – and perhaps you too – is into themselves and beyond. It is to extend their reality, and to claim a power that is not a power, and yet is beyond all powers, which is theirs to have and to hold in the present, the everyday. As with all powers, it brings responsibility. It is a development that will radically transform their relation to our world and all others.

Fine words. But how do I know what I am saying? I know because I've been there. And, over and over, showed the way to others too. More than a dozen years ago I was a successful media professional. A serious television reporter and presenter. More, I had also developed another strand in management consultancy, specialising in communications, and been blessed with two children as well as an affluent lifestyle. You might be forgiven for thinking I had it all. But I was tormented. I fought it in one form, and then in another. Divorce, moving home, changing jobs. Still, no peace. It was as if the peace I craved would never come.

Finally, on my own and exhausted, I gave up. As a single parent, I worked out the family's finances and decided I could afford to take a six-month sabbatical to finally beat whatever spectre it was that was haunting me. Or at least find out what the problem was! And that's just what I did.

In *The Pool of Memory: the autobiography of an unwilling intuitive*, my previous book, I wrote the story of the years that followed my decision. How my world, my notion of the world, reality for me was utterly and absolutely, irreversibly exploded. How, after an extraordinary process of inner teaching, I became what you might call psychic (though I dislike the word, 'intuitive' suits me much better) and a healer (again, no longer the right word, but it will do for now).

Word got around quickly. Clients came, first in a trickle, then, quickly, in great numbers. I was reluctant, to begin with, to see them. I did not know how I did what I did, or indeed whether it would continue from one session to the next. But the early clients were insistent, and all accepted that I made no claims for what I could, or could not do. Soon my clients ranged from the famous, to entrepreneurs, Jungian analysts, teachers, business people, the very wealthy, alternative practitioners, psychotherapists, devout Buddhists and Christians, transcendental meditation specialists, and a fair representation of everyone else – they all sat in front of me. I was booked for months ahead.

But that wasn't the end of the story. The process continued. Now, I want to share as much as I can of what I have learnt, and learnt to teach, about experiencing, understanding and claiming spiritual reality, and its relationship to intuition. In the process, I'll tell you about the role that 'energy', for want of a better word, plays in it all. And I'll try to make the explanation as simple as possible. But also one that satisfies your intelligence, and mine – as well as explaining my experiences.

You must understand, though, that this is different to telling you 'The Truth'. I don't have the one and only Truth. As far as I know, no one has The Truth. Though surprisingly some claim they do. What I do know is my view of the truth. It is my metaphor for the truth at this time in our history. Which, actually, is as much as I think anyone can ever claim to know.

Of course I will be addressing phenomena that have been addressed before, and saying things that have been said before. But it will be in the words and concepts of our immediate future. Each age invents the truths it needs to hear.

Think about it. Hold the words for a while. In the final analysis, the choice whether to accept or reject it, part or all, will be yours.

To think about and to do

1. Think about any case where you can see two or more different explanations for the same fact. This could be as simple as noticing that your colleague is not eating lunch. It could mean that: (1) he or she is not hungry; (2) he or she is trying to lose weight; (3) he or she had a late breakfast and isn't yet hungry; (4) he or she is suffering from a serious medical

condition; (5) he or she is saving money, and so on.

2. Are the explanations mutually exclusive?
3. Can you see that there is more than one way of explaining the same situation?
4. Think of how your own experiences and psychology might incline you to accept one explanation before the others. This is what I call your bias. For example, if your weight is a problem, might you be inclined to think that your colleague, by appearing not to eat lunch, was dieting?
5. Think of how it would feel to suspend judgement on the causes for the situation you are seeing. And how there might be a number of different causes.
6. Think how different people might describe or explain the situation differently.
7. In other words, think how many different ways there are of explaining the same situation, and think how your own personal experience plays a part in deciding which explanation you accept.

Chapter Two

My Journey

I want to tell you, as briefly as possible, what happened when I took my sabbatical, and signed off from my ordinary life. It's important not because my story is special – everyone's story is special – but because it is how I came to know spiritual reality and, later, help others to claim it too.

I secluded myself, alone, at home – a housebound single mother, the day ordered by the school routine and nothing else, my pain started to ease. But only a little. I knew it was just a breathing space. I had to find the real solution. I was prepared to try anything. Even, out of a sort of desperation, meditation.

Now, meditation was not a process that had ever appealed to me. I was the sceptical sort. As a journalist, and in life generally, I had always been driven by a desire for social justice, and what I called, or believed to be, truth. I had worked as a current affairs reporter, up and down the country and abroad, fighting injustice, exposing what seemed to me to be scandal – multinational drug companies, hospital accidents, social security scandals, international

17

adoptions, the sexual abuse of children (which I had covered in some depth, repeatedly) and a host of other subjects. That, I felt, was worthwhile. Mysticism and spiritualism just didn't seem particularly – relevant. To me, I would have added, tolerantly. And meditation just seemed . . . boring. But when you are sufficiently desperate, it's worth trying anything, as perhaps you may know.

So, clutching a small set of instructions, thinking I would probably prove to myself, by trying it, that meditation wasn't a cure for me, I sat down on the edge of my bed to give it a try – and the world as I knew it dissolved.

A new reality – another level – opened before me. Very quickly I came into contact with presences who seemed to want to 'teach' me, if that's the right word. I certainly didn't know what they were teaching me or, often, how to make any sense of it. Also, calling them 'beings' makes it sound too much as if I thought they were like other 'people'. Perhaps spirits of people long dead, or creatures from another level of existence, 'guides'? All of which I didn't think to be the case. But I didn't know what to think. Then. (See Chapter Eight for what I think now.)

Clearly, I had embarked on a journey. Even if I had no idea where it was going. Once I had begun, I had to continue. I meditated sometimes for hours each day. Early, early in the morning before the children were awake and in the evening once the house was quiet. And I kept a diary. It seemed I had the curious power of complete recall after each session – every word seemed burnt on my memory – and that it was very important to write it all down. So, steadily I filled my notebooks. While suspending disbelief.

I was very ignorant. I knew nothing about meditation, little about religion, nothing about Eastern spirituality, or even Western mystery traditions. I had never read about spiritual journeys. I did try to find out what was going on. Did my experiences make any sense in any orthodox terms? But I quickly gave up the endeavour, as it appeared to infuriate the forces I had contacted.

It seemed my body was being altered, particularly my spine. My energy was changing, though I barely understood anything of the significance of that to start with. My vision too was being altered. It became clear fairly early on that I could see something in or around other people. It was a force or a quantity I could not describe – only the word 'energy' seemed to fit. Perhaps 'subtle energy'? And then I had to realise that my access to knowledge was no longer the same. I began to receive information about others, and I began to be able to slide into their reality, in meditation, to feel that I was really standing in their shoes, able to feel what they would feel, know what they would know. Or at least to think that something like that seemed to be going on.

But was it all fact, or fiction? Was I imagining it? Was I weaving private fantasies, or even, as I confided in one of the very few people I discussed it with, a psychotherapist friend, going nuts? My friend reassured me. She told me that some of what I had described was almost textbook descriptions of Buddhist rituals, only, of course, I had (and have) almost no knowledge of Buddhist practices. She re-assured me I was not 'going nuts', as I put it, but experiencing something very special. And very pro-found. I couldn't accept that, but I couldn't stop what I was doing either.

Not long after, I met a high Buddhist teacher who asked me for healing. Something I had no idea about. I had no knowledge of healing, and didn't, for even a moment, think I could offer it. When I demurred, he insisted, telling me that I possessed the ability to heal. He also asked me for clairvoyance, and to my amaze-ment, I found I was able to speak to him, at length, about himself. Whether what I said was true or not, I will never know. But it seemed to please him as great-ly as the whole process astonished me. It also marked a turning point in my journey.

The question, 'Was what I saw fact or my own fiction?' was soon put to the test. Soon after the inci-dent with the Buddhist lama, others began to clamour to see me, all wanting me to use my gifts, whatever they were. This fact soon put paid to any question of validity. Using my intuition I was able to offer my clients new ways to understand their situations and the options the future held. At the same time I was given internal instructions on how to offer healing, the effects of which were plain to see. Some clients wanted to come again and again, or as often as I would let them.

All the time I tried hard never to be directional,

always to avoid encouraging dependence, to be careful not to counsel those who needed psychotherapy rather than my input, and not to allow anyone to use healing as a substitute for proper medical advice. Above all, I tried to do my best to empower those who came to see me. At the same time I was learning. Hugely. My own process simply rolled on, changing form, shape and direction in its course. But never stopping. My own understanding continued to increase.

Then, a few years later, I saw signs in my own energy which, had I seen them in a client, would have led me to urge them to go straight to their own doctor. I saw darkness, on my right-hand side. Darkness which I could shift, but which always came back. From that I knew it was not merely in my 'subtle energy', it was in my physical body. But what to do? Of course I went to my doctor; in fact I went to several doctors. None found anything serious the matter with me. Some seemed hostile in their attitude towards me and my unorthodox work. As the months rolled on I developed a tic in my eye and my mouth, and became weaker and weaker. I stopped working. Somewhat disdainfully my own family doctor gave me a certificate stating I had 'post-viral fatigue', and suggested rest. As if there was much else I could do! I saw a huge range of alternative doctors and practitioners too. None helped – some were even dangerous. All wove their own stories around my 'problems' – none came remotely near the truth.

Finally, I felt death approaching. My nearest and

dearest were simply perplexed. Medically there was no real, treatable problem, I had been assured. But I knew otherwise. Then my inner world, which had up to that time simply offered encouragement and urged me to continue looking, began to whisper a new message. 'Go back to the place you were born, there you will find the way.'

I was born in Cape Town, South Africa. It was hard to book flights and arrange to go. A few weeks later, however, I arrived in the glorious sunshine. It gave me strength. But I knew it alone was not the answer. Was I going to die where I was born? Then the message in my head changed. 'The orchid grower, find the orchid grower,' it insisted. So, I asked my kind hostess, my aunt, also a doctor, to help me to find medical help, which she was very willing to do. But who, she pondered. Tentatively, I asked if she knew an 'orchid grower', expecting her to laugh. To my enormous surprise she seized on my suggestion and immediately arranged for me to see 'the orchid grower' – a well-known gastroenterologist, and old friend of hers.

It was that wonderful doctor, in his open-necked shirt, that hot late summer's day, who, by listening, looking and keeping an open mind, saw the tic in my eye for what it was. A sign that the relevant nerve was under severe pressure. In fact, I had already begun to lose sensation in my eye as a huge tumour pressed on my facial nerve.

A few weeks later, with death pronounced as literally weeks away, I was operated on in Los

Angeles for an acoustic neuroma. A benign tumour on my acoustic nerve – probably originally caused by the experimental radiation therapy I received as a young child – that had grown to the size of a peach, pressing on my brain stem, and about to take my life.

Fortunately, it was removed and my life was saved. But at a cost. I lost the hearing in my right-hand side, and today, after a nerve graft, one side of my face is still partially paralysed. But I am very well.

Recovery was a slow process. Were my 'powers' lost, or to be lost? What to do now? Had the tumour caused my extraordinary abilities? So many questions besieged me. In short, my powers were not lost but intensified. I could find no evidence to support the theory that all had been 'caused' by my tumour, and my journey simply continued! Clients continued to come, and I saw as many as my slowly returning strength would allow. But, as I recovered, something else happened. Again, I did not understand the significance or the consequences of it at the time. Over and over, I did not understand my journey, as you will not understand your journey, at the time I was experiencing it. Only afterwards.

Some of my clients pressed me to give 'teachings'. I refused. I felt I had no special knowledge to pass on, other than what came in sessions. 'Try,' they insisted. Somewhat reluctantly, I agreed to give first one, and then a series, of 'intuitive' talks. Talks where I would simply open myself to whatever words came from the deepest levels of my consciousness, without censoring what I said. Basically, the talks came through me, but were not prepared or thought out by me. In fact, as with an intuitive session, it was essential to let the words simply come. When I have given intuitive talks, like my sessions in the early days, I have been as surprised as anyone listening to hear what I am saying.

Others, giving talks that are apparently similar, have called them channelled talk. But I am not happy with that label. For two very important reasons. First, channellers often believe they are allowing a spirit or some other being to talk through them. I did not believe then, or now, that I was allowing some other being or spirit to speak through me. Equally, I was always very concerned, both in giving a talk of that sort, and in seeing clients, to stay responsible for what I say. (Which, if you don't know what you are going to say till you say it, can pose problems.) But channellers, particularly if they are working in a trance, sometimes claim that they do not know at all what they are saying and, it follows, can't be held responsible for what it is they express.

The first intuitive talk I gave was held at a local community centre – the Tabernacle. I wasn't keen to do it. I didn't feel that I had anything particular to say – and I was afraid, to put it bluntly, of simply depending on the words to come through me! I needn't have been.

A particular focus seemed to take over and the words flowed. In the first talk the subject was the organisation of society and the changes that are taking place in our inner and outer worlds. Answering questions from the well-informed audience, I realised how deep and sure the source of my knowledge and understanding seemed to be. Though it didn't seem extraordinary. Just, perhaps, unusually coherent. A new way of putting ideas together. Albeit in slightly convoluted language. I agreed to do the next, on relationships, then more followed, on a range of subjects.

Initially, I didn't fully understand the value of the talks. Those who came seemed to think them very interesting. We tape-recorded the talks, and the tapes sold well. Then I began to see that they were being studied, and that the wisdom they contained – which I almost took for granted, it seemed so matter-of-fact – was very profound. It was not the same as 'the ancient wisdom', as the core body of esoteric knowledge is called, but more like an approach to it. Or, sometimes, simply another way of saying it.

I began to understand how each age says the truths it needs in the idiom of its time, and that what I had said was perhaps best understood as knowledge that was particularly relevant to our age. It was, and is, elements of essential spiritual knowledge, but especially appropriate to our dilemmas and situation at this point in history.

The talks also pushed me to recognise that I was seeing the patterns that these crucial elements in spiritual and intuitive development formed. They were presenting new ways of thinking. Offering a fresh approach for a far wider understanding of the universe and key aspects of ourselves and our relationships. Also, tools for thinking in a new way, a way oriented towards developing into a different space, and broadening our perspective.

At the same time I began to understand and accept that the talks came from no more and no less than a deeper level of myself. In other words, I was accessing my own wisdom. I realised that I didn't want or need to consider them as simply 'intuitive talks' anymore. I didn't need the 'intuitive' process. I had become intuitive. In the everyday. I was owning the extraordinary, far-reaching power of my spiritual intelligence and intuition in a much wider sphere.

It was a crucial point. It offered me huge additional power and understanding. Needless to say, I no longer give intuitive talks, and haven't for some years. Obviously, I don't need to. I can say outright all I need to. Sometimes, teaching, I am surprised at the explanations I give to questions! I had not thought of the answers before – but they simply come. And they fit. Which is intuition, and spiritual intelligence, in the everyday.

Now, the nub of those teachings that came in my original talks, along with the wider patterns I have learnt to see, is what I want to offer you. They are not the solution to everything. But if you allow it, the intelligence of this book is part of the solution to the ache that masquerades as countless different agonies – the social, the physical, the sexual, the mental, the material.

It can be the key to learning to see differently – and when you see differently, you begin to have a different sense of the universe and yourself in the universe.

Which is the route to reclaiming your spiritual self, and the power of your intuition, as an added bonus. In other words, your spiritual intelligence. Which will revolutionise your relationships to yourself, all others, your work and our universe.

There are places where what I have to say may seem very simple. Forgive me, but also don't be deceived. You may also find places where it's difficult to make immediate sense of what I am saying. Again, forgive me – I'll do my best to tell you what I need to in as accessible a form as possible. But if you don't understand immediately, stay with me; the shape of the whole will help you accept the parts. Your journey will not be simple. Like mine, at many points you will not understand it. Once you begin, though, the compulsion to continue will carry you through. And transform your consciousness.

And help you play your part in transforming our world.

Part II

Your Journey

Chapter Three

Emerging

So much for my journey; what about yours? Well, you have to start, we all have to start, in the same place as I started – with ourselves. With yourself.

Why now?

When my journey became more intense, I did not understand that it was spirituality, in some form, that I was turning towards. Perhaps you do. Or you wonder. But why should anyone feel the need to go in search of spirituality now? What does it mean anyway?

We all know that religion has, in so many cases, lost its hold; that different versions of self-development vie for our attention; that it's hard to know how to balance self-advancement with some notion of greater good – hard even to know if that is desirable. At the same time the pressure on performance is intense, demands on our time and resources are huge, and in the West anyway, as we start the third millennium, personal wealth has increased enormously, without necessarily bringing happiness.

For so many of us, our own perception is that personal misery is also on the up. Statistics say the number of one-person households is steadily rising, as is the number of one-parent families. Many of us know sadness and loneliness only too well. Whether we know those states more or less than our forebears, or have more or less to cope with, is not really relevant. What is relevant is the prevalence of stress, and worse.

Pundits cite the breakdown of the family, religion or society as the cause for our ills, to differing degrees. On the ground an increasing number of us begin to search for some explanation, some understanding of our malaise. I did not realise, when I experienced the breakthrough that came to me, that I was simply conforming to my age. Now, I know that my experiences were only a variant of what faces us all.

Subjectively, what many of us know is that life, in some way, is less certain than we once thought or expected. Which is more than simply a dispelling of a childish belief in certainty. More than can perhaps be ascribed to 'the breakdown of society'. Many of us recognise that we are plagued, increasingly, by a need or desire for a different understanding. Which may or may not come with a growing concern for our environment and the future of our world.

Increasingly we feel that there is more than what we know, or more even than is known. Often, we feel that whatever we have, or do, is somehow not enough. And that perhaps these symptoms are not simply our own psychological so-called problems but that they relate, in some way, to aspects of our world. There is an ache, an unspecific pain that hovers. The cause is both inside and outside of us.

Human consciousness is changing

Human consciousness is changing. It is expanding to incorporate a sixth sense. Beyond sight, smell, sound, taste and touch there is another sense, a sense that responds to another aspect of our environment. A dimension for which we have no word because we cannot describe it – save by ascribing certain functions to it. It is a particular sensitivity. Intuition is the word most commonly used. We are facing the possibility, for some – maybe all – of us the eventual certainty, of expanding our intuitive functioning.

At the same time the often uncomfortable realisation of some other, perhaps greater, reality begins to emerge. But quite what isn't certain. It can be the opening for spiritual development. It may also lead to the rise of superstition of all sorts, or worship of ritual, or a retreat into rationalism in the face of the unknown.

It is not simply that as individuals, or in our private lives, we are registering those changes. Certain sectors of the scientific community are aware of change and there is a growing attempt, particularly in physics, to explain or expand on the situation we face. But there is more.

I worked as an intuitive for some years before the notion put itself into specific words for me. Looking back I can easily see how it was a reality I lived, and even taught, but I would not necessarily have formulated the words as clearly as I now know them. Now, I know that understanding this change in direction is the first major step in embracing spiritual intelligence, the wider spiritual reality and the development of intuition that goes along with it. The core of the explanation came in my first intuitive talk.

A new approach

The change that we are experiencing is not simply a new way of ordering our old experiences, or a call to undergo a new set of experiences. It is a change in our perceptions that is needed to recognise and understand this new vibration in our consciousness.

The new vibration does not signal the need for a search for new meaning. It is new meaning. It is a connection with a greater, deeper sense of order. And it is not an order that is being imposed from outside. It is an order that is coming from within each of us. A form of knowledge that is being revealed from within. Which is why it is so pressing, why it helps cause the ache.

In other words, there isn't some new parcel of knowledge that we have to learn. It is almost as if knowledge or information has little to do with it. But there is a new approach, a new way of understanding and acting that we must find. It is the approach of spiritual intelligence. When we achieve that, what we crave will be revealed.

Spiritual intelligence, with its wider perceptual understanding, will allow us to see and know what we haven't been able to see or know – till now.

Meeting power in a new form

Imagine you had never driven a car before. In your village all you have are horses and carts. A car appears one night in a field. No one knows quite what to make of it. Eventually, seeing it has wheels, people decide it must be a vehicle of some sort. So, they hitch it to a team of horses and drag it around. The folk driving the horses are proud to have cracked the problem, and to be 'driving' the car! But of course they are not doing anything of the sort.

Driving the car needs quite a different set of skills. In the beginning, when someone suggests that, no one else wants to listen. It could be dangerous. It sounds crazy when all you're accustomed to is horsepower. Developing spiritual intelligence is the same as learning to drive the car, activating its own, inner horsepower – rather than dragging it around like a cart.

Remember, you are not concerned with just learning lessons, but with altering the nature of your experience. Recently I had a letter from a psychiatrist, who put that point rather well, in another way. He wrote following a seminar I had given. He told me that he had appreciated the seminar at the time as fine and clear. But, over the last few months he had found some of the words – simple words – returning to him. And he had realised that though he had always tried to live a good life, doing good, learning about good, he had never really stopped to consider what sort of a person he was. Or given any attention to the quality of his inner reality. He had just concentrated on trying to perform good acts, or learning about supposedly the right things to do.

But despite material and professional good fortune, he had become increasingly discontented, and puzzled by his discontent. He had come to the seminar searching for some sort of further spiritual explanation, or knowledge. Now, something seemed to have changed. He felt the seminar had pointed him towards learning to focus on himself in a different way. He became concerned not simply with the external mechanics of good, but rather with being good at a fundamental level. So that goodness might come to be an expression of his very being, not something he did when he thought about it.

It is an issue we all see played out in the world around us constantly, and in our own lives. We can all do good actions – particularly in the public eye – and then, metaphorically speaking, go home and 'kick the cat'. But being good, knowing spirituality from within, fundamentally alters our perceptions of ourselves, others and our world. It makes it much more difficult to 'kick the cat'.

What you know and what you do

You do not need new knowledge. You don't need me, or anyone else, to repeat the spiritual truths that have been written in so many different ways in past ages and our own. Learning to act on them is different.

At the very start of my journey, my meditation spoke, saying that I already had what I needed to know. My problem was to bring the knowledge within me to consciousness. I believe the same is true for all of us. Listening to spiritual truths being repeated may be a good beginning. But, important as they might be, listening to them won't, alone, transform your ability to act on them. It will not make you able to integrate the spiritual side of your world, or enable you to operate from truly spiritual principles within yourself.

Learning spirituality, from books or study, does not make you able to apply what you have learnt. It will not change your behaviour and deeper feelings significantly. Learning to experience spirituality as part of yourself, and consequently acting from the perspective of spiritual intelligence, is the only way to do that.

Through time, countless terrible actions have been performed by people quite sure they were doing the right thing, according to what they had learnt, acting for the forces of good and even of spirit. But they were not using their own spiritual intelligence. They had not integrated the principles of spirituality.

It's a phenomenon most of us are very familiar with, on a different scale, in our own lives. Acting on the basis of what your peers say is good, or what society would like you to believe is right, is not the same as acting from the perspective of spiritual intelligence.

Then, how often have you been confronted by someone claiming to be acting with the best of intentions, when consciously, or unconsciously, it seems to you they are doing something quite different? We are all aware that behaviour exists on many levels. Clearly, what motivates behaviour is something quite different from book knowledge, intellectual learning or even, sometimes, choice. Only developing spiritual intelligence, which necessitates a change in your perception, provides the key to changing feeling, understanding and behaviour. This inner change has begun for many.

Outer as well as inner changes

At the same time as the shift in your perception, the background of our society has changed, and is changing. Not only is there a new vibration stirring in our consciousness, but the old order of our external reality is being altered, radically.

In the old external order there is a hierarchy. 'God', or some ultimate authority figure, sits at the top, followed by his 'church', the priest, the institution, men, women, children, animals – in that order. To relate to 'God' you must go through a priest, and a church. But that is no longer the case. We are all being urged to connect to spirit directly.

For example, in society at large, we all know that men are no longer automatically awarded a position above women. In the business world many organisations acknowledge that old hierarchies are no longer appropriate, and they are looking for new ways to organise themselves. In the family and the courts, the rights of children, and the responsibilities of adults towards them, are a major area of debate. How we relate to the animal world – the way we use animals – is coming under scrutiny in an unprecedented way. Environmental organisations are gaining wider support as we realise the importance of our relationship to the inanimate world. More and more of us no longer take our environment for granted, or assume we have the right to exploit or pollute it. All these are examples of the way the old order is crumbling.

Goodbye to gurus

Now, apply that to how we relate to spirituality. Instead of relating through the old triangle, the old hierarchy, we are being asked to connect directly with God, or the force of spirituality, or the force of the creative – however you see it, the words often confuse the issue. That means that as well as dramatic changes in your relation to spirituality, the role of the priest or the guru is also changing. Altogether. They are no longer your link to spirituality or God.

Of course, that doesn't mean that you can't learn from anyone else. Or that you don't need anyone else's help, or that you can't benefit from anyone else. But your relation to that person will be very different, because they won't be 'above' you (see Chapter Thirteen, Teachers and healers).

For example, when I work with others I am in the role of teacher, but I never forget that the role is merely that of enabler – not imparter of knowledge. Over and over again I have said to clients that if they resonate with the things I have to say, it is because they already know them. All my words are doing is bringing their own knowledge to the surface. Or taking them a little further. Helping them ask more questions and consider more answers.

My own meditation journey reflected exactly those principles. I wasn't taken on my spiritual journey to some outside leader. I was taken within. My teaching, that is, my connection with a spiritual reality, didn't come from words of wisdom that I read. In fact, my inner reality was insistent – no books and don't go looking for anyone to validate the process. Which was, in some ways, a relief to hear since I didn't have much, or any, specific spiritual knowledge at the start of my journey. And no one I consulted seemed able to really help. So, my spiritual and intuitive development didn't come from a wise man (or woman!) leading me to knowledge. It came from within. And allowed the process. It will be the same for you.

I see the same thing over and over with my clients. Peter was a good example. Trained in the law, he had turned his attention to his spiritual life several years before coming to see me. When he came, it was in despair. 'I don't know where I am going, not really,' he confided. 'It seems as if the more I do, the less it seems to work for me. I keep telling myself I ought to be finding peace, or it ought to be becoming easier, but actually it's not. All sorts of other people come to me for advice about everything from meditation to the nature of the universe, and they seem to find what I tell them useful, but I am completely stuck. None of it is really doing me any good.'

It is not often I meet a client whose esoteric and spiritual knowledge is as deep as Peter's. He knew a great deal about all sorts of areas where I knew nothing. As ever, knowledge, book learning, was very different from the ability to act on the principles behind the knowledge. A devout and spiritual man, Peter had studied with a well-known guru who was clear about the route to 'enlightenment' and the path his disciples had to follow. He gave detailed teachings which his students did indeed follow – to the letter, in Peter's case.

It was obvious to me that Peter had lost the ability to hear his own inner voice. He was so good a 'follower' that he had lost the ability to do anything other than follow. He could no longer really take any initiative unless it was prescribed for him through his guru. Worse, he was in this condition because he felt he was doing 'good'! He felt it was the right thing to do, for the world and for himself.

Once he began to understand this view of his situation, Peter decided to slowly detach himself from his guru, and the organisation he had supported for so long, and started gradually to feel his way. When last I saw him, both his business and his private life were growing in new and vigorous directions. But it isn't easy. Learning to grow up, and opt for independence, never is.

It is the same for all of us. We have lived through the age of the guru. There are many who have played guru, and many who have followed gurus. Often, but not always, to good effect. And there are probably lots of people who still feel the need or desire to do so or who benefit from doing so. Each of us chooses our path and when, or if, we become ready we change. (And that may happen repeatedly.)

But right now there's a call that all of us can hear. It is a persistent call. A call to grow up, almost an evolutionary demand to move towards spiritual maturity. And it's a demand that dictates, first of all, that we move on from the age of the guru or priest. Of course, though all can hear this call, only some, the first few, are ready to listen to it. Some wonder what they hear. Some will not hear. Yet.

Religion and old-fashioned ideas of God have lost their place; the rest of the picture doesn't fit together any more either. You don't need a priest or a guru to connect you to a spiritual reality. You have to learn to reach out, touch it, know it and be prepared to re-define it, yourself.

Often, I see clients who are looking for a guru to follow, or who want me to tell them what to do. How things are. It's a very human desire. And one I try hard to resist. The message of this time is clear: the moment has arrived for you to forge your own con-nection to spirit, or the light, however you choose to understand it, which at the moment may be very vague – but will become clearer.

Concentrate for now on the fact that you will not

look for a guru to take you to spirit, and try to understand what it means for you in your life to give up the notion of the old hierarchy. In many ways it is like the process of leaving childhood behind. As children, we have parents to guide us and help us learn the ways of the world – how to be and how to think. Many traditional concepts of religion award 'God' a paternal role, and the officers of God likewise are 'heavenly' parent figures, guiding us, children. Substituting the word spirit, or the light, for God, often makes little difference. Try to come to terms with the implications that there is no one standing between you and an enlarged reality. It is your personal responsibility to connect to that reality. Accept your power to develop your spiritual intelligence. You can and you will.

To think about and to do:

Here are some questions and exercises to help you in reaching for that power.

1. Think about how the hierarchy that I have described operated in your family, and your place in that hierarchy. Do you have a residual sense that there is someone who knows more than you, is more important than you, and will tell you how it 'really' is? Being able to accept that you have the power to connect directly to spirituality, that there is no expert or guru who can take you 'there', is crucial, and often relates to how far you have been

43

able to give up childhood feelings of dependence, or inferiority. Which is not the same as saying you don't need anyone else, you can't learn from anyone else, or that you have to be totally independent. None of that is true. But you do have to accept responsibility for yourself, your actions in the world and your relation to the world.

2. Do you feel you have grown up? And if not why not? And in which ways have you not grown up? We all, as adults, from time to time feel that we are children. Maturity is not a constant state! In fact, life would be very boring if it was. But one of the big things about being grown up is accepting responsibility. Claiming your spiritual intelligence, and moving into spiritual maturity, requires you to face life as an adult and accept responsibility.

3. Consider how far you still subscribe to an old-fashioned hierarchy in your personal and family life now. Remember that it is necessary to guide and sometimes even to restrain children, but this is simply to help them to grow into adulthood and independence. To help them become able to take responsibility for themselves and those who need to be looked after. You are an adult now. What role do you play in your personal and family life? Think how applying the principles of spiritual maturity – the responsibilities that the

downfall of the hierarchy implies – would affect your personal life. What does being a spiritual adult mean to you?

4. Think about your relationships with your peers. The most satisfactory ones are where the give and take is equal. In your relationships with your peers you want equals who can give and take. You don't want others who make you feel inferior, play power games, or make themselves dependent on you. Which does not mean that your friends will all be the same as you, or will all have the same gifts, powers or responsibilities. You will be different. But as humans, you will be equal.

5. Think about your job and workplace. How far are you allowed independence in making a contribution and how far are you dominated by a hierarchy? A healthy environment will use a chain of command for practical purposes but at the same time will encourage you to retain your dignity and the ability to act independently, to take responsibility. Many business corporations have come to this same conclusion and actively implement ways to circumvent hierarchies, or develop chains of command that promote a greater sense of individual responsibility and equality.

6. When you ask someone else for their opinion, or guidance, do you feel you retain the responsibility for making the ultimate decision, or do you try to give it up to them?

7. Can you think of a situation where you have had to decide between conflicting opinions from experts, and what has this taught you? Have you learnt that the ultimate responsibility for most decisions lies with you, and that reputable authorities will frequently hold opposing views? There may not be a single right path, though you will have to choose to go with one opinion.

8. Can you think of a situation where you have felt it correct to give up your power to another or others? Remember, there are situations where it is important to allow others to take command – you don't go into surgery and tell the surgeon how to do his job. But nor do you necessarily accept the first opinion you are given about a medical condition, for example. You may well seek a second or even a third opinion and it will be your responsibility to choose between them. That is being an adult. Developing spiritual maturity demands some of the same ability to suspend judgement and consider situations carefully.

9. In your job, if you work with others, you deal with clients, whether they are co-workers you interact with or outside customers. You might even work with patients. All relationships where you are called on to display your competence carry the possibility that you can be made into a guru of some sort – the one

who 'knows', the one who has the power, the one who will take the responsibility from the other.

Whilst leadership is necessary, and there are many situations where it is essential to take responsibility from others, consider how you handle the possible role of guru. How do you use the power?

10. Can you accept that you have exactly the same ability to connect to spirit as the 'holiest' person you can think of?

11. Can you accept that we all, however apparently flawed, have that potential?

12. Remember that important as all the above are, without joy the effects are all diminished. Think when you last really laughed.

Chapter Four

The World of Energy

All of your development will be influenced by energy. But what does that mean? Energy can be a difficult word, when it's used outside a strictly scientific situation. Einstein's famous definition of energy is $e = mc^2$. Energy equals matter multiplied by the speed of light, squared. Energy in the everyday is easily understood – 'he made the bed energetically.' But the New Age has taken to using the word widely – with rather confusing results. And it's a staple in alternative or complementary medicine. I wish there was another word, or words, that applied specifically to that subtle quality I want to describe, but there isn't. In time, physics – not I – may be able to describe more accurately the quality I am talking about.

Everything has 'energy'

From an apple to a rock to a human being. From sound to pressure to temperature: all involve energy in some way. Science describes energy as a spectrum made up of frequencies. There are different sorts of energy. Looking at the body, at the heart, for example, there is electrical energy, which cardiologists measure with an electrocardiogram (ECG in the UK and EKG in the USA). But there is also electromagnetic energy, which only some cardiologists can measure, using a much more sophisticated technique. The heart's electrical energy is a signal that can be picked up from any cell of the body. Much more advanced and more recent techniques can pick up electromagnetic energy eight to ten feet away.

Frequencies and indestructibility

All types of energy merge into one another as frequencies, including, for example, those for chemical, magnetic and electrical energy, cross over. Within particular frequency bands there is great variation. Take sound. A dog whistle at one end of the spectrum of sound is inaudible to humans. The frequency of the energy is simply too high for our perceptual apparatus – our ears in this case – to pick it up. But that doesn't mean the sound does not exist. Dogs hear it loud and clear.

Science's understanding of energy is constantly developing. Whether energy in the sense I use the word corresponds exactly to some scientific category, I can't be sure. But neither can science. For example, exactly what the role is of electromagnetic energy as related to the body, or how it develops, or what affects it, medical science cannot say precisely. Yet.

At the same time it's important to remember that energy cannot be destroyed. It can be transformed, deflected or distributed, but it cannot simply cease to exist. That applies to all manifestations of energy.

Energy and information

Energy carries information too. For example, Morse code is an energy-generated signal which, by its pattern, carries information. Speech is a combination of frequencies in differing patterns. The traces or pattern generated by an ECG machine give medics information about the functioning of the heart. Many expressions of energy carry information. But, ways of picking up and reading those messages are poorly understood at the moment. For example, a key challenge facing science in understanding the functioning of the body is how to chart the relationship between energy, the information it carries and the matter it influences – our bodies.

Through my own journey, I learnt to access information from and about the subtle energy that I see in a particular way – and I am certainly not unique in having done so. There are healers and practitioners all over the world who work with energy and the properties of what's loosely called energy in many different ways.

For me the experience of seeing and reading energy began with seeing some sort of force around people – perhaps what has been called auras – and also the energy, in some form, within people. It was soon supplanted by the experience of seeing images that related to what I learnt were called the chakras, the supposed energy centres of the body, known for centuries in Eastern disciplines. As I saw them, I simply understood what I was seeing – particular issues connected with the different chakras. Today, whilst I can still see chakras if I 'look', usually I find that all the information I need is given to me without my necessarily being directly aware of what in particular is carrying that information.

I feel it's very important, though, that I – or anyone else – never 'look' at another person's energy without a specific request from them. And I regularly refuse, even if asked! At the same time, in everyday life, I usually choose to deliberately 'shut down' in, for example, social situations, for obvious reasons.

So, while science works to come up with a complete explanation of the forces of our universe, the forces of human understanding press ahead. Which makes the label or metaphor of 'energy' necessary. But why is it important to spiritual development? Or spiritual intelligence? And how does it relate to intuition?

Sensing the new

Developing spiritual intelligence goes hand in hand with extending your perception of the world and its inhabitants. Evolving spiritually means – among other developments – learning to sense, see, hear or feel what you can't (yet) always sense, see, hear or feel. And there's a pattern to that progression. It is an energetic progression with each stage offering a wider perspective than the last until, ultimately, you reach the place where spirituality rules and the values of spirituality are self-evident.

Chief among the qualities of spirituality, the very essence of the place you reach, and the real understanding that informs you, is love. It is a new understanding of love, though. Love whose magic attracts all, but which we routinely misunderstand and misuse. And this new understanding of love brings with it the real ability to stand in others' shoes – the essence of intuition.

Which is why coming to know the reality of spirituality is about widening your perceptual senses, and why intuition, which is simply another means of perception, engages as your perceptual senses unfold and develop.

And that's where energy comes into the picture. The growth and refinement of your energy occurs in parallel with the development of your spirituality. Understanding the role of energy is crucial. Fortunately, there are ways of working with your energy, and your perceptions of energy, which will help you on your journey.

Perceptual leaps

My own spiritual development was punctuated by huge leaps in the development of my perception, specifically my perception of energy. For example, it was shortly after I began to receive 'teaching' in meditation that I began to be able to see energy in others, if I 'looked'. And, to learn what that energy meant. At the same time, for many months my spine was 'worked on' – I don't have a better way of expressing it – in meditation. Physically, it felt in some ways like the effect of a visit to a cranial osteopath. It might, or might not, have corresponded to what Eastern traditions describe as 'kundalini rising' – which is a complicated notion related to the progress of energy up your spine and over the crown of your head.

To me, my energy was being developed, or worked with. And, crucially, I came to realise it was all a part of what I now see as the development of my spiritual intelligence. My understanding and integration of love.

In the years that followed, I have worked to share the knowledge accumulated from this process. Now, I want to pass on as much as I can of my experience to you. Understanding the workings of the energy you encounter in the world is the start of understanding and developing the energy of your own body.

The Energy of the Universe

Astrology

Astrology is the ancient science of how the different influences, or energies, of the planets and their movements affect us. As well as long-standing historical support for astrology, there is a growing body of scientific work supporting the basic premises of astrology. Physicist Will Keepin, now of the Colorado Institute for a Sustainable Future, made news when he announced his 'conversion' to astrology in 1994. But whether or not you believe, or how much you believe, in astrology – and many people today accept that there is something in it, it is worth remembering some basic facts.

The sea is the largest body of water known to man. The sea is moved by the movements of a planet, the moon. Tides rise and fall in response to a lunar ryhthm. Similarly, our bodies are largely made up of water. If a planet, the moon, causes tidal movements in the sea, what does it cause in human beings? (Studies show that suicides are greatest at the full moon, also incidence of mental illness.) And if the moon has this effect, what about the other planets – astronomy suggests there are at least some similarities between them: is it only the moon that causes these effects?

Clearly there are a variety of energetic forces operating in and on the universe, some better understood by science than others. Just because a force, or a theory of a force, is not entirely understood, it cannot be dismissed.

Shamanism

According to Leo Rutherford, probably Britain's leading shaman, shamanism is the oldest way in which humanity has sought connection with Creation. A shaman is an indigenous healer, or visionary. Evidence of shamanic practices exists all over the world, dating back as far as the Paleolithic period. Many different forms of energy are recognised by different shamans – from the energy of individual plants to compass directions, to spirits and a huge variety in between. Shamans often use trance as a way of reaching heightened energetic states. Modern studies, in South Africa, for example, are increasingly interested in researching shamanism, and are drawn to conclude that it is effective in some cases, and its efficacy cannot be explained by Western science.

Feng shui

The Chinese practice of feng shui is based on complex theories of the organisation of the forces of the universe. Feng shui is essentially about the energy of places, and over the centuries it has built up an elaborate system of knowledge about those energies and the most propitious ways of using them, changing them or avoiding them. Of course there are various feng shui theories, many of them conflicting and confusing. However, Western feng shui expert Sarah Surety argues that whether or not you are aware of the forces of the universe, be they magnetic or cosmic, they are real. She repeats a story, told by one of her Chinese masters, to demonstrate this fact.

Once upon a time a little fish was swimming happily in the sea at one of the poles of the earth. One day, unknowingly, he swam into the current. Unknowingly. But it was easy being there. Food was plentiful, he was comfortable. So, he continued to swim along with the current, and didn't try to move out of it. (Though, of course, he didn't know he was in it!) In the end, he found himself in the warm bountiful sea at the Equator. Now, did he have free will or not? Was he influenced by subtle energy forces or not?

Well, though the fish, or you, may have thought he made all the choices that brought him to the place he ended up, he was in fact influenced by the currents, or energies, that he cooperated with. So, the story may show that whether or not you believe in forces beyond your own free will, they exist, and they influence the direction of your development. More. You can learn to sense and cooperate better with those forces or energies.

Your immediate energy environment

The places you choose to be, the people and objects around you affect your energy. It's common sense that we feel more comfortable in some places or with some people than in others. So do our pets. Places, people and objects all have a feeling about them.

Energy of objects

A little while ago I visited the Holocaust Museum in

Washington. A chilling, sad place. One of the most terrible and touching exhibits for me were the piles of clothes that gas chamber victims had been forced to remove. Looking, I could see a low grey haze around them – what I knew to be the 'energy' of those clothes. At the same time that exhibit gave me the most terrible sensation. Though, of course, it was by no means the only exhibit to do so. The entire day was a very sobering experience. But not just for me. I am sure most people visiting that museum are deeply touched. And whilst they might say it was the knowledge and explanation of the events that touched them, I am sure it was the energy of the place and the objects it contains, too. In fact, I can't see how those sets of qualities could be separated.

Objects often have significance for us. A vase is prized because it belonged to a favourite aunt. A picture frame is special because it was made by your father, as a boy. Those objects are not special just because they make us think about the people connected to them, but more because they carry some of the energy of those people. Like the clothes in the Holocaust Museum. Other experiential evidence seems to point in the same direction.

It is not chance that mediums, for example, often ask for an article belonging to their sitter. Or if you were seeing a medium who claimed to connect with the dead, they might ask for an article belonging to that person. Not everyone believes in mediums, though. I am not a medium, nor do I have an interest in promoting that sort of work (on the contrary, sometimes), but feeling an object often tells me something about the person to whom it belongs. However, it doesn't have to be an object. I can have a sense of someone, or some circumstance around them, through their name. In other words, names, mere words, contain something beyond their literal meaning. Again, I am not alone in having this ability.

Energy of thoughts and feelings

The relationship between our thoughts and feelings and our physical well-being is a major area in complementary medicine. Dr Alan Watkins, editor of *Mind–Body Medicine*, states categorically: 'The health of any individual not only depends on physical health, but also on the unique mental, emotional, and spiritual aspects of that individual.' In other words, thoughts and feelings – or the energy generated by thoughts and feelings – play a part in health.

Biologist Rupert Sheldrake recently published a book on the psychic powers of animals, *Dogs That Know When Their Owners Are Coming Home And Other Unexplained Powers Of Animals*. Among much interesting data, he found, as a result of hundreds of experiments, overwhelming statistical evidence that some dogs knew in advance when their owners were returning home, when there was no conventional way to explain their having this knowledge. One dog, he found, even appeared to respond – in repeated experiments – when his owner phoned a taxi to bring her home. So, what were these pets responding to? Intention, or some energy signal, would be my answer.

What you think or feel is important to the well-being of your own body. At the same time, the energy messages you transmit to the universe by your thoughts and feelings can and will be picked up by at least some others – in one way or another.

Joy

Joy, or pleasure, deserves a separate paragraph to itself. It is that important.

Laughter is infectious. Joy lights up a face. Happiness radiates. We all use those phrases without thinking. What they say is a reflection of reality. And vital to our well-being. The strictest adherence to energy 'rules' is of little use without joy. What gives you joy, though, is worth considering carefully.

The others around you

The situations you are exposed to, or choose to expose yourself to, are part of the energetic environments you literally take in. If you have ever stood in a crowd, remember how powerfully the feeling of the crowd can affect you. Mass hysteria is a well-recognised phenomenon. Crowd behaviour is well documented and studied. Feelings and behaviour can be infectious.

In the same way, being, for example, in a harsh environment where language and behaviour are abusive will have an effect on you. Whether you want to say that effect is caused by example, conditioning or whatever is not important. However that effect is evident, it will leave its mark in your energy, as well as on your actions and disposition.

You may be able to avoid your surroundings directly affecting how you behave, but it will be at a cost, and the cost will show. For example, if you work in a setting where abuse is constantly hurled around, you may be able to avoid responding with abuse while at work. But exposure to that atmosphere will affect you. It will lodge in your energy, where you will continue to feel it. You may find yourself giving way to anger or tears in your private life. Similarly, being in a very calming, soothing environment will of course have an effect on your behaviour, and will also be evident in your energy.

'No man is an island'

Your surroundings are important. You are influenced by them, even if you do not want to be. Be careful where you place yourself. Remember, the behaviour of others in your environment will affect you. Even if you want to, it is impossible to consider yourself as altogether separate from them. Be careful what you think and be aware that your feelings have significant implications.

All this may even begin to suggest a moral dimension to energy. For example, standing in a place where terrible things are going on around you – for example, others being hurt – will affect your energy even if you do not participate in those actions. It is as if you will be infected by the circumstances – even if you fight the infection, it will leave a mark. Peacekeeping forces in war-torn corners of the world are well aware of the terrible effects on them of their involvement, even when they are not fighting. The scenes they witness, alone, are deeply damaging.

But it is not simply the overall effects of places, people or actions that you need to consider. Every aspect of life that you encounter has an energetic counterpart. You have the chance to use some of these forces for your benefit.

Energy of colours

We all know different colours have different effects. Red is known throughout the world as a 'beware', 'watch out', 'stop' signal. Everyone recognises the power, or energy, of its effect. It is always a colour that draws attention to itself or the situation where it is being used.

Most of us feel the calming effect that the sky or a large expanse of still water can have. That, in part, is because of the energy of the colour blue in all its shades. Green means nature. The effect of green will often, but not always, be related to the effect nature has on the individual who is perceiving the colour.

Whilst colour therapy is a relatively specialised and alternative practice – using coloured lights or silks for healing – the use of colour in hospitals, industrial environments and schools has long been established. And art therapy is a strong discipline, used in treatment of mental or nervous conditions and also to promote well-being. All these therapies include the assumption that different colours have different effects, and therefore energy, in my terms.

In some colour therapy the energy of paler colours is considered to be more sensitive and that of stronger colours more vigorous, or even less refined, but not always. Use of the colour black is always interesting. It can reflect negativity and a desire or need to avoid the emotional entanglements of colour, or it can represent a degree of protection. Or something else. I often use the power of colour in stirring feelings in my seminars, and you will find some suggestions at the end of this chapter.

Energy of sound

Sound has long been held to have power. The bible has a number of references to sounds. Perhaps the most famous being the statement that, 'In the beginning was the Word.' In other words, sound came before anything else. Then there is the Old Testament story of the walls of Jericho being destroyed by the sound of trumpets. Again, in the Old Testament David played the lyre to Saul and he was 'refreshed, made well and the evil departed'. Tibetan bells (more like metal cups), which are used for healing, are an expression of ancient Tibetan belief in the power of sound. Modern medicine today suggests that music releases endorphins, the brain's painkillers.

Individual variation plays an important part, though. It is not possible to say that sounds higher up the scale are more powerful than those of the lower reaches. Or that softer sounds are more powerful – or less powerful – than louder sounds. In some circumstances it may be one way, in others it is another. What is clear is the power of sound itself.

Music therapy is built on this notion, therapists using rhythm and different instruments to deal with physical, mental and behavioural difficulties. From time to time reports emerge of miraculous cases where individuals, thought lost in their own private worlds, are drawn back to reality by the use of music. Like the case of Sophie Stewart Jones, born in the early 1990s in England with cerebral palsy and brain damage. Though unable to speak, Sophie was roused from her private world – where she had been diagnosed as never being able to communicate or to hear – by the power of music. Now, it holds her in its thrall, particularly blues. Not only can she write, but she shows a fierce intelligence in her writing and a determination to study music.

Energy of foods

It may seem superfluous to say that food has energy. I don't mean calorific energy. Foods carry the energy, or vibrations, of the places they come from. While it might at first seem a strange notion, many of us know something of that, instinctively. When you go abroad, part of the experience may be enjoying, or trying, the local diet. We recognise that eating native is one way of finding out about a place, or assimilating with it. In the same way, a dislike for foreign fare is often part of not enjoying the experience of the place. That is, the energy of the place or people.

Food carries the energy, or vibrations, of the place where it was grown. If you go to the Caribbean and eat locally grown sweet potatoes, you will be harmonising with your environment. If, on the other hand, you live in Europe and you eat imported Caribbean sweet potatoes, you will be taking in a little 'Caribbean energy'.

Exactly the same notion is part of the macrobiotic theory of diet. Energetically we are best suited to eating locally grown produce. With the minimum of chemical or genetic interference, of course. Locally grown food will carry the vibrations of the region, which will help us harmonise and literally connect with the earth of the place where we are. Also, local herbs and spices often play a part in helping the body to deal with local conditions. (Though, of course, particular spices may be used largely to make the boring, unvarying fare of a poor area more interesting, and there is no reason to make a virtue of what resulted from necessity.)

Food has always had a special place in culture and history, with rich people usually eating better than the poor, and culinary traditions forming another aspect of social divisions. Take the British Raj in India, for example. Members of the British ruling class stuck rigidly to their own style of food, and disparaged the native cuisine. Perhaps they preferred the taste of English food, but at the same time it was a way of maintaining their culture. Of course, because the produce they were eating came largely from India, they would not have been able to avoid the Indian 'vibrations' of their food – however hard they were trying to do so.

Some healers today believe that the digestive problems that are rife in the Western world are due not only to intensive farming methods and interference with seeds, but to imported foods and the moving away from local produce. Recently I heard a healer from Eastern Europe speak movingly about how traditional foods in her country were being replaced by American imports or the American style of eating. She saw that as responsible for the digestive problems plaguing her people, problems found whenever there are similar patterns.

While I don't agree with that argument entirely, there are important respects in which it is valid. The difficulty of harmonising – digesting – the energy of foreign places is considerable. You are always best able to digest locally grown food, often prepared in a local manner. That will 'earth' you best, and help you harmonise with local conditions best. However, if travelling, remember it takes a while for your body to acclimatise to local flora and fauna, and that traditions of hygiene vary, which results in very different resistances and tolerances being developed.

Then, given that locally grown produce is best, freshness matters too. Storage of any form inevitably effects the energy. And whilst storage may be necessary, it may also be avoidable, by reclaiming the notion of the significance of the seasons. Seasonal food, quickly transported from producer to consumer, is energetically superior to frozen or canned alternatives. And it harmonises with the time. If this seems a strange notion, you might like to try it out.

In each season you need different qualities. Those qualities are best supported by the produce of that time. If your aim is to strengthen your links with the energy of the earth, and your sensitivity to the energetic influences around you, eating imported lettuce in winter will not be supportive in the same way as eating, for example, locally grown cabbages.

Organic and GM-free food

At the same time, it goes without saying that genetically manipulated food may be very difficult for your body to digest; chemical additives may be similarly harmful; so obviously organic, GM-free food is best. Equally, for those who want to eat meat, the provenance of the animals they eat will be important. The Dalai Lama is sometimes quoted as saying (wrongly or rightly, I am not sure, but I applaud the sentiment) that he feels that ideally everyone should be a vegetarian. But his own health suffers if he cuts out all meat. Therefore, in eating meat he gives thanks to the animal which laid down its life for his sustenance. It goes further though. The circumstances of the life and death of the animals killed for food will all play a part in the effects on your energy of eating their flesh. Which means being as careful as possible in choosing and buying meat or fish; consider how those creatures lived and died.

Energy medicine and its practitioners

It's not just the taste or freshness or provenance of what you eat that is important. Food can be used as medicine too. Major developments are under way in treating physical ailments with diet or supplements. This is an obvious way of trying to balance the body's energy by using the energy of food or nutritional supplements.

It is a huge and growing area, which recognises that a change in your energy, or the energy around you, can be used to improve your physical and emotional well-being. And those changes can be effected by methods that vary from hands-on healing to using light itself as an energetic tool. Of course, all remedies – pills, potions and therapies – are in some way energy transfers.

There are a wide range of practitioners, from healers to osteopaths to homeopaths to shamans to acupuncturists to colour therapists and feng shui consultants, who believe that they can work on your energy or environment, and indeed may be able to do so – with excellent effects in some cases. For some years I worked as a hands-on healer myself. But I reached a point where I felt I could more usefully teach others how to change and develop their own energy rather than act as a conduit for energy for them.

Some energy practitioners may believe that their understanding of energy, and therefore your energy, is superior to yours, and consequently will require you to entrust your body or home to their hands and greater knowledge. Don't. Not without certain safeguards anyway. Remember the principles relating to the hierarchy in our age, and be very careful about putting others 'above' you.

For example, not long ago I saw a young woman in her early twenties who was starting out on a career of which she was enormously proud, where she was dealing and coping with considerable stress. Her life was moving very fast and she was working at maximum capacity to keep up with it, and to stay whole. She went to see a homeopath about her health, and was seriously disturbed by the consultation.

The homeopath told her that she was in the wrong job and that she would not stay there for long – her destiny was elsewhere! She was hugely concerned – did he know something she did not about the job she was so pleased with? Could he see ghastly consequences that she could not? Could I explain? Now, perhaps my client misunderstood. But hers is a story I have heard before, often, in various forms. If that was what she was told, it was highly irresponsible. The homeopath was fortune-telling, or 'playing God'.

'Playing God' is an expression that used sometimes to be applied to the attitude of some members of the medical profession in relation to their patients. It suggested they were taking the mantle of medical power that has been, historically, so often awarded to 'the doctor', and using it to reinforce their position as superior to the patient – all knowing and all-powerful.

In this case that could have been what happened. The homeopath had no right to tell his client she was in the wrong job. His job was to help support her in her chosen path and, if her choice changed, or she faced a change, to help her deal with that. Even to tell her that her choice was having a destructive effect on her health, if it was. But not to ordain or foretell change for her – like a fortune-teller. Practitioners who feel they have insight into clients' lives have particular responsibility not to try to direct their lives. Of course, as clients we have to accept responsibility for our own lives and not expect our practitioners to direct our life choices.

In choosing a practitioner it is always your responsibility to discriminate and to choose whom you want to work with, what you will and will not take from them, and for how long. All our bodies are different. Not all of us are developing in the same way – there are many directions open to us.

Certain individuals specialising in specific skills

become enormously proficient in using them to excellent effect for their fellows. We are hugely lucky that there are today increasing numbers of wonderful masseurs, chiropractitioners, healers, homeopaths, reflexologists, acupuncturists, Alexander technique teachers and a host of others. But sadly there are others with limited knowledge, dogmatic notions, the desire to play God, or simply inadequate skills. Particularly early on in your journey, it may be difficult for you to discriminate.

Carefully check out anyone you may want to see. Above all, listen to your own body. When it comes to any treatment or changes in your environment, be open to the possibility that the practitioner you have come to may not be right for you, may not be right enough, or may not continue being right. If in doubt, ask for a second opinion. Often therapists or practitioners are excellent for one client and not for another. Listen to yourself if something in you feels you want to stop the treatment, or not to follow the prescribed path. Don't take anything as gospel truth.

Above all, watch the effect of the treatment or suggestions on yourself and your energy. If it feels good and you can see it doing you good and you want to continue, excellent. If it feels bad, or you are unhappy with the effects, or you have a doubt about continuing – pause.

Allowing anyone else to enter your energy field is a serious choice. As soon as a masseur puts his or her hands on you, not only are they entering your energy field but they are putting their energy into you. To be blunt, in the transfer of energy you are taking on their issues – the unhelpful as well as the helpful. An osteopath, reflexologist or chiropractitioner is doing exactly the same. As are any number of others, many of whom recognise this and do their best to protect you, and themselves. Some acupuncturists, aware of this problem, believe they guard against aspects of this energy exchange by using their needles as a barrier between you and them.

It is up to you to protect the energy of your body, and the energy around you. Choose carefully whom you want to work on your energy. Or advise on your environment. Allow yourself to change that choice whenever you feel it necessary. Don't become dependent on the energy input of another. And remember that though someone may have been a great help in the past, or have been fantastic in helping a friend, that does not mean they can be helpful to you, now.

Finally, a good practitioner can be a real boon. Or can skilfully guide you through a particular problem. But no course of massages, no pills, potions, remedies, herbs, acupuncture or any other therapy will achieve spiritual intelligence for you. That's your responsibility. Only you can do it.

Alcohol and drugs

Both affect your perception, and your physical body.

The effects of a moderate intake of alcohol are not important. But at many stages in my own development, drinking alcohol was quite impossible – I had no ability to tolerate it. Others have told me they have had similar, (fortunately) usually short-lived experiences. Now if I choose to, I can have the odd glass of wine without ill or lasting effect.

Recreational drugs are a very different matter. I have never seen anyone whose energy they did not adversely affect, for quite some time after being consumed. How long seems to depend on the individual. But they seriously impede perceptual ability. They enter an individual's energy, and stay there.

Of course, many societies, including our own, have used them for exactly this purpose. Hallucinogenic drugs were used to go on 'trips'. Unfortunately, as with any chemically induced state, afterwards you have to come back to reality. I have not seen evidence that insights obtained by the drug route have lasting benefits. Others, however, may have different evidence. Indigenous people such as the bushmen of Southern Africa are famous for using drug-induced states for particular spiritual purposes. Obviously it is hard to comment on the results for their development. On the other hand, I have never seen an ecstasy user's development positively affected by a couple of tabs.

Medicinal drugs are likewise very capable of affecting your energy and perception. Most drug manufacturers issue warnings to that effect. Clearly, in developing your energy you are advised to avoid use of any except strictly necessary medicaments. Our growing realisation of the dangers of some medicines is part of the reason for the search for other, less intrusive ways to deal with physical and mental problems. Fortunately there are several to try – starting with the basic recommendations that follow here.

Suspend disbelief

Ultimately, the less obstructed your own energy, and the clearer you are in upholding your own perceptions, the easier it will be for you to be aware of the forces of the universe, and to respond appropriately. In other words, the development of your intuition will be strengthened, and the growth of your spirituality best supported.

But if the notion of energy that I have been suggesting sounds all-embracing, or even implausible, stop a moment to consider the germ theory of disease, developed by Louis Pasteur in the mid-nineteenth century.

Before Pasteur's theory, notions of the forces that carried illness varied widely. In the 1850s and 1860s Pasteur put forward the idea that disease is caused by germs attacking the body from outside. This was strongly debated by physicians and scientists who argued fiercely that germs played a secondary and unimportant role. The idea that tiny, microscopic organisms could invade and kill vastly larger ones seemed ridiculous. We all know what followed, it's a familiar story. And today, as the wheel of knowledge continues to turn, medicine is coming to a new understanding altogether of psychoneuroimmunology that goes way beyond Pasteur's discoveries.

Almost all new theories on the nature of the universe meet the same scepticism, or opposition, to begin with. In time, they may be accepted, or modified, even eventually superseded. I can't claim that the vibrations or energy I am talking about are an absolute quality that will be proved and measured by science. But I am saying that this concept of energy is a powerful metaphor, with important implications. It may also come to have scientifically provable correlates.

Don't feel you have to accept it. Just suspend disbelief, and listen to your own experience. It may help to open another dimension of reality to you. At the same time, the following suggestions will help you to develop and purify your energy. The greater your sensitivity, the more you pick up on the energies around you. And the more sensitive you are to the energies around you, the easier it is to allow your perception to extend, to develop your spiritual intelligence.

This is a case where some simple rules really apply. They are the only 'rules' I suggest. Then, the questions at the end of the chapter will make you think about the situations you choose to put yourself in, and their effect on you.

Energy Basics for Health and Development

1. Wash daily

This sounds so obvious, but it is surprising how many people think 'a lick and a promise' or an extra splash of deodorant will do. Water washes away old vibrations, or the old energy. You want to wash away the experiences and emotions of the old day before starting on the new. Also, for the best results, particularly when you are relatively new to the process, if you are going to meditate, contemplate or try to look within yourself, I strongly advise washing away as many outside influences as possible.

In some cultures Westerners, with their love of baths, are regarded with utter astonishment: 'Fancy relaxing in your own dirt!' However, I am not against baths, but I am in favour of washing all your body every day, bath or shower. If you like to bathe, sometimes adding sea salt or even an essential oil can be helpful, in moderation. (Just a tiny drop of an essential oil, occasionally, as it can be very powerful and must be used with great caution.)

Baths are great for relaxation, cleansing and focussing, especially at the start of a process of spiritual unfolding, or at crucial times. Then, it can be helpful to light a candle – I like three – on the edge of the bath, to switch off the bathroom light, and then to lie peacefully in the gloom with the candles flickering in front of you. This can be very powerful, evoking early experiences of being in the womb, in water, in the dark. Concentrating on the candles in front of you is a way of affirming your desire to connect with the light.

2. *Smell*

Be careful in your use of perfumes and strongly scented toiletries. If you are trying to allow your senses to expand, overwhelming them with artificial odours gives you yet another barrier to penetrate. Be very careful of burning essential oils in vaporisers – I can't overemphasise how powerful they can be.

3. *Clothes*

Change your clothes. Again, it seems very obvious, but is often overlooked. In trying to increase your sensitivities, be open to all the ways in which you may hold old energies to you. Like the clothes in the Holocaust Museum that so affected me, your clothes hold the experiences you encounter while wearing them.

There is a good energetic reason for wanting to wear again exactly what you wore when something special happened to you. Or to feel that you can sense another through a piece of their clothing. Many a parent has give a child an article of his or her clothing to assure their offspring of the parent's continued 'presence'. And lovers frequently swop clothes. Like swopping identities. 'I hugged her T-shirt when she went to take a shower,' one very happy young man told me of his new love. Wherever possible wear clean clothes every day next to your skin. Preferably of natural fibres which help the body to breathe more easily. Air suits, coats and other outer garments, which can't be changed every day, in the fresh air and send them to the cleaners regularly – then air them well to get rid of any chemical residue.

4. Environment

Keep your own environment clean. Being tidy in your home isn't the same as being clean! Given the choice, I go for clean over tidy every time, though both can be important. Household dirt holds old experiences. Clean it out. So do old possessions that have outlived their function and no longer please you aesthetically. It matters to consider the role of all your belongings in your life.

The wider environment is crucial to our well-being too. There is much debate about sources of electro-magnetic pollution, even chemical poisoning. Personally, I would try to avoid living beside an elec-tricity pylon, a power station, any kind of nuclear processing station, multiple electrified railway lines, a chemical factory, or in any other situation where the environment was likely to be exposed to electrical or chemical waste.

5. Air

Allow plenty of clean air to blow through the space you live in. Regularly. Also, make sure you have enough opportunities to breathe fresh air. (Or as fresh as possible.)

Spend time every day outside. You need to expose yourself to the sunlight, the wind and the weather. If you live in a city, then you may, of course, face more environmental challenges than someone who lives in the countryside. But it remains important that you spend some time, every day, outside.

Spend regular time out of the city, in the countryside. Where or when the opportunity presents itself, in a summer garden or at the beach, walk with your bare feet on the earth.

6. Exercise

Keep your body as mobile as you can, and in good shape – that means good working shape, not to some aesthetic fantasy. Body shape, strength and mobility are a very contentious area. My prime interest is sensitivity, function and balance.

The aim is to set the energy in your body in motion, gently, and to be conscious of the effects that moving or using your body creates. So swimming uses the muscles of your body and at the same time alerts you to the resistance of the water you are moving through and the way in which your body interacts with that resistance. T'ai chi, yoga, some martial arts, dance, even cycling, might all offer similar opportunities. Once you are aware of your body, and have a good sense of how your limbs move, it becomes easier to begin to notice factors affecting your balance.

Balance is a crucial aspect of energy development, because it affects perception. Only when you are truly balanced can balance in your heart be achieved (see Chapter Twelve). To be in balance, physically, means that your weight is equally distributed on either side of your spine, your feet are equally firm on the earth, and your arms and legs are easy and equal in their movements. Then, there is a good chance that you will be able to achieve energetic balance.

Our bodies are very sensitive instruments. What suits one body does not suit another. All bodies can be developed to be more sensitive. How to do that in each particular case varies. Some don'ts are clear. Be careful of over-muscling. Through working out, or a similar repetitive action, you can develop particular muscles to the point where they can actually interfere with your body's sensitivity. They become a sort of body armour. In the same way as excess fat can dull senses, and being too thin can sometimes leave you too vulnerable. However, the opposite is also true. Too little muscular strength can leave you feeling exposed and inadequate.

Don't be harsh on your body when it comes to exercise. I am unhappy about notions like 'If it doesn't hurt it isn't doing any good,' or 'You have to go past the pain to do any good.' Just the opposite is often true. You need to be gentle with yourself. We all have different exercise needs, and different needs at different times. Developing a supple and sensitive body is not the same as developing a well-muscled one. Though the two may coincide, up to a point.

7. *Pleasure*

Whatever you choose to do, it's important that you turn your attention to how you use your body, regularly, until it becomes almost second nature. You will be surprised how much you learn. But there is a final point that influences all the above. Pleasure. You need it.

Rigorous attention to all aspects of purifying or developing your energy can pay dividends. Pleasure will multiply those dividends many times. Is what you are doing pleasurable? Change whatever it is if it doesn't give you pleasure. Seek out pleasure and really enjoy it. Find pleasure in all you do. Which doesn't mean give up your chores. We all have chores, of one sort or another. But do them lightly. Walking – looking at the sky, enjoying the wind on your face, gardening, doing the shopping lovingly, enjoying cycling to work – all and any of those can be put to excellent use in allowing all your limbs to move, and then to settle afterwards. At all times, joy is your aim.

Questions to think about, practices to try

1. Make a list of half a dozen different places that make you feel differently. Try to pinpoint what you think the differences are, and any factors that you feel are involved in those

differences. See if certain kinds of places always make you feel well, and others often make you feel bad, or less happy. You may be able to identify a pattern, or you may not. Don't be disappointed if you can't.

2. Try holding an object that belongs to someone else. Notice the feeling it inspires in you. See if you can, in any way, feel someone else through something that belongs to them. Now, put it down and pick up something else, belonging to another person. Again, see if that feels any different. Don't look for a huge difference, or a very noticeable sense of the object's owner. Be aware that what may come to you may be very subtle, like a shade of a feeling. Again, don't discount any sensation, and don't be disappointed if you can't feel anything in particular. If you try to suspend disbelief you will be more successful.

3. Give yourself a bath, by candlelight, preferably with three candles, every evening before going to bed, for a week. You can shower in the morning if you like, but see how it feels to clean yourself of the day's vibrations before you go to bed. Make sure your sheets and nightclothes are clean at the beginning of the week, and change them after no more than a week. Or oftener.

4. Take up a practice to help move your energy. It could simply be doing what you already do, but becoming more conscious of your body in

its everyday routine. Or it could be another discipline altogether.

5. I often advise clients to work with colour, as a way of working with their emotions. Whilst I think colours have very particular meanings, I don't think that trying to understand exactly what your use of a particular colour means is as important as allowing yourself to experience the feelings that a given colour can inspire. So, my suggestion, especially at the start of a new phase of life, or a place where you feel stuck, is to make it a habit, every day for a week, or even two, to take out a box of crayons and do this exercise:

a. Choose two colours. Any two that you feel like. Use those two colours on a sheet of paper. Form is not important. You are not trying to draw anything in particular. In fact, you are not trying to make any shapes at all. Everything is second to putting the colour on the page, just where you feel like it, and in the way you feel like.
b. Cover ten sheets of paper in this way – quickly.
c. Then put down your two colours, and choose one colour. It can be one of the two you have been using, or a separate colour. Using that one colour, more slowly if you like, put the colour down on three pages, in succession. Again, form does not matter. But this time, allow yourself to work more

slowly, still without 'thinking'. Just do exactly what you want to do.

You may be surprised at the power this exercise has to loosen up your emotions. By your choice of colours, you are expressing yourself emotionally. But without having to analyse what you are expressing, or even to put a name to it. Putting the colours down is simply another way of giving vent to your emotions.

6. Think carefully about the sounds and particularly the music you subject yourself to. Wherever possible, do not tolerate 'junk' music, or continuous external sounds, but consciously choose the sounds that you experience. If you are listening to music, note how it makes you feel. If there is a lyric, think about what the words are saying. Even if you feel you are not consciously registering them, they will be making an impression on you. Do you agree with what the words say? Do you want to support them?

   Think about how the sounds you encounter in the everyday make you feel. Do you want to feel that way? How can you increase the component of sounds that support the way you want to feel, and decrease your exposure to those sounds that make you feel uncomfortable or worse?

7. Spring-clean the place where you live, and work, regularly. And your car.

8. Start noticing how and when you feel different. Not just because someone else has said something flattering to you! But because you are in a particular place. Or you are doing something that makes you feel good. Or there is an aspect of your environment that is affecting you. Begin to tease out these differences. And don't be surprised if your preferences change. They will.

Chapter Five

Your Energy Body

Renaissance paintings often show haloes. Wonderful circles of light around the heads of chosen individuals. It seems unlikely that Renaissance men and women were commonly able to see energy, but clearly the notion of light around the head, particularly of a holy person, has a long history. Traditionally, esoteric literature talks about auras, and the energy around the head. Perhaps they are the same quality?

Medical science confirms that, for example, electrical energy can be measured eighteen inches from the heart, and electromagnetic energy eight to ten feet away from the heart. And, of course, the pattern of that energy conveys information. Like many others, I have had experience in reading the subtle energy in and around others. It is possible to see, or sense, feelings and much more – including elements of the past and the future, in energy.

Everyday language easily acknowledges this reality. We describe someone as 'bright and cheerful', 'full of energy', 'a really dark character', 'in a black mood', or having 'a sunny disposition'. These are very accurate descriptions. Looking at someone who is in a gloomy mood, it is often possible to see, literally, a dark shadow over their features. In just the same way as someone who is in great spirits can radiate their good feelings.

Looking specifically at the energy around the human body, experience teaches that it conforms to a particular pattern, and that pattern is important. I can't give you the specific correlates – say, at what frequency which sort of energy appears – but I can show you by an example from nature what I mean. You can take this example as a model for a metaphor, or as a model for reality. In either case it is the sense of the different energetic functions that is important.

The energy around the body divides roughly into three bands, plus a fourth, the energy in the physical body. Lightning gives a clue. When lightning occurs, a series of energy events takes place. The first one is on the electromagnetic level; you don't usually see or hear anything. It's followed by the sound – a crackle – a different energy frequency, and is often clearly perceived by an observer. Then the flash follows, the manifestation of yet another energy frequency. Finally the effects on earth, if it strikes the ground, display yet another energetic process. All under the heading of lightning.

Human life can be divided in the same way into different energy bodies, with different characteristics. It is as if running outside and around the physical body, like three overcoats in ever increasing sizes, are three separate energetic layers. The emotional body, the mental body and the spiritual body. And, energy moves from the outside to the inside – from the spiritual through to the physical.

The Subtle Bodies

The spiritual body

Remember, energy is a spectrum and one state bleeds into another. Furthest away from the physical body is the spiritual body, the subtlest of the four. The energy and interchanges here are of a particular sort. It's the realm of intuition and spirit. The finest and the quickest. Intuition is far quicker than the speed of light.

The mental body

Next comes the mental body. Thought takes place here. The more developed the brain, the quicker the energy here. Trained minds often (but not always) deal with the thinking process much· more quickly than untrained ones.

The emotional body

Raw emotion is very different from thought. And slower. Often you may decide not to hold a feeling any longer, but it persists. That is because the energy of feeling is slower than the energy of thought.

The physical body

Finally, there is the physical body, the densest form of energy of the four. Matter. And the slowest. Energy here moves quite differently. As it is the last of the bodies, the energy from the other bodies eventually filters through to the physical body. That means problems that are registered, but not resolved, at the other levels can, eventually, create physical problems. This is where energy imbalances or issues may become part of the scope of medicine. And where conventional and complementary medicine have much to learn from one another. What is the effect, for example, of repeated emotional trauma on the physical body?

The development and interaction of the energy bodies follows a pattern.

Development and Workings of the Energy Bodies

Infancy and the energy bodies

The foetus growing in the mother's womb is bathed in her energy. Similarly, the mother experiences a unique relation to the foetus's energy. Medical science bears this out. A single pair of electrodes placed on the mother's stomach records both the mother's cardiac energy and the foetus's developing cardiac energy.

It is not until the early teens that a child's own subtle energy is fully established. Until that time, the child is very largely surrounded by the mother's energy. Which is a good reason why the mother's well-being, in all respects, is so important to the child's development.

As we grow up, the development and working of our energy body follows the same rules as our psychological and physical development, in broad terms. We all start by knowing the physical body and, at much the same time, the emotional body. We express and hold feelings from infancy, or before. Broadly speaking, mental constructs develop from feelings, or are imposed by social conditions or educational processes, and become part of the mental body. Particular problems that we encounter, and do not resolve, register in the affected energy and form obstacles, or issues, which may well spread. If we are to grow and achieve balance, they have, sooner or later, to be dealt with.

If you have unresolved emotional issues or troubles in your relationship with your parents, for example, they will affect not just the emotional body but the mental body too, and so your access to the spiritual. And, it goes without saying, they will interfere with the development of your intuition.

Likewise if you have a mental block – for example, you won't consider the reality of anything that cannot be logically proved – then your access to and attitude towards the spiritual will be severely affected.

In growth we aim to widen our perception, and consequently to purify and expand our energy body. This leads to change in the physical, emotional, mental and spiritual bodies. It is can be a fundamental part of 'the ache'.

The ache is often the result of your dissatisfaction with the limits of the mental and the emotional bodies. It is when the solutions of the mental and emotional bodies don't work. When the balance begins to shift. When you sense you don't know what. When you feel the pain and confusion that comes with all growth. You are being pushed into your spiritual body.

Recognising and dealing with bias

It is a process that will bring you face to face with the problems held in each layer of your energy body. In recognising and dealing with them, we have to consider one fact first – bias. It's a problem we all encounter. We are all biased, and it affects us in different ways.

Your mother may have curly hair and because you love your mother very much you may find you are biased to respond favourably towards women with curly hair. Life predisposes one to bias. Growing up always produces biases. Widening your perception involves overcoming your biases, which are usually a mixture of emotional, intellectual and even spiritual or physical issues. Of course, in energetic terms, you hold them in the various subtle energy bodies to begin with. Most are easy to perceive and overcome. Experience helps to detect bias and put it right.

For example, at a seminar recently the group was

working with colour, and I held up an offering in two colours. It was 12.45 p.m.

'What does this make you think of?' I asked. To me, the picture in red and green showed the artist to be very attached to the natural world but also to hold strong feelings or opinions. A second's silence. Then, an answer shot out, in a hopeful tone: 'A ham sandwich?'

It was nearly lunch time. The bias was clear. The physical body was overriding the evidence or input of the others.

Sometimes bias is not so clear. We often don't realise we are biased until something happens, or someone points it out. Then, of course, the healthy response is to address the bias. (Eat lunch.) In pronounced cases, if your experiences have left you unable to deal with your bias, even when it comes to your notice, the problem in your energy body is so severe that it is necessary to find help of some sort.

For example, in an extreme case, an overwhelming and vindictive parent figure could cause a child to grow into an adult whose emotional and intellectual bodies are so damaged that they are unable to deal with, or see clearly, authority figures. Obviously, the damage there would go beyond bias and would need treatment of one kind or another.

But in many cases, experience, thought, observation and practice help us overcome our bias, and reach towards an ever wider, more balanced perspective. In the process you are, of course, recognising and resolving issues held in the energy bodies. Each body presents particular challenges.

Resolving issues in the physical body

Many physical problems are not simply physical. For example, if you are experiencing an undiagnosed, unrecognised illness it will affect your feelings and thoughts. When you know your physical condition, you have the best chance of achieving emotional and mental authenticity, leaving the way clear for your spiritual development.

I say 'authenticity' because what is important is not resolving every physical, emotional or mental situation that faces you – that's impossible, but knowing and acknowledging exactly where you stand. You may not be able, for example, to heal completely the chest weakness you have had since infancy, but acknowledging its existence, and persistence, is crucial. Not only will it aid your physical healing, but, at least as important, it will help resolve your approach to the problem, and how you deal with it in your life.

Of course some, but not all, physical problems will be the result of energetic issues filtering through particularly from the emotional and the mental bodies. Many medical scientists believe that certain personality types are more prone to cancer. So, for example, if you internalise emotions repeatedly, creating an emotional pattern held in your energy, you may be more liable, depending on a huge selection of other factors, to develop a cancer. Emotional response could also play a part in, say, a heart attack (see Louise Hay's book, *You Can Heal Your Life*) and, in fact, most conditions.

However, you are not directly responsible for every physical condition that you face. For example, you are not directly responsible for an illness caused by drinking water that was accidentally polluted by the water authority. The people of Chernobyl were not individually guilty of thoughts and feelings that produced the contamination of their city. Notions of total responsibility for physical well-being can produce terrible, unnecessary guilt.

At the same time, healing your body does not necessarily mean overcoming all damage or illness. It means clearing the mental, emotional and physical energy of the body of any obstacles that could create or compound physical problems and opening the way for the fullest development of the spiritual body. Death, after all, is the failure of the physical body – but it can also be the flowering of the spiritual.

The emotional body

Dealing with emotions and emotional development brings many challenges. To begin with, feelings are characterised traditionally as belonging to the 'female', or 'feminine' domain. In a male-dominated society, our history inclines us to avoid feelings, and treat them with suspicion. Learning to balance emotions appropriately is a multi-layered task, which most of us work on through our lives.

As with all problems, emotional problems need to be recognised before all else so that they can be dealt with. Sometimes, it is relatively easy to do this. Or it may come with time, experience and practice – we have a particular problem, know it, and a peaceful, if sometimes painful, way forward emerges. That is usually the process of maturation, and it is why relationships are so important (see Chapter Nine).

Spiritual development will be governed by the extent to which you can resolve your emotional and mental issues, before really approaching, understanding and knowing spirituality. I say resolve, not solve, because, of course, not everything can be 'solved'. Resolving an issue is sometimes acknowledging it, and coming to live with the reality that it cannot be completely solved, or put to rights. But that acceptance, provided all the facets of the situation are accepted, is the place where we face ourselves, authentically, and the issue is resolved.

Of course, we all have good and bad patches where we feel our underlying issues are better or worse resolved, and wonder whether we need emotional help, or are really facing an issue of spiritual development. Emotional issues *always* need to be dealt with at a fundamental level before spiritual development can take place. Unfortunately this is sometimes not well understood, or may be confused.

Theories of self-development can suggest that developing your spirituality is a perfectly reasonable way to deal with all sorts of problems. And that is true. Awakening your spiritual intelligence changes your attitude to many aspects of your life. As well as the way you behave and interact with others. But achieving basic emotional well-being and competence is different.

In practice, usually it is not hard to recognise the difference. Take, for example, the case of Sarah who approached me, saying that coming to grips with her spiritual life and developing her intuition were the most important issues in her life.

As I talked to Sarah, it became clear that she had a very poor relationship with her husband, who was also not able to keep a job. Sarah herself did not work outside her home (nor did she have children) and was supported by her wealthy father with whom she had a very troubled relationship. But Sarah did not want to talk about her relationship issues, or her work/financial issues. She firmly believed her solution lay in progressing in the spiritual realm, and developing her intuition.

Emotionally, and practically, it was clear that Sarah had important issues to resolve. Basic issues. In attempting to focus on the spiritual she had convinced herself she had found a better or higher way of dealing with her problems. Actually, it was an attempt to escape the taxing, difficult and in some respects ordinary problems she needed to confront in the everyday.

I had to suggest to Sarah that spiritual development should not, and could not, be her primary focus at this time. First, she needed to deal with her emotional body and the issue of her family relationships, and find a means of supporting herself in the world. Needless to say, she found this very difficult to hear. She was determined to find a way to 'become more spiritual' without focussing on her emotional issues. Or her practical problems.

This approach is dangerous. All development needs a firm basis. In the days where religion was a creed, to be learnt, and belief was the cornerstone of spirituality, it mattered little how much attention you paid to, for example, the emotional aspects of your life. As long as you behaved in accordance with the tenets of your faith, which usually included obedience to religious authorities, you would be 'saved'. Which, of course, in many ways relieved believers of considerable responsibility, and led to situations where even murder and torture could be carried out in the name of spirituality, as they were, for example, by the Spanish Inquisition.

Spiritual intelligence results in a quite different relationship to the forces of spirituality. It starts with the understanding that you need to connect with spiritual forces yourself, not through a guru or priest. By accepting that tenet, you accept a new degree of responsibility.

It goes on to require that you deal with your emotional and mental issues – from watching for bias and correcting it, to acknowledging more serious problems if necessary. All this is essential to develop the perspective necessary to own spiritual intelligence, and also strengthen intuition. Of course, your spiritual intelligence will alter your relationship to emotional and mental issues – which continue to be part of all our lives, for life. But it is not a substitute for, say, psychotherapy. To acquire spiritual maturity, and its gifts, is to step into the place that requires you to be able and willing to deal with emotional issues independently.

Recently I had a letter from Robert, a man in his fifties who felt that he wanted guidance in going further in his spiritual work. Robert wrote that he had worked with his energy for several years, in meditation and practice, but for the last two years he had been stuck in a place where he was unable to interact with the outside world. He said he spent much time alone, in contemplation. He had a number of ways of describing his state, telling me for example that 'the kundalini has risen [an Eastern description of a form of energy and its supposed progress], leading to extreme sensitivity and often tears.' He made many references to complex esoteric texts. He said he could not bear to be with others. Nothing in his life had meaning any more. He asked for my help. At the very end of his letter he told me that his wife of thirty years had died two years ago.

Two years ago was when he said his symptoms started. It seemed clear that, before all else, Robert was suffering from grief at losing his long-term companion. It was also clear that he had great difficulty, a residual difficulty, in dealing with the emotional. It was much easier for Robert to display a 'stiff upper lip' – a traditional male response – to his emotional problems and translate them into issues of so-called spiritual development, rather than acknowledge his grief.

I debated how to suggest, gently, that – above all – he needed to deal with his feelings. Old-style religion might offer him comfort for his grief. To embrace spirituality through the route of spiritual intelligence, he needed to take responsibility in a different way. He had to deal with his emotional energy. Which means he had to acknowledge his grief before he could go further into his spiritual work and exploration of energy. He might choose to do that by working with it in meditation, finding others in a similar situation, accepting help from someone else with appropriate training; or perhaps simply acknowledging his feelings and 'allowing' them would enable him to work through the situation.

In both Robert's and Sarah's cases I felt they were looking to spiritual development to solve a range of problems, which perhaps was not appropriate. Sarah needed a job, and perhaps psychological help to sort out her relationship with her father and her husband. Of course she could – should, even – start to work with her energy, preparing the ground for spiritual development. But that meant, first and foremost, addressing the practical and the emotional. Robert needed to face his grief, not deny it by trying to concentrate on the development of his energy.

On the other hand, Howard, a family doctor, came to see me on his wife's recommendation – she was already a client. He was rather doubtful as to whether I could help, but he put his problem anyway. Howard felt an ache that he couldn't really define, and had doubts about so many aspects of reality. He wondered whether, despite marriage, two children and a good job, he needed psychoanalysis.

Now, it was absolutely clear that Howard had no more than the usual emotional ups and downs that afflict us all. I advised that he certainly didn't need psychotherapy – it was spiritual development he was craving. Shortly afterwards he took up a meditation practice that I suggested with great success. Three years later, he is making enormous strides, and his marriage in particular has benefited.

Understanding about psychotherapy

There is one more point about emotional issues. It relates to psychotherapy. Many forms of therapy rely on the patient using the therapist as a mentor, guide or even parent type of figure. This can be important and useful. However, opening to the spiritual development that I am outlining needs you to move beyond this stage.

Moving into spiritual maturity meant letting go of the old hierarchy. The first step is to realise that your connection is through yourself, not some guru. And this is a great deal more difficult to do than it seems, because the role of the guru, guide or parent figure is so deeply established in our psyches. And society. Of course, it goes back to childhood.

As a child it is very important that you have the security and guidance (sometimes more) of parents who are, in a sense, wiser and more powerful than you. But in reaching towards spiritual evolution, like maturity, you have to take responsibility for yourself. There is no 'father', 'mother' or 'guru' figure to turn to or rail against. You carry the responsibility for yourself. Of course there are teachers, but they are human and, essentially, no more or less than you (see Chapter Thirteen). In fact, we are all one another's teachers and healers.

Now, many psychotherapeutic situations depend for their success on the client submitting to the authority of the therapist. The therapist becomes a mentor whose interpretations steer the patient. In many therapies, accepting the therapist's interpretations is a crucial part of the treatment. To refuse is to 'resist'. Whilst this may be useful in treatment, that is where it belongs. It is directly at odds with the kind of independence needed to develop spiritual intelligence and come to spiritual maturity.

That means that while you are in psychotherapy, concentrating on the emotional body, it may not be appropriate to try to push forward your spiritual development, which requires a different sort of independence and responsibility. Of course, the point of therapy is to reach a more integrated state, and that would leave you well prepared for the next stage: extending into the spiritual. Provided you have reached a balance in the mental body.

The mental body

Western civilisation places the greatest importance on

the mental body. Our culture and our educational systems are geared to developing our mental faculties, over and above all others. The male dominance of recent centuries has led to the pursuit of science and reason – part of the mental body – at the expense of so-called female qualities, feeling and intuition. That is now changing. Though it is essential that what we aspire towards is balance. The mental, the emotional and the spiritual all have a role to play. Giving the emotional, say, dominance over the mental would only create yet another, further problem (as the dangers of superstition can make clear).

Meanwhile, the dominance of the mental has brought for many of us the great advantage of trained minds and the ability to handle a high degree of mental information. Vital qualities in dealing with superstition, and equally useful in handling the wider perspective of spiritual intelligence.

Problems of the mental body

Physicist and Nobel prize-winner Richard Feynman (1918–88) said in *The Meaning of It All*: 'Knowledge is of no real value if all you can tell me is what happened yesterday. It is necessary to tell what will happen if you do something – not necessary, but fun. Only you must be willing to stick your neck out.'

Unfortunately some clever men and women find the possibility of the current and coming expansion of human consciousness into the fields of spirituality and intuition enormously threatening. We all have experienced the disdain or derision of others attempting to ridicule, or destroy, our expansion in these areas. It is the response of fear. And it is a great pity because development in any area of the subtle energy body is an indication of the possibilities of development in others. So, a well-developed mental body is an indication of the depth available for the development of the emotional and spiritual bodies too.

Because of the approval and acclaim our society has awarded to mental achievements, a well-developed mental body often presents another problem. Power. Those who are especially intellectually able may take their ability as a sign of superiority and of an especial merit that entitles them to hold power over others. Or even bestow it. This is a problem both for those wanting spiritual development and those who intellectually deride it.

You cannot translate intellectual prowess and success into spiritual achievement by knowledge or will-power. It requires emotional development. Not just some emotional development. But the profound emotional development that opens the way to the understanding and values of the spiritual realm.

However, the mental body alone does not understand this. Significant intellectual development often goes hand in hand with emotional underdevelopment, making it very hard for those with a well-developed mental body, and the pride and ambition that sometimes go with it, to recognise and embrace true emotional development. Let alone the development of spiritual intelligence. They will often be fooled.

Simon was a university teacher of considerable status, with a brilliant mind. Mid-career, he had become interested in esoteric philosophy and began to incorporate it in his work. Soon his time became largely devoted to teaching spirituality and spiritual practice. His students and colleagues, dazzled by his intellect, quickly came to consider him an authority on his new field.

Unfortunately, his emotional development lagged behind his mental. Though his learning was immense it was book knowledge. Observing his practice, it was clear that he was unable to put into action the essence of what he taught. A problem for us all. But particularly puzzling for some of Simon's students, who sensed a discrepancy between the high standards he taught and the methods, attitude and tactics they saw him display. Others, of course, were not yet able to make this distinction.

However, because of Simon's position, and the respect he was held in for his mental prowess, few were willing to question his authority. And he himself probably had little idea of the problem, particularly since, like most people, his intention was to do good.

It is a common scenario with many clever people. The old adage – practise what you preach – is very true. But understanding what you preach is the first issue, and a skilful mind can often be an impediment. Where there are issues in the mental body, the subject can be completely unaware. More, their mental power inclines them to fight tenaciously and cleverly to retain or increase their position in the old hierarchy which they understand so well.

Of course, where significant mental development is combined with deep emotional experience, spectacular progress can be made in spiritual understanding; and this is exactly what is increasingly happening.

The spiritual body

This is the finest of the four bodies. Many of us are not even aware of it until the mental and the emotional are sufficiently developed, and we begin to feel the lack or the need for something – else. Others are luckier, and hold on to the sense of its presence which childhood often acknowledges automatically.

We know it by its quicksilver qualities. Some of its qualities become ours long before we understand, or even begin to own, the whole. The flash of inspiration. The intuition to do or not to do. The sense of knowing in an action or a feeling. The scent of magic. The knowledge of unity. The understanding somewhere, somehow, of a greater love than human passion. Those are the province of the spiritual body.

All aspects of the body, the physical, the emotional and the mental, are linked to the heart. But the spiritual body is particularly closely linked to the heart. It is only at a certain stage in the development of the heart that the way into the spiritual clears. Einstein wrote: 'A person who is religiously enlightened appears to me to be one who has, to the best of his abilities, liberated himself from the fetters of his selfish desires and is preoccupied with thoughts, feelings and aspirations to which he clings because of their supra-personal value.' Swop the word 'religiously' for 'spiritually' and those are all qualities of the perspective of the spiritual body, when the issues of the emotional and mental bodies have been dealt with. They are activated through the heart, and the development of the heart is part of the next chapter.

For you to think about and to try

1. Draw an outline of a figure, and around it draw three lines to represent your own emotional, mental and spiritual bodies. Don't consider where to draw the lines, simply put them down in the first places that come to you. When you have completed the drawing, think about the way you have spaced the lines and what that might indicate about your own beliefs about the comparative strengths and weaknesses of your emotional, mental and spiritual bodies.

2. Think of a way in which you have been biased in the past, how you discovered that bias and overcame it.

3. Think of a way you could be affected by bias now. Can you relate the issue to your emotional or physical bodies? For example, you may have had difficulty learning a foreign language or languages at school. Are you now hesitant about travel to foreign-speaking

countries? That could indicate a problem in the mental body, which infected the emotional body and left you with a mental and emotional weakness when it came to certain sorts of foreign travel. Does it perhaps make you feel vulnerable, inadequate or diffident? All limiting emotions. Think how some people, without a foreign language, handle travel of that sort without any misgivings. (Which does not mean you should not make every effort to learn to speak a foreign language!)

4. Identify one issue in your emotional body that you would like to change. It could be a fear of dogs. Or feelings of professional inadequacy. Or feelings of not being loved. Whatever, they will be specific to you – but probably any number of others will have the same feelings! Consider how these issues have 'bled' into other areas of your functioning.

5. Identify one issue that initiated primarily in your mental body, and that you would like to change. Again, consider how this has 'bled' into your wider functioning.

6. Choose a friend or member of your family and identify one predominantly emotional issue and one predominantly mental issue that seems to you to limit their functioning. Remember, because energy bleeds into other frequencies, it is unlikely that you will find issues that do not have an impact in all the subtle energy bodies simultaneously. Also,

remember that it is much easier to see problems in others than in oneself. You may well
be seeing a problem, or problems, that apply
to yourself.

7. Think of how you could expand first your
emotional energy, and then simultaneously
your other faculties. By a new experience,
perhaps? Listening to some music you would
not normally listen to, or going somewhere
different that would help expand the range of
your feelings – an exhibition, or even a new
country – or in some other way.

8. Try the same exercise for your mental energy.
Bearing in mind all the time that the effects
will not be solely mental, but emotional too,
perhaps even spiritual. Try going to a play
you would not normally choose, or reading a
book about an area that's new to you, or a
similar exercise. See how much you can draw
from the experience. You're aiming to expand
your understanding.

9. Find one new pleasure. Emotional, intellectual, spiritual, or any combination. It could be
a new taste, a sight, a feeling or something
quite other. Find it.

Chapter Six

Head, Heart and the Rest

When I reach this point in teaching a group, the effect it has can vary, but there is usually one constant. 'It's curious, it's like I know it, but somehow I wouldn't have put it together this way,' is how one management consultant described it to me. 'Of course, the stuff about energy is new to me, but most of it seemed, well, sort of obvious. I've been uneasy about gurus for a while. And the idea of the breakdown of the hierarchy that you started with, it really seems so obvious. It's easy to see in organisational terms, of course, that's what's happening. It was almost as if I knew what you were explaining – but I didn't.'

'But you did,' I countered. 'What I am saying to you is buried inside you already. All I am doing is helping you bring it to the surface, pointing it out to you so that you can see it – when you are ready. This isn't book learning in the usual sense that I am passing on to you. It's a deeper layer of organisation, one that is already contained inside you.'

(Some who follow modern physics might see this as a parallel to the idea that, at a deeper level, organisation is implicit in apparent chaos.)

We finished the session at the start of this book – the one that Jamie the journalist came to – with a short creative visualisation. I led the group through a series of images – I don't use meditation until later. At the end two of the participants were in tears. One of them, a highly skilled therapist, asked, through her sobs, 'Why is it so powerful? I'm used to group work, and we haven't really done anything but I feel utterly blown away.'

I smiled and explained that, working with a small number, my energy, and the combined energy of the group, is very powerful. My aim is to help everyone to raise their energy. Whatever it looked like – simple though my words often are – I had been working hard. It was as if I had been giving the entire group a healing session. I had been offering the clearest, purest vibration I could, trying to help all the group to awaken to a 'finer' energy, to enable them to move into their spiritual bodies.

'Many of you,' I continued, 'will be exhausted tonight – this will have stretched you in a way you may never have experienced before.'

'I can't imagine that,' exclaimed another member of the group. 'I feel so excited, you're putting words to everything I've had lurking in the back of my mind for years – but couldn't express. It's like coming home!'

And in case you are wondering, Jamie, the journalist, was hooked by the seminar and went on to complete the course – asking any number of direct, and increasingly profound, questions on the way. He was deeply affected, and is continuing to develop his spiritual intelligence.

Voice vibrations

Those who come to my seminars have an advantage, and a disadvantage, over those reading this book. I ask that before all in-depth seminars, if it is relevant (sometimes it isn't), participants listen to a tape of me teaching. The reason for this is partly to begin to familiarise them with the ideas and themes we will be talking about, but also because by listening they have to engage different faculties to, for example, reading.

When you listen to something, it is not just the sense of the words that you are assessing. Something else is happening too. You are being affected by the voice, and the frequencies of the sounds. What I would call the resonance, or the vibrations, or the energy of the speaker. By listening to a tape, those coming to seminars expose themselves to the vibrations of my voice, which will help them to go beyond their brains, and come to a different, more complete, understanding of the material.

It will be felt, and register not simply in the brain, or the mind, but in the entire energy system, which includes the emotional body, of the listener. I don't want those who come to my seminars simply to engage with their brains. Just as you would be missing out if you only engaged with this book with your brain.

Book learning is fine. But only up to a point. Often it develops only the mental body. Integrating the material, really making it part of you, is quite different. I want those I work with to integrate the work we do. To make it part of themselves. (See Where Do I Go from Here page 353, for where to buy tapes of my teaching so that you can experience the work in a wider way.)

Your Response

In responding to what I am saying, of course, I want you to use the power of your brain, or mental body. To think about it, examine it intellectually. I would! But I also want you to use your emotional body, to respond to the images the words convey, and the meaning they conjure up in you. Sooner or later, perhaps immediately, your spiritual body will also come into play – with your intuitive and higher response. If or when that happens, it will indicate that your heart is engaged. When the heart's energy comes into play appropriately, it shows that the rest of the body's energy is engaged too. That's not just the energy bodies, but the energy centres in the body, which are commonly called the chakras.

The chakras spell out in much greater detail what the energy bodies simply indicate. In fact, you can trace your development through the chakras (which doesn't necessarily mean you have to believe in them;

just use the idea to further your understanding, for a start).

The Chakras

Much has been written about the chakras – the supposed energy centres actually within the body. There are seven main chakras, to which most attention is directed, and several smaller or other ones too. My explanation of their functioning comes from my own observation and experience. Others have come to similar conclusions – though there may be some differences. (See Caroline Myss's work in Further Reading, page 355.)

I don't believe there is one definitive, correct version of this information. In my work, I find the one that I hold is correct for me. But if someone else told me that something slightly different seemed right for them, I wouldn't contest it – but I wouldn't want to use it either.

Real or not?

Indian and Chinese texts have recorded the existence of the chakras for thousands of years. They are an integral part of the traditional medicines of the East. Interestingly, the Indian and Chinese theories differ slightly. But that does not seem to affect the efficacy of the systems – which include acupuncture – based on their existence.

Fundamental to acupuncture is the idea that the

body is criss-crossed by meridians, or lines along which energy travels. These so-called meridians cannot be seen or measured by any Western scientific method. Because of that, for many years acupuncture was dismissed by Western medicine. The argument ran: science can't establish or measure meridians. Therefore they do not exist. Therefore acupuncture has no status, and should not be considered. But the argument has disintegrated because acupuncture was shown to work in so many cases. Studies prove, for example, that anaesthesia can be achieved by acupuncture, and a whole range of curative effects too. Real effects, not just placebos. But, of course, it does not prove the existence of chakras, or meridians. Only that they provide a communications map through which acupuncture works. And the map and reality should never be confused.

Western mainstream medicine has not embraced the notion of the chakras in any way. However, medicine today incorporates certain relatively new findings which, in some ways, could be seen to relate to various aspects of chakra functioning. To explain.

Each of the seven main chakras is located in and related to a different area of the body. So, the third chakra relates to and is situated around the middle of the body, in the area of the stomach. The fourth chakra, the heart, is located in the centre of the chest, and relates to some of the attributes of the heart. These chakras do not necessarily govern all the physical functions of the areas where they are located, but they have connections to many of them.

In the same way, modern medicine recognises that the functioning of various areas are not simply organised or allocated by or from the brain. For example, the 'brain in the gut', or 'the mini-gut enteric brain', is a well-accepted view that means exactly what it says. So, gut functioning is seen as governed by an organisational process, or brain, also lodged in the gut. (See *The Second Brain*, page 356). A parallel, perhaps, in some ways, with the third chakra?

When it comes to the heart, neurocardiology embraces the concept of the 'little brain of the heart', which attributes cognitive and sensory – that is, feeling and thinking – functioning to the heart. Again, this suggests a comparison with the heart chakra. (And in considering the all-over defences of the body, Ed Blalock working at the University of Alabama has gone further than the chakras and come up with the concept of the immune system operating like a sixth sense.)

None of that means there is any kind of medical proof of the existence of the chakras. But what it does suggest is that modern medicine may be coming towards recognition, in its own terms, of features of the functioning of the human body that could relate to observations and descriptions made in other cultures, at earlier times – different metaphors.

But whether chakras represent physical reality or not is relatively unimportant – what matters is the highly significant role that chakras, or the metaphor of chakras, play in understanding the development of spiritual intelligence.

The overview

The chakras are like junction boxes. They take in, send out and process energy. Each centre concentrates on a different range of the energy spectrum. Which means they take in energy of a particular frequency, generally getting 'higher', or 'finer', as you progress up to the crown chakra at the top of the head.

At the same time, the different frequencies that each chakra works with also correspond to a different area of experience or functioning in our individual lives. Also, to a different area of functioning in our collective or social existence.

Perception, and perspective, are crucial. The wider and more able to open the chakra, the greater your perspective on the area that it relates to. In other words, you will see and understand more of the issues related to that chakra's functioning, which will go on to affect your view of the whole. Obstacles in or around a chakra affect your relations to the area governed by that chakra, spiritually, mentally, emotionally and physically too. For spiritual and intuitive development, and physical health, the chakras must be as free of obstacles as possible, and as open as possible. And in balance.

Also, the more open the chakras, the more able you are to respond to the changing vibrations coming from the outside world. Most importantly, the change in vibrations that is causing the downfall of the hierarchy (see Chapter Three).

Understanding the chakras can offer a route map to developing spiritual intelligence. Though, of course, your spirituality can develop without your having ever heard the word 'chakra'. And you can achieve, and keep in, excellent health without understanding anything about chakras either.

Most of the lower chakras function in some form, perhaps blocked or partly open, most of the time. But in some cases they may not function at all. The functioning of them all changes significantly as the fourth chakra, the heart, becomes increasingly involved and open. It enables the others to open even further, which changes their perspective in the areas they govern. A change of the same order takes place with the involvement of the crown chakra, on the top of the head. In development, one or other chakra usually plays a dominant role. As spiritual intelligence grows, that changes.

The base chakra

The lowest main chakra on the body is the base chakra, situated on the perineum, between the anus and the genitals. All issues of home and fundamental stability in the world reside here. It is about your base in the world. In a collective sense it also relates to your connection with a small, intimate, interdependent group of individuals. Your immediate family, for example. If primitive man functioned as a very small subsistence-oriented group, he would have been largely focussed on base issues. If that was so, his behaviour could have been dominated by the base chakra, the need to survive and protect his base.

Similarly if today, for example, you are concerned about creating or moving home, or unable to settle to a job to give you the basic means of supporting yourself, those are the sort of issues which would, or could, be taking their toll at your base. Disputes within your family, or separation from your family group, would also show at the base chakra.

Jane came to see me deeply distressed about the state of her marriage. She and her husband were talking about moving home and at the same time about separating. They were debating whether to try living in a new home together, or to move to separate new homes. 'I don't feel as if I have a home anywhere,' is what she said. In Jane's view she no longer felt she had a base.

It was a very clear example of base chakra issues, relating to marriage and home, coming together. Of course other issues and other energy centres were also involved, but because the base was so crucially implicated Jane felt particularly destabilised and unsure where she belonged.

Physically in the human body, base chakra issues often, but not always, reveal themselves in problems related to the legs, and sometimes the hips and buttocks. Recently I saw a woman who had seriously injured her foot. The injury came at a time when she was considering a move of home and job. It was compounded by her being offered a job that she felt she ought to have been very pleased by – it would improve her standing in the world – but that really she did not want to take. Her injury meant she was forced to take some rest – not to stand at all – and rethink the direction of her career and position in life. In other words, her base.

Another professional who came to a seminar I was giving was unable to sit down comfortably. He had been in the same job for several years and had accumulated much expertise. But he felt a growing concern about the work he was doing, and a sense of not knowing where he belonged any longer. Partly to deal with that he was investigating a spiritual path – trying to give himself a sounder base in life. The particular spiritual path he was trying to follow required that he meditate sitting cross-legged on the ground, for long periods of time. Though he followed this programme assiduously, he had not seen the results he longed for.

At around the same time his hip joints started to hurt, particularly when he sat down, and he began to find sitting, in any situation, very difficult. It seemed to me he was being urged to move! To take his weight – metaphorically and in reality – on his feet and move. With regard perhaps to both his job and his spiritual search.

Overall, a strong base chakra will mean you are comfortable in your work, and the place you live. It will also govern your relationship with your immediate family. A strong base chakra helps put family relations on a firm footing. If, however, your base chakra is far stronger or more important to you than any other, you will consistently put your family's welfare and well-being above any other concern. You will not be able to empathise with a significantly larger group, or indeed show real concern for the welfare of others outside your immediate family group.

The functioning of this chakra, and therefore the entire individual if it is allowed to take a dominant role, is governed by the primitive fight or flight response. It will subject the individual it rules to the dichotomy of power or powerlessness. They will experience their feelings in relation to others in terms of being powerful or powerless, and when challenged will respond in fight or flight mode – driven by fear.

As with all the chakras, the smooth functioning of the base chakra is essential. Of course, obstacles or issues occur from time to time. Growing spiritual intelligence helps in understanding and resolving them from an ever wider perspective. As we gain greater energetic clarity, base chakra functioning is increasingly influenced, and with the application of spiritual intelligence, it can be harmonised with the whole to bring out the best aspects, and allow the others to recede.

Then, chakras are associated with colours. I usually see the base chakra as yellow. However, different individuals work with different series of colours, and yellow may not be the appropriate colour for you. If you choose to try the meditation I describe in Chapter Seven you may find yourself working with another colour that suits you better.

The second chakra

The second chakra is called the sexual chakra. It is situated halfway between your genitals and your belly button. As the name makes clear, all sexual issues are dealt with here. In following sexual desires, you will be led by the second chakra. But that's not all. Friendship, possessions or material gain, a peer group or interest group, are all concerns of the second chakra, and may dictate behaviour accordingly. Think how often material success or involvement goes hand in hand with particular attitudes towards sexuality or increased sexual activity.

The second chakra corresponds to a larger group than the immediate or extended family. It is concerned with the interests of the group or groups you choose to identify or unite with. This could be a club, a profession, a society, a political party, even a support group of some kind. With the power of communications today, membership can range from less than a dozen people to a significant percentage of the population in certain circumstances.

It is a chakra that is enormously important in our society today. This is the chakra, or power centre, many people work from when their lives are dominated by a particular interest group, as well as by their own sexual and material interests.

In some cases we are happy to admit, or even proud to claim, that our actions are driven by a group. For example, if it is a professional group, or a support group. We feel it is quite legitimate to confront the outside, greater world through the organisation that represents us, and it can be very useful indeed. History shows endless cases where group action has played an important part in re-balancing interests – take much (but not all) trade union activity, for example.

At other times it is difficult to admit that we are being led by a group interest, that we are doing something because it is in the best interests of a 'club' we belong to. Usually, in that case, we will claim that at the same time it is not really against some more general interest. Or, indeed, that our 'club' even serves the greater human interest.

Again, history abounds with examples of ruling cliques who believed or claimed their actions were for the greater good, while simultaneously, of course, serving their own interests first. The Ku Klux Klan is one example. The behaviour of the white ruling class in South Africa during the apartheid regime is another. It is a good example of a 'club', the whites, acting to protect their interests and claiming it was in the interests of 'separate development' – the greater good. It is not uncommon.

Voters, and particularly women in the USA, faced a real dilemma, which many of them were only too aware of, in the character of President Clinton as revealed in the Monica Lewinsky affair. Because of his personal behaviour and the attitude it revealed, could the example presented by the president be regarded as going against the interests of women? If that was the case, the problem deepened for

Democrats. Was it better to have a Democrat – 'one of us' – although he disrespected women, than a Republican in the White House?

For those largely influenced by the second chakra, the needs of the interest group would have meant that above all else it was important for Democrats to keep a Democrat president in power.

They might also, of course, have felt that his over-all records and abilities justified this course. Many Democrats argued that his actions on behalf of women in general outweighed his behaviour in his personal life. (It's OK to mistreat your own dog as long as you support animal welfare charities.)

People join together in 'clubs' for wide and varied reasons of self-interest – often from the desire for commercial power, political power or support in varying ways. This need not be detrimental. On the contrary. But all too often, when the second chakra takes command, it puts your interests and your group's above all else. And, usually, the group plays a part in your personal success.

This can put friendship, and relations with a peer group, for example, before issues of truth or justice. Some groups even appear to make this explicit. The Mafia, for example. Or perhaps the Freemasons in Britain – though their strict rules of secrecy make it difficult to know. Just as many communities, on the basis of social status, ethnicity, income or even aspiration, protect their own.

Friendship is very important. But when ties of friendship or loyalty come before those that support a greater Truth, an impartial Justice and Love that is dispassionate, it is always clear evidence that the second chakra has taken control and is imposing its limited vision.

In the same way desire for sex or material gain may come before all else. And because, like the base chakra, the second chakra is ruled by the primitive forces of power or powerlessness, the second chakra's methods may be quite ruthless. Something we are loath to admit.

Anyone with any knowledge of a dealing floor in a financial trading house, or the history of Wall Street in the 1980s and 1990s, will know only too well the stories of great consumption and acquisition, often linking money, sex and food too in a very basic way. The year 1999 ended with a typical sex and money scandal, with a respected Wall Street figure, also a supposedly happy family man, being accused of passing insider information to his porn-star mistress – who then passed it on to another lover too.

But we need all the chakras to be in good functioning order and balanced. When a balanced part of the whole, the sexual chakra has wonderful power to add to our joy, fulfilment and well-being in life. And to order our relationships in the groups that are essential to the smooth running of society.

That's as a balanced part of the whole. So often today people speak of acting 'from the heart', justifying or awarding many actions with that epithet. Unfortunately, much more often, it's the sexual chakra and the interests of the sexual chakra – their group, or the ideas or interests of their group – that are really in command.

At the same time, what is also true is that, in some way, so many of us recognise the need to act from the heart. Though, often, we don't know what that actually means – let alone how to do it. So we may cover self-serving actions with a sentimental blanket, and say they are done 'in love', or 'from the heart', when, in fact, they support only a smaller group, or (a part of) your family, and/or are directly aimed at increasing your interest group, personal possessions or power. The wider perspective that so many of us aspire to can transform this position.

Not long ago, I was consulted by a client, Paul, who had been through an acrimonious divorce, and had then married a much younger second wife who presented him with a baby son. A conference organiser, specialising in environmental work, he repeatedly emphasised the good, disinterested work he was doing. He spoke in flowery terms of his love for mankind and desire to better the common lot.

He said he wanted to be 'working on his heart' and his relationship with 'mankind' and 'the forces of the universe'. When I asked about his former wife, who I knew had suffered greatly in the divorce and now lived in reduced circumstances, he would not discuss the subject. His new young wife confided that she was concerned because her husband was working so hard to provide for the future and education of their baby and, of course, the sibling they were hoping for.

Now, this is a good example of being dominated by the second chakra. Though Paul might feel his 'love for mankind' to be sincere and from his heart, I would contend that his main motivation came from his second chakra. He was driven by love and sexual ties to his new wife and their baby, and a desire to provide for the new family's material comfort.

He had been able to close his mind entirely to his old reality – his former wife and former family unit. I suggested it was easy to claim love of mankind, but much harder to love those immediately around you. Especially in cases where sexual ties have broken down, and compassion – the true province of the heart – must guide relationships.

It was hard for Paul to understand that his desire to expand his notion of spirituality, and his intuition, could relate directly to practical issues, like concern for his ex-wife, mother of his older child. He had been hoping – innocently – to further his material position in the world using spirituality as if it was a sort of marketing device. Again, it seemed a case of the second chakra masquerading as the heart.

'Old boy networks', trade unions, and any group who come together for mutual benefit, can show the traits of second chakra dominance. On the other hand without an active, well-functioning second chakra, sexual balance, part of living in the world and not just the act of sexual intercourse (see Chapter Twelve on balance), cannot be achieved. And, as we are all both male and female, achieving balance is crucial. Just as our relations to groups are crucial, living in society. And our material well-being. The introduction of the heart, and the heart's wisdom, has a profound effect on the second chakra, widening and transforming it.

As for colour, for me, the second chakra is a medium blue.

The third chakra

The third chakra is the digestive chakra, and I work with it as red. Here more sophisticated issues – ideas, emotions, situations – are taken in and digested, as well as they can be. Ideas can often be 'indigestible'. Feelings can cause physical indigestion. Fear can 'sit on' or 'grip' your stomach. Situations can be more than you can 'stomach'.

Situated where it is, covering the stomach, the third chakra focusses on all matters that are taken in, which makes the digestion of food and drink an important physical correlate of the third chakra's functioning. Again, this chakra responds to the primitive emotions of power and powerlessness, which arouse fear. For example, overweight or physically large people sometimes use their size to exert power over others. But the opposite is also true. Some people are compelled to cultivate body mass as a protection – they overeat and put on weight basically because they are afraid and need to feel well covered. We sometimes call it comfort eating.

Grief, or the first flush of romantic love, or emotions that we cannot, or do not want to digest, or that overwhelm us, often prevent us from taking in and digesting food. All the province of the third chakra. Interestingly, as social complexities multiply, food regimes, food fads, diets and food-related illnesses all mushroom.

For example, malabsorption is considered a relatively common problem in some circles. It is the notion that the sufferer is not able to extract the necessary nutrients from his or her food, and it may be a relatively new diagnosis. Whether it is accurately applied or not, the number of people who feel it might apply to them is significant. They represent a group who believe that however rich or well-supplied their environment, they are no longer able to absorb what they need from it. And, of course, being a third chakra issue, fear and feelings of powerlessness could also be present.

Then, the third chakra relates to a much larger group, a city, state or even a nation. This is the place where ideas come to be considered as valid for more than the immediate interest group – which could still be a relatively small number of people, or a much larger one.

Bree, an experienced alternative practitioner, came to see me complaining of, among other things, digestive problems. She was from Eastern Europe and there was much racial fighting in her homeland. Bree's own loyalties were deeply divided, with relatives from different regions. As she was expansive and warm-hearted by nature, her instincts were to love all her fellow countrymen, but she felt compelled to choose sides and could not. Along with her distressing dilemma came a range of 'stomach' problems. To me, it all spoke of the third chakra being particularly affected.

Introduction of the influence of the heart chakra changes the functioning of the third chakra very much for the better. We all know that a solitary meal eaten in sadness has a very different effect to a happy meal shared in joy with others.

Which brings us to the heart.

The heart chakra

The fourth chakra is, of course, the heart, which I see as green. So much is attributed to the heart and so little is understood. To begin with, the heart chakra is closely related to the organ, the heart.

The heart and medical science

In the past, medical science has suggested that the role of the heart is little more than a dumb pump. When the prospect of heart transplants first provoked some reaction, medical science rejected the so-called philosophical objections it aroused. And the advances in organ transplants, with the prospect now even of transplants with animal hearts, seem to confirm the view in many quarters that the heart is an interchangeable spare part, whose real function is to pump oxygen around the body. It has, some assume, nothing to do with, for example, emotions, values or any other higher functions.

Poets over the centuries have thought differently:

> *My heart aches, and a drowsy numbness pains*
> *My sense, as though of hemlock I had drunk.*
> John Keats, *'Ode to a Nightingale'*

Keats expresses what our language has always acknowledged – emotions as seated in the heart. And the role of those feelings in affecting our entire body and well-being.

New medical research is beginning to challenge the traditional scientific view of the heart, suggesting that perhaps there could be more to poetry's view. For example, the heart has been shown through measurement to produce forty to sixty times more electrical energy than the brain, and about a thousand times more electromagnetic energy. The electrical activity from the heart can be measured in every cell of the body. In other words, not only does the heart pump blood, carrying nutrients around the body, but it pumps patterns of energy, and therefore information, to every cell as well (see *Advances: The Journal of Mind–Body Health*, Russell and Schwartz, page 355).

Some scientists are beginning to think that because it is the strongest power force in the body, the heart may coordinate many other body systems, operating in tandem with the brain, with which it is in close communication. As an organ, the heart may well set the tone for the actions, output and health of the rest of the body. This notion is a radical departure from previous theories which suggest that the brain alone largely controls body.

It could also be support for the role of the heart chakra, and the crucial part it plays in spiritual intelligence. Of course the heart chakra is not at all the same as the organ, the heart. But in the same way as there is a close relationship between the third chakra and the stomach, and between the second chakra and the sexual organs, so there is a close relationship between the heart chakra and the heart. The heart chakra can affect the functioning and the well-being of the whole body, just as it is beginning to be argued the heart can.

In *The Heart's Code*, author Dr Paul Pearsall explores the stories of heart transplant patients who appear to take on some of the characteristics, and indeed memories, of the donors whose hearts they received. Drawing support from the new science of energy cardiology, he paints a picture of the heart as thinking, feeling, remembering, loving, even hating. Certainly communicating information and memory to every cell in the human body. It is a model far closer to the heart chakra than the 'dumb pump' many have long accepted.

Dr Pearsall does not only argue that these effects take place within the body, but that the heart's energy can be passed on to others. In a similar way, the heart chakra affects relations and energetic links with others. In fact, one of the most important characteristics of the heart chakra is its relation to all other living creatures.

The heart's domain

The heart chakra's domain is the world. That is the real key to understanding the heart chakra. Its affiliation goes beyond the particular, the small group, or the interest group, or even the city or the nation. The love and understanding that the heart offers extends to all. The heart chakra does not love one group at another's expense, or one individual whilst at the same time blotting out everyone else. The wider the heart chakra, the wider its ability to affect the functioning of all the other chakras, and so all your attitudes and actions, particularly your relations and connections to other people. Which is why it is the root of spiritual consciousness, and it offers the gift of a true spiritual perspective.

The heart chakra has nothing to do with sexual love. Romantic love can play a role in opening the heart chakra because it can open the eyes to the world – not just to the loved one – with the vision that is special to love. An open heart chakra does not mean being able to love one other person. Love – from the heart chakra – is not about a connection to another for your simple mutual or personal benefit. At its widest broadest level, which is the spiritual level, love is the quality that exists connecting the whole.

But remember how the feeling of being 'in love' often leads you to feel 'in love with the world', and everything seems wonderful. Which is exactly why love for another may play an important role in opening the heart chakra with its connection to the universal group. It is a quality that recognises 'God' or spirit in the other and reaches out to that quality, at the same time seeing it everywhere. In doing so it goes beyond the confines of 'the twosome', usually the domain of the second chakra or the base chakra. The heart loves the whole. And the way in which it loves is very particular.

Qualities of the heart chakra's love

The heart chakra is ruled by compassion – the essence of love at the spiritual level. But what does that mean? It's not sympathy, in the way it's usually understood – feeling sorry for someone else. It's closer to empathy, and more. It will do its utmost to do no harm. The heart can stand in the other's shoes and know what they are feeling, and yet retain a quality of detachment and along with it wisdom. Which is why it is so closely linked to intuition.

It is not sentimental. The heart chakra sees a wider picture. It has no place for ambition, rivalry, arrogance, greed, pride, judgemental attitudes and a host of other qualities, which plague us in the day to day. The words are easy to write: 'The heart chakra has no place for ambition or rivalry.' Living the reality is quite different. So often we think, or even claim we are acting 'from the heart' or 'in the best interests of all', or some other lofty expression, when it is simply ambition, or another, lower set of aspirations.

And the heart chakra does not need recognition. The heart is content to do and to know its own action. The heart knows humility. A hard lesson. It does not need the reinforcement or satisfaction of others' praise or recognition. Flattery can't touch the heart chakra. Which makes it particularly powerful. The values the heart knows are the values it must, and will, follow.

The heart chakra also knows the powers of discipline, patience, perseverance, endurance, wisdom and generosity. Old-fashioned virtues, not easily achieved. And then it knows joy. A light magical joy that is not attached to material success, recognition or achievement. It's a joy that goes beyond emotional attachment to another, that's present in the quality of the air, a view, the energy of the morning, the silence of the night, a colour, a leaf in the wind. And more.

But they come together. Joy without discipline is of little use. It's not effective, its actions are not appropriate, and its results will not bear fruit. Likewise, endurance without joy is a stony road that will not deliver the blessings of the heart chakra. All of which is why opening, or standing in the place of, the heart is so rarely achieved.

Many years ago I attended a workshop on spirituality – one of the few I went to in my search. It was at the time that I was trying to come to terms with the opening which had brought another dimension of reality flooding into me through meditation. The workshop didn't make much sense. Perplexed, but always open to the possibility that I simply didn't understand, I asked the leader a question. (I forget what now.) To me, his answer seemed garbled and, well, puzzling. But I said nothing further.

At the coffee break that followed, my neighbour came to speak to me. I was glad to talk to a fellow searcher, as I assumed her to be. And someone whom, from her few comments in the morning, I took to be well intentioned. She started, her voice trembling slightly, by saying that she was a healer, and had been for several years. Then, her tone rising slightly, she asked me what I knew about spirituality. When I replied, 'Very little,' it seemed as if it was the opening she was waiting for.

'I'm going to tell you this, in love, from the heart,' she announced, her voice stronger now, 'it's for your own good. You are in a dark place! You're here to learn from Martin [the workshop leader], you can't go asking him questions like that! You have to listen, to be humble – it's terrible the way you were talking to him! Questioning him! When you don't have a fraction of his knowledge, not as much wisdom and love as he has in his little finger! I'm telling you this in love – you're going very wrong.'

Needless to say, this onslaught left me utterly per-plexed. But, even then, I was quite sure that it was not 'in love', and certain that it did not come 'from the heart'. Now I know that it was probably the second chakra – allegiance to the group – that was in command. However good my neighbour thought her intentions to be.

Applying reason and logic can never be wrong. Being led only by those qualities is a grave shortcoming, though. Using the love of the heart chakra does not mean abandoning any form of reason. It is a love that is not opposed to the 'brain', or the power of intellect or understanding, but knows it, and a wider reality too. In the same way as some scientists are beginning to suspect that the organ, the heart, may work with the brain, not under the brain, in communicating with and ordering the functioning of the rest of the body.

Increasingly I am hugely gladdened by the number of others I see really trying to come from the heart. Trying to link to the values of spirituality for the benefit of all, not simply for personal advantage. Or personal advantage disguised as 'for the benefit of all'. All through history every religion has taught love and compassion. But usually only towards friends or believers – a very different behaviour has been displayed towards 'enemies'. The challenge of this millennium is to move into the heart chakra, that observes no boundaries. To learn and display the love that is universal.

Freedom from fight or flight

Because of the qualities it knows, finally, when the heart is truly engaged, we are liberated from the crude mechanism of fight or flight, power or power-lessness, and the fear that drives it. The heart does not respond by needing to fight, or to flee. It responds with compassion. It has a breadth of vision, with a love and a detachment that those who do not know the heart's deeper reaches often do not understand. Occasionally, the heart chakra's compassion might indeed mean fighting, especially if it is to protect others – but it will be a different choice to the primitive fighting response of the lower chakras.

Open versus closed

As with all the chakras, it is not a question of the heart chakra being simply 'open' or 'closed'. Rather, as it opens or widens, your perspective on the issues that it governs increases, and as your understanding grows, your behaviour changes. It's very unlikely that you will be able to foresee or predict the extent of this change.

As with all shifts of perception, you cannot see what they reveal until the shift takes place. Which is why you can talk about the process, read about it, even teach it and satisfy those who also do not have personal experience of it, but that is quite different from knowing it because you have been there. And in some sense, once you know it you always know it.

The heart chakra's effect on the lower chakras

As the heart chakra widens and clears, so it affects all

the lower chakras. It changes their perspective by introducing a breadth of vision and compassion. So, for example, an open heart might actually strengthen the marriage and physical relations of a couple by its effect in transforming the second chakra. But at the same time, it would inspire a sense of connection to, and concern about, all others. Not just their colleagues, family or social set. In the same way, an academic, who worked previously from the third chakra, would find when the heart chakra opened that his attitude to the world and his fellows significantly altered. The quality of all his important relationships would be affected, and the underlying assumptions would be subtly changed.

The heart chakra and intuition

Because of its qualities, the heart chakra cannot but contribute enormously to intuition. Intuition can vary from a sudden inspiration to take a different turn, to knowing the workings of another's mind, to understanding a situation without studying it, to knowing what to do in a given circumstance.

In all cases probably the greatest problem in using one's intuition is the question of whether it is simply bias operating. Does 'My intuition told me it was time to come home' really mean 'Actually, I was afraid to go on but couldn't admit that'? Or does it reflect a deeper sense that knows your presence at home is vital now? Likewise, in thinking about others, do you have an intuition that someone you have met has malignant intentions, or are you simply afraid of her or his competence?

The heart chakra brings the surest resolution of these issues. The more fully the heart is engaged, the deeper your compassion, the surer your ability to be detached, the wider your love. The clearer and more developed your energy below the heart will be, the greater your ability to respond to the information in the energy around you. The development of your intuition is the natural result of these qualities, and at the heart chakra comes the start of the real breakthrough.

A warning on intuition

In the early stages, before the heart chakra is properly engaged, it is easy to become muddled about intuition and the need to find or advance oneself in various forms. As in Anne's case.

Anne had no job and was lost. She wanted to develop her intuition to be clearer about herself, where to go and what she wanted in life. She was receiving social security and had given up looking for work. She had convinced herself that if she developed her intuition, she would know exactly where to go for work, and what kind of work would suit her.

I suggested that this was in fact a delaying technique which prevented her from taking responsibility for the basic building blocks of her life. At the same time it diminished her self-esteem and was making her the responsibility of society, that is, the rest of us.

All circumstances that were likely to prevent, rather than support, the development of her intuition and spirituality.

Anne had not thought of her situation in that light, though she bitterly resented the humiliation involved in receiving social security benefit. But she had persuaded herself that it was necessary while she developed her intuition.

Intuition cannot be deliberately cultivated for 'self-advancement', or even to help you know yourself better, though that is a great side effect of coming to know the values of the heart. Similarly, I was never pleased when clients tried to make me use my intuition to give them business tips, or 'winning information' – in other words, information to help them advance materially.

Intuition is a part of spiritual intelligence – which is itself an evolutionary step in knowing and dealing with the universe. Inevitably, developing spiritually and intuitively leads to knowing oneself, what one wants, what to do or where to go, better. Or differently.

Material gain sometimes occurs. What almost always happens, though, is a change in attitude towards the material – which the involvement of the heart chakra would predict. As a result, you may become more aware of your material responsibilities and better able to fulfill them. Or, less driven by material concerns and more centred on other aspects of your existence in the world. And the ache will leave you.

The throat chakra

Above the heart chakra is the throat chakra, which plays a very important role in expressing the feelings of all the chakras. It's the channel through which the consciousness of the energy you are working with is given a voice. In other words, your throat chakra can express some very basic ideas if you are driven by the base chakra, and some sublime ideas if you are driven by the heart. In physical terms, throat troubles are almost always related to the truth, or authenticity, of what you are expressing.

At the same time, when the throat chakra is clear and wide open, it has another role in 'speaking your intuition'. You can sometimes find your throat chakra surprising you with what you say!

Like the third eye which follows, the throat chakra is not tied to the primitive fight or flight response. It is simply tied to the chakra or chakras that are driving you.

The third eye

Above the throat chakra, midway between the eyes on the brow, is the famous third eye. It is the centre of a more developed form of intuition – almost always best used for the benefit of others. Some of us are led to do this work, others are given other gifts. Like the throat chakra, the third eye has no values of its own, but reflects the values of the heart below it, and the crown chakra above it.

Which is, in part, why there are particular dangers associated with the third eye. Some of its qualities can, as with all the chakras, be accessed without reference to the other chakras. To open your third eye without first opening your heart puts you at risk of doing great danger to yourself, and to others, by the misuse of your intuition.

It is the use of intuition for power. Especially power over others. Power and fear are the primitive currencies of the chakras below the heart. When the third eye is open, or open enough, and you are driven by the lower chakras alone, you will have the potential for the misuse of intuitive power, particularly playing on the fear of others. You become vulnerable to the desire to misuse the third eye because of a desire for power. Others are vulnerable to you because of their fear. This dynamic is the basis of the so-called dark arts, or black magic.

Only when the third eye is accessed via the heart, in the orderly progression of opening the chakras consecutively – making sure that each is properly supported by those below it – then, and only then, will the third eye work in the service of the Light, the positive forces of spirituality.

Sadly, I sometimes meet people who want to develop their intuition, which they see as a special skill that they can cultivate for their advantage, separate from their spirituality. When the heart chakra is really engaged, you may choose to explore the third eye, although it is difficult to do so unless you are directed to take that course. (Then you will have little other choice!) But by this stage you will not have the desire to master some special 'intuitive skill'.

Holding your heart open, you will know that you already have access to the skills and intuition you need to find your way in the world. You will be able to harmonise much better with the changing vibrations of the universe, and to use those changes to strengthen your intuition. Knowing and developing love, along with spiritual intelligence, will be your overriding concern.

If your intuition – almost always for the benefit of others – sharpens at this point, well and good. However, intuitive power is not something you'll want to cling to. You will understand its part in the whole, as a step in the onward and upward drive to open your crown chakra and allow as much spiritual energy as possible to flood your system.

The crown chakra

On the crown of the head is a centre known as the crown chakra. It is the centre that receives a particularly fine form of energy. It is a higher level of energy, and individuals vary in their capacity to 'tune in' – that means to absorb, integrate and use this frequency. It means different things to different people too. The extent and the form of the vibrations that you respond to dictate your perception of the forces behind spiritual reality.

But working to purify and strengthen your energy from the base chakra upwards makes you more able to receive crown chakra energy, and better able to open the crown chakra to receive more of it. The more open the crown chakra, the wider your perspective. Those who reach this point will know the far-reaching changes it brings. It is a high point in spiritual understanding, and the mastery of spiritual intelligence. And you will know that there are chakras beyond the crown.

The journey out and the journey back

The process of developing your chakras, and simultaneously owning your spiritual intelligence, falls into two parts. I call the first the journey out. It is the journey to the heart chakra, the place that mankind, as a group, must reach. And then onward, as far beyond as you can, or wish to, go. But you can't jump to the heart. You have to cover the ground to get there. And in the process, you must neither abandon your intellect, nor your emotions, nor be ruled by them.

At the same time, in the course of the journey, it is very difficult to understand the full implications of a given stage before you reach it. For example, when you are driven largely by the second chakra, you may think you understand the heart chakra, but in reality your vision will be limited by the second chakra's perspective. Just as it is very difficult to 'see' or understand someone who is working on a higher level. Often too we will be very uncomfortable with their energy, because it will be significantly different from our own. But as we begin to open to change, we may, on encountering someone on a higher level, be strongly drawn to their energy, as a forerunner of our own.

Of course, in the early stages the energy of spiritual development and mental power are easily confused. All too often we collect information about spirituality, read wise diatribes on the subject, go to esoteric lectures, even call the knowledge we accumulate in this way 'wisdom', but don't be fooled. It has nothing to do with the evolution of spirituality, or knowing spirituality. Any more than do sentimentality or emotional liability. Neither has it anything to do with the unfolding of your intuition.

With the perspective of the heart chakra you will know the fundamental principles for humankind in this millennium. The values and behaviour of the areas below the heart will be in the process of transformation, integrating with the values of the heart. An advanced goal and an extraordinary journey to have achieved.

It is then, and only then, you may choose consciously to go on. And only a few will wish to do so, to complete the journey out. For most it will be time to make the journey back. To concentrate on consciously integrating the wisdom and love that has been experienced back into the everyday.

At this point the three higher chakras have probably already been open to a certain degree, and all who reach the heart chakra will feel greatly increased contact with the crown chakra energy. Among those who choose to go on, the third eye calls only a few. Intuitive transformation has already occurred with the opening of the heart chakra. If the third eye calls now, that process will deepen greatly. But for those continuing the journey out, it is the crown and beyond that will draw you, linking you with the highest forces of the universe. You will know the most extreme vibrations of the spectrum, and, knowing them, will see them everywhere. Not only in the extraordinary, but in the ordinary too.

This point is not reached by many. Almost inevitably it means leaving everyday life. Some of those who reach it choose to stay there. Apart, or detached, from the issues of the world. Some, even fewer, decide sooner or later to make the journey back. To bring their knowledge back and put it at the service of their fellows, and themselves. To confront again the issues of the lower chakras, marked by where they have been.

The all-important ego

Eastern religions are often understood as advocating that their followers give up, or rise above, their egos. Buddhist clients, for example, have spoken to me of the noxious effects of the ego, and their attempts to become ego-less. This has often caused me some concern. I can think of several occasions where I have been struck by the low self-esteem and general doormat-like quality of those who are trying, usually with excellent intentions, to give up 'ego'.

Of course, it is difficult to understand exactly what is meant by ego in these Eastern teachings. Generally it is explained as rather different from the usual concept of ego which most of us use in the everyday – 'He has a big ego.' However, the precise Western translation of the Eastern notion of ego is not clear. But what is clear is that the simple concept of losing your ego is not to be recommended. At the same time, understanding the workings of energy suggests a new understanding of the notion of ego.

Ego can be seen as a process, not an entity. It is the process of organisation working in you. Ego is directly related to the functioning of the chakras. It reflects the dominance within the chakras. It relates directly to the strengths and weaknesses of the way your chakras are working. It dictates your attitude towards others, your needs, drives and how you hold them. It provides the basis for your values, beliefs, your conscience and your moral decisions. In other words, it reflects the energetic level at which you are functioning.

That means that if you are dominated by your first chakra (I doubt you would be reading this if you were), then your ego would be concentrated on having enough food for yourself and your family, and a safe home. It might include having a job. First chakra values would also dictate the scope of your 'caring'. Whatever you said, it would be highly unlikely to take the well-being of a larger population into consideration, and would have no understanding of any values related to, for example, compassion. But neither would it be very sympathetic to, for example, licentiousness. The base chakra isn't driven by that need. Procreation, yes, but it's not likely to indulge in the excesses that can dominate the second chakra.

In the same way, when the second or third chakras are dominant, they play a dominant role in shaping your ego. Most people, of course, are a mixture, and that mixture changes, which the ego reflects. Then, when the heart is sufficiently open, it transforms the ego process, which acts for the benefit of mankind, rather than from a personal perspective only. A trickle of people, which is steadily swelling, are reaching these levels now, and the number is set to increase dramatically.

Meanwhile, one of the major problems associated with the ego process is that, almost inevitably, we do not understand those whose egos are organised predominantly on the principles of higher chakras than our own. We cannot understand their motives, actions or feelings as they come from a wider perspective, one that we have not yet mastered. Sadly, sometimes we dismiss them as failures, or worse.

To someone struggling with the ego processes of the second chakra, the actions and concerns of someone working to gain a wider perspective at the heart, and more deeply connected to the fundamentals of the material and spiritual whole, make little sense. They will probably be seen as 'weird', and will be pitied, disregarded or even feared. Certainly they are unlikely to be understood, or appreciated. Examples abound.

In his lifetime, poet, artist and mystic William Blake was not understood, but was subject to considerable abuse. It was only well after his death that his stature was recognised. In the earlier part of their lives, and by the authorities they threatened, Nelson Mandela and Gandhi were both seen as subversives, and were punished. Of course, both were working from the heart chakra. The painter Van Gogh was another who worked closely with the essence of reality and received no recognition while he was alive, but quite the contrary (which must have contributed to his mental state). Keats, now probably seen as the greatest lyrical poet bar Shakespeare, and a deep and profound thinker concerned with fundamental issues, was relegated to a minor position in his lifetime. All were motivated by a higher understanding than many of their peers, and suffered accordingly. Needless to say several others, both famous and unrecognised, are or have been accorded the same fate.

By the same token, on your journey it can become increasingly difficult to find others 'on the same wavelength' as the process of change takes charge. At the higher levels there may indeed be few others working with the same perspective as you are. Whatever pain that will cause, you will also understand. It will not be the old ache that will trouble you; your connection to the greater whole, and joy in the process of life, will be greatly strengthened.

With the coming of spiritual intelligence the ego process in us all is changing, slowly but surely – and in the face of the inevitable backlash. Instead of being a process rooted in second or third chakra values, for many ego will become a process largely based on heart chakra values – a blessing for our relations to each other and to our planet, and our passport to a future for our species.

For you to think about or try

Many of these exercises work well if you do them with a friend – if that appeals.

1. Sit comfortably in a chair and very slowly explore the space around you, from say six inches to twelve or even eighteen. Can you feel any difference in the texture of the atmosphere surrounding you? In fact you are exploring your energy body. Think about the feeling you have when you say, 'He, or she, stood too close.' You are actually talking about their energy body impinging on yours and the discomfort that causes. Likewise, you are happy to be physically close to people you are very comfortable with.

2. Think of at least one thing that you believe to be true, though you have no rational reason for thinking that way.

3. Think of three examples of areas or issues where you know you are biased, and try to

think of why that is. You may need a friend to help you here! Ask your friend to suggest issues you seem biased about – see how far you can make sense of the answer you receive. Remember, your friend's suggestions may not be absolutely true – they could be influenced by bias on your friend's part.

4. Think about any physical symptom you may have. Is it located in the area of one of the major chakras and could it relate to the functioning of that chakra? If so, can you see a connection with the relevant issues in your life?

5. Consider your own energetic journey – how would you rate the functioning of your own chakras? Where do you think the blockages or limits are?

6. In your journey into the heart chakra, make a list of the following qualities: compassion, discipline, perseverance, endurance, wisdom, generosity, appropriate effort, joy. Under each quality, list examples of your own performance that demonstrate that you understand and include this quality in your life. If you feel you can, and would like to, swop lists with a friend to consider one another's contributions. Your friend may not understand, for example, compassion in the same way that you do. Where do you feel the truth lies?

7. Think about the application of the heart chakra's values to the world. Think of the

ways in which the world would be changed if more people used these values as a yard-stick for relating. Socially, politically, eco-nomically, environmentally – what changes would you anticipate?

8. Think how you can consciously apply heart chakra values in your work. What changes could you make? And what effects would they have on any colleagues, clients, or the wider world?

9. What about the application of heart chakra values by organisations of all kinds? Who do you see proclaiming any heart chakra stan-dards? And how far do you see them being put into action? Don't simply list those organisations that respect the environment, for example, and avoid furthering pollution. But which organisations actively promote the well-being of the world and her people?

10. Can you think of any way you could encour-age the businesses you deal with to apply heart chakra values? For example, by spending your money or using your influ-ence with those who follow a policy that pro-motes the well-being of the world?

11. Joy deserves a separate space because it is so important. List as many examples as pos-sible of incidents, places, people, objects, images, sensations, smells, dreams, visions, flora, fauna, tastes and events that have given you joy recently. Did the sound of the

rain last night please you? Practise recognising, appreciating, exulting in and being thankful for every tiny instance of joy you encounter – not just the big ones. If you and your friend are still happy to swop lists, look at one another's lists and see how many different examples of joy you have listed. Why not each try to experience some of the examples the other felt but you did not?

Chapter Seven

Finding a Way

So, the progress of your energy and your spiritual development are part of one and the same thing. Clearing your energy – helping to free your chakras of obstacles, and purifying your energy body – is part of your spiritual development. But how to do it when, for most people, 'energy body' and 'chakras' are only a little better than metaphors! Few people are really capable of seeing energy – and even if they do, are they seeing a personal metaphor, or an absolute concrete quality?

The answer to that question doesn't matter, because I know there are ways of bypassing it. Repeatedly, I have seen the effects of actions aimed at clearing, and raising, your energy. I know they work. So, whether they work because the picture I have painted behind them is accurate, or whether they work just because they work – doesn't seem important.

Choosing a practice

The physical practices and rules related to developing

and purifying your energy outlined in Chapter Four are important. They help. But a practice that frees your mind and allows you to reach into your depths is very important too. In that way you can directly access the obstacles or residues in your energy. Without needing to go to someone else who can supposedly 'see' energy and asking them where your energy is blocked, or asking for their input in freeing it.

Of course, someone else can be tremendously helpful. In many different ways. Massage, for example, might well move blocks in your physical body and because the physical and the mental are so closely connected, it could also help purify the mental. After a good massage people often tell me they feel, for example, 'a weight off their shoulders' or 'really relaxed'. Not just a physical sensation, but a mental one too.

Accepting someone else's help in, for example, psychotherapy or reflexology can help enormously with all sorts of emotional, mental and physical issues. But I am not talking about that here. Here I want to concentrate on what you can do for yourself. Which becomes far more fundamental.

All practices are most effective when undertaken regularly. Not necessarily year in, year out, but for a while. You need to find something that you will work with regularly, perhaps daily, to help you penetrate your own depths. You are looking for a route to a deeper level of reality than the one you encounter in the everyday. You are looking for a tool that will help you enter into the deeper levels of yourself, where the knowledge you hold is of a different order. Where the blocks in your mental and emotional bodies, in particular, are easier to see. Where your intuition is not shut out by the chatter of the everyday. Where you are open, in the greatest degree possible, to the spiritual body and energy of the highest order.

Meditation is the obvious candidate. It's the technique most often advocated. But a bewildering number of meditations are offered, claiming to do all sorts of different things. So, what sort of meditation? How to do it? And what to do when it doesn't or won't work for you?

Meditation

The meditation that I find most useful to start with is meditation on the chakras. It is the way I started, which eventually led to another practice that took me on the journey I wrote of in *The Pool of Memory*. But I think my own development was greatly helped, maybe even made possible, by the chakra meditation which was important in the process of clearing my energy. So, I am going to explain the technique I used, and what to do if meditation is not for you, at the moment.

The chakra meditation

This technique worked for me, and I have seen dramatic results from it with many others, including psychotherapists. But I cannot tell you it will definitely suit you. Nor can I tell you it will definitely 'do you good'. Or that it is either quite safe, or very dangerous. I can only say you must take responsibility for yourself, your well-being, your decisions, and use your own judgement. It can be very powerful. If you are in treatment, or need treatment, or are in any doubt, check with your practitioner or doctor.

To begin, choose a quiet place, and a good time of day where you will not be disturbed, or can eliminate disturbances. It is best to choose a time and place that you can return to regularly. Find a wooden chair to sit on, and a candle, or three, to light. I say a wooden chair because wood helps absorb fear. Light the candle, or candles, a little way in front of you, in your field of vision. It is your allegiance to the light.

Three is a number of particular unity and power. It is important in many systems of thought. In Buddhism, it symbolises the three forces of mind, body and speech. In Christianity, the holy trinity. In esoteric thought, it is the basic symbol of the fruitful union – two which becomes three.

Sit as square as you can on the chair. I don't advise sitting on the floor – most Western bodies are not well adapted to being balanced and grounded sitting cross-legged. By sitting square I mean try to distribute your weight equally between the two sides of your body. Let your spine – the structure that developed from the first bundle of cells that was the foetus – act as an axis. Allow your body to settle equally on both sides of that centre line. It is balance that you are try-ing to achieve.

At the same time, nothing can be done by force. In time, following the path, you will become straighter and straighter, and balance will permeate all areas of your life, the physical and the non-physical. Close your eyes and say a prayer. It is a form of dedication and acknowledgement of a power beyond and greater than your individual self. I don't mind what sort of prayer – sometimes making up the words yourself feels most comfortable, sometimes using a prayer learnt in childhood works best.

Concentrate your attention on your base chakra. The area on the perineum, between your genitals and your anus. (See the figure on page 158 to show where the chakras are located.) Now switch the base chakra on. You may do that by visualising a device like a light switch, which you switch on. Or you may simply think the base chakra 'on'. When it comes on, aim to see it as a yellow light. If the colour is not yellow, that doesn't matter. Another colour may be more appro-priate for you.

For different individuals, different colour ranges seem to be relevant. Eastern religions seem to bear this out with various religions awarding different colours to the chakras. In my experience none is 'wrong'. However, people seem to group around different colours. This may reflect allegiance, experi-ence, aspiration, ability or something different.

It can take several attempts to light the chakra. That doesn't matter in the least. Allow yourself the

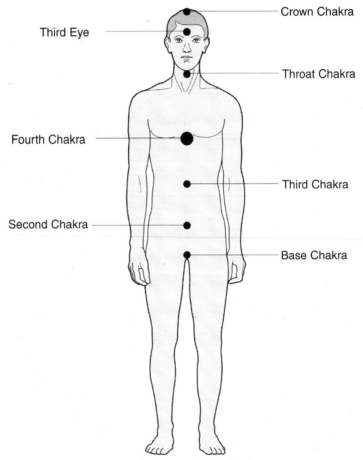

Third Eye

Crown Chakra

Throat Chakra

Fourth Chakra

Third Chakra

Second Chakra

Base Chakra

Position of the Major Chakras

benefit of the doubt. If you have a sense of a colour, take it that you have lit the chakra and can proceed. Above all, don't plague yourself with doubts – have I done it? Is this it? Can I do it? Just go on.

Move the light up your body, or an image of your body, in your mind's eye, to the centre of your forehead. When you reach that place, stop. Make sure the light is now held outside your body, and look at it. But not with your eyes. Concentrate or focus on the yellow (if it's yellow) light from a point in the centre of your forehead.

Allow whatever thoughts come into your mind to come. Don't try to exert any control at all. If you find yourself thinking about what's for lunch, simply go with the thoughts and let the flow continue. If after a while you feel you are simply drifting into a reverie about, for example, work or domestic issues, try focussing back on the yellow light but then, immediately, releasing control again. If your mind goes back to the area where it was previously, let it. And stay with those thoughts. Don't judge them.

There is no way of knowing the significance of the thoughts that are coming to you. You cannot label some important and others trivial. Anything or everything may have crucial significance. Above all, don't try to analyse what comes to mind. Just let it be.

Finally, when you feel you have reached the end of a train of thoughts, or the end of your desire or need for this exercise – and that could be after five, fifteen or even fifty minutes: time is no measure of virtue – it's time to stop. Bring the yellow light back to the middle of your forehead. Then, return it to the place it came from on your perineum. At this point you must switch it off.

Switching off the light is very important. Use the device of seeing a switch, if it worked for you before. Or simply 'see' the light as going off. When you have cut off the light, next make sure your chakras are all closed. Or you could think of it as making sure you have switched off the electrical activity. To do this, see a white light above your head. Move it swiftly, like an arrow, down through your body, passing through all the main chakras, from the crown down to the floor. Repeat this at least twice more. Make sure all is peaceful, and no lights occur.

Next say your thanks, inwardly. Then open your eyes, and write down, briefly, what occurred. No need to dwell unduly on details, but be careful not to censure events because you judge them 'unimportant'. The whole exercise of recording events is not so that you can go back and analyse or, equally bad, gloat over them, but to acknowledge, or 'fix' them. Going back over your notes can be seriously counter-productive. You can't analyse your journey while you are travelling. Focus your attention firmly forwards. Leave the past behind. Acknowledge events – as far as possible. Take responsibility. Then move on.

Make this meditation a habit. Perhaps once a day at the same time of the day, or even twice a day. Twice a week is possible, if it is all you can manage, but you lose the intensity of the exercise. When you feel you have exhausted the need – and I don't mean simply desire – to concentrate on the base chakra, it's time to move on.

Beware the role of desire. It is a real snake. We all tend to be so achievement-led that it's hard to resist a feeling that 'getting ahead', moving upwards to the heart as quickly as possible, is the aim of the exercise. It matters to reach the heart chakra. But only when you have cleared all the ground leading up to the heart, and you are really ready to occupy that space. Otherwise, it's not very difficult to fool yourself into moving up to the heart, and imagine the journey. Of course it's disappointing when you proclaim you have reached the heart chakra, because there is and has been no real transformation on the way. There couldn't be. So, don't move from one chakra to the next until you are absolutely sure you are ready to do so. Sometimes you will even experience some inner prompting, urging you to move on to the next chakra.

When you're ready to go to the second chakra, the method is equally precise. (See the figure on page 158 as before). Go into your meditation as before. Switch on the yellow light. But, instead of raising it up, go on to the next place, the sexual or second chakra, which is located about halfway between your genitals and your belly button. When you reach it, switch on the chakra. The light should come on a mid-blue colour (unless you are working with another colour range).

Now go through exactly the same procedure with the blue chakra as you did with the yellow. Raise it up to the middle of your forehead, listen to it, allow whatever comes to come. Again, go on for as long as you feel you want or need to. When you are finished, return the blue chakra to its place. Then switch it off. Next, go down to the yellow chakra and switch that off.

When both are dark, turn your attention to your crown. Visualise a white light, in the shape of an arrow, above your head. See it sweeping down through your body, through all your chakras, exactly as before, at least three times. Then, repeat the rest of the exercise, your thanks, and your record, exactly as before too.

You may work with each chakra for a matter of days, weeks or months. There is absolutely no virtue in rushing. To reach the heart you need all the chakras below the heart to be clear enough. If you move from a chakra before it has emptied itself, you will not be able to deal successfully with the one above.

Also, you may on occasion find that a lower chakra wants your attention when you have been working with a higher chakra. For example, you may have reached the digestive centre, the red chakra; then one day on entering your meditation you might feel that the yellow light wants to rise. Allow it. Recognise that the base is telling you it needs your attention. And you must give that before you move on.

When you reach the heart, the lessons of this book will really begin to make sense to you. Meanwhile, aiming towards your heart chakra will build a crucial series of steps in strengthening your intuition and understanding. As you release the obstacles at each chakra, your perception of the issues governed by that chakra has a chance to alter. As you move towards the heart and embrace the values of the heart, your sense of yourself, and of yourself in ㄴ... ance, becomes stronger. Along with that, your ability to widen your vision to see more clearly is greatly strengthened – an important step in developing your intuition.

A word of warning, though. Unless you have good reason to think you are secure in understanding energetic development differently to the way I have laid out, don't improvise when following this meditation. The steps are quite precise and specific. There is nothing arbitrary or optional (unless specified) about the process. If you want to try it, stick to the instructions.

However, perhaps the chakra meditation hasn't been effective for you, or you haven't wanted to try it, or you are not drawn to meditation. What then?

Contemplation

According to the poet Milton, in *Paradise Lost*, God made man: 'For contemplation he and valour formed,' and woman: 'For softness she and sweet attractive grace'! I agree with Milton on contemplation – for man and woman. It is essential. At times. In a less well-known work (*Il Penseroso*), Milton expressed an even more profound sentiment:

> . . . *And Wisdom's self*
> *Oft seeks to sweet retired solitude*
> *Where with her best nurse Contemplation*
> *She plumes her feathers, and lets grow her wings.*

For me that says it all. Contemplation is a space in which it is possible to sink into the deeper layers of the self, the deepest layers of one's own wisdom. I acknowledged the need for contemplation years before I ever tried meditation. And now, years later, again it is not meditation that is central to my own practice, but contemplation. And what's the difference between contemplation and daydreaming? Very little – only that contemplation isn't 'just fantasising', but real, core-level thinking – letting the mind roam freely.

Or try ironing!

There's another route to contemplation. This isn't a joke. It's any action that is repetitive and does not require much conscious attention. Painting a wall could fall in the same category. Or perhaps ploughing a field. Or vacuuming a floor. The key quality of the action is that you should not have to hurry to do it. Because you do not have to pay it much attention, it should leave your thoughts free – allowing you 'private space', to go into yourself, and engage in contemplation. Both contemplation and using a repetitive action to inspire contemplation, are regular exercises that can be used instead of meditation, or as preliminaries to meditation. But there are other routes too.

Sound and colour

In Chapter Four I went into ways in which sound and

colour can be used to access your energetic body and your emotions. This, of course, is in part what meditation on the chakras is doing. It follows that working with colour can stand in for meditation of this kind, up to a point. Sometimes, making actual pictures or creating music can have a similar effect too.

Creativity

Creativity in all forms has a very special relationship to the meditation I have outlined. Meditation, or contemplation, can offer an access to a deeper layer of yourself, and an opportunity to transform those depths. In a similar way, creativity can reflect your access into your depths. It can also interact with them.

What do I mean by that? Well, there is a great deal of debate about the nature of creativity today. Take, for example, modern art. Is an unmade bed a masterpiece in the same way as a Van Gogh? Obviously this is not the place for those discussions. But I am bringing it up because my use of the concept of creativity is quite specific.

One way of describing creativity is to say that it is the reworking of what you know – but perhaps do not always know you know – to form new solutions. Some novelists, for example, say they do not know what a book is about until they reach the end. Or a painting can reveal to the painter, and its audience, aspects of the reality it is depicting that were never deliberately intended or foreseen.

The parallel between this and the intended or possible effects of the chakra meditation can be striking. Both aim to penetrate the body's energy or, to use a different expression, consciousness. Both look to address issues held there. However, there are two main areas of difference between them.

The meditation that I have outlined aims to release the issues held in the energy. Consciously or unconsciously, creative endeavours may repeat those contentious issues, perhaps over and over again, or release them. The role that organisation plays emphasises the difference.

Creative endeavour may mean that you put the constraints of the project you are working on above the true working out or resolution of the material, which is often a reflection of the issues in your energy. What I mean by that is simple.

Suppose you are in pain and you write a song. The words that you write instinctively please you deeply. They seem to encapsulate your pain and, in expressing them, you feel you move beyond your experience. You are so pleased that you put your creation to a music publisher. He likes it too, but suggests that it will only be commercial if you change part of the words and the music in a way that he is suggesting.

Now, commercially this may be excellent advice and you might well hurry to take it. However, the song is no longer the same as the original song that released your pain. It's a commercial product. Creating products to meet a commercial market is not the same as allowing your authentic, deeper self to surface. Though it may follow from that.

Exploiting creativity commercially may well need you to master the form you have chosen to express yourself in, and, according to your aims, take account of market forces.

Meditation, purifying your energy and releasing obstacles, never takes account of a market force. However, paradoxically, the very process of focussing on yourself in the way produced by the chakra meditation, for example, also strengthens your intuition. Quite simply, you know yourself and what you feel more clearly, and at a deeper level. At the same time you become better able to tune in to the vibrations of the world around you. This in turn helps release your creative forces, encouraging you to bring new life, or creations, out of yourself in a variety of different areas.

Contact with deeper levels of consciousness, specifically in the form of attempts at reaching other levels of reality, has a long history of association with creativity and the written word. W. B. Yeats, for example, was much influenced by the activities of his wife, a medium who used 'automatic writing' to contact another level. The work of a number of others, including William Blake, Francis Bacon, William Shakespeare and poet Ted Hughes, in our own time, have all been claimed to be linked with the quest for another spiritual reality.

In visual art the idea that the artist should see into the spirit of things became particularly prevalent with the modernist movement at the end of the nineteenth century. It helped inspire artists like Kandinsky, Mondrian and others to move beyond the stage of representing life in a literal or even an impressionist mode. Instead they attempted to find a way to show some more fundamental or abstract, inner essence – perhaps what could be called spiritual essence. In music the search for the spiritual has always been especially active. In the modern age, pieces like jazz supremo John Coltrane's 'A love supreme' epitomise a spiritual search, and reach right outside jazz.*

When I first began to meditate, I often used the words 'the will of the Creative' to mean the governing force of spirituality. It was the best way I had of expressing the organising powers of the universe, and it is apt in many ways. Repeatedly I have seen the effects of accessing the deeper levels on the creativity of individuals who have come to me.

A psychotherapist was led by her meditation to take up music, formerly an important part of her life that had been left behind. She was rewarded by great joy and a whole new dimension to her life. A journalist found the need, and the ability, to begin to write plays. I could go on. As for myself, I was teaching a seminar dealing with these issues, when I was so deeply stirred that I had to make time to write a work of fiction. It is a story (not yet published) about the power of the force of creativity in accessing deeper emotions and the altogether surprising consequences this can have on life (*Lost and Found*).

---

*My thanks to Neil Spencer for sharing his learning in this area.

Suggestions for you to think about or to try

1. Choose a practice. Even if it is just to say that you will take ten minutes, sitting on the train on your way to work every day, and make that a time for contemplation.
2. If you are not already playing with colour or sound (see Chapter Four), try it.

Chapter Eight

Other Worlds?

My own meditation practice took me on many journeys in life and in meditation, with the two often meeting and finally coming together as one. The meditation journey was like a story – with many different characters and locations. But were they real? Were the characters 'real'? Or what was going on? How to explain them? Figments of my imagination? Or an esoteric reality of angels, guides and ghosts?

Angels, guides, ghosts – past lives, for example, are all parts of some contemporary spiritual beliefs, as well as history. What to make of them? What reality status to give to the idea of beings from another world? Or help from beings from other worlds? Or, indeed, what about other worlds? What about the idea that we have 'guides'? Or perhaps guardian angels? Or that those who are no longer alive watch over us and try to help our progress on earth? Or the notion of reincarnation, that we are born again and again? My own journey brought up these questions and answered them.

'Guides'

My meditation brought me into contact with many so-called beings – from another layer of reality. On 20 February 1991, my journal records:

There is a presence with me. He is from God, not God. I am to know him as the Disciple, for now. He is a relatively young man, thirty to thirty-five. Very kind. I am shown the world above the clouds. The message is 'You are to love everyone, that is an important part of your work.' I see flickery pictures, like old movies or negatives, lots of people walking.

The Disciple tells me I am to speak to many people. I am to teach 'the wisdom of the ages, you have the ability to communicate it'. 'What's the wisdom of the ages?' Then it's over. I go back to my body, reunite with it, splash into the pool, and emerge the other side. *

On the face of it, it seems that I came into contact with beings from another realm. The Disciple was not my 'guide', but perhaps I met him or her later?

In fact, I met many presences. For example, a skeleton-like figure who represented death, a female figure who stood for all the feminine qualities, a male presence who was with me for much of the journey,

---

*Edited and abbreviated extracts from my meditation journals were published in *The Pool of Memory: the autobiography of an unwilling intuitive*.

whom I identify as V. Then another, apparently much more important presence entered my meditation. It was often difficult for me to see him, and his shape and location usually baffled me. He is known as T. A snake in many forms plays a large part. Non-human shapes in various frightening guises also feature. Later, so do images of Jesus and Buddha. I have the experience of seeing and interacting with relatives no longer alive; and others still on earth.

At the time, when these visions or this journey started, I held no view about the reality or nature of the images I was encountering. The entire process was so remote from anything I had even envisaged, let alone wanted to be associated with, but also, once begun, it was so essential. I clung constantly to the need simply to allow whatever happened to happen – to try to avoid judging, or interfering in any way. And to record as much as I could. (Which seemed a great deal.)

While the experience, at the beginning in particular, was very strange, what made it compulsive, and so deeply satisfying, was an almost overwhelming, extraordinary quality of love that permeated all the exchanges. Even those that were deeply terrifying. I felt loved, and connected with love, in a way beyond any I had experience of. In a totally different sense. Love that was complete, unconditional and curiously impersonal, while at the same time altogether embracing. Now, I know it was the love of the heart chakra that was being unlocked in me, and enfolding me.

But there were other aspects of the interactions. Many deeply perplexing, if I had allowed myself to

dwell on them. One in particular is especially important. It concerns location. For example:

*Thursday, 11 April. I am happy to see V. I ask for his
help to do the will of the Creative, and then relax,
lying on the grass in front of him. Casually I look at
him. It is unusual for me to see his face clearly, or to
focus on it, but this time I look and look. Something is
happening. I look away, but he tells me to look at him
again, into his eyes. I do, and am pulled right inside V.
We are one, or perhaps two in one.*

Issues to do with location become increasingly confused.

*Monday, 15 April. Later. Meeting with V there is an
odd phenomenon – I feel that I am both facing him
and he is simultaneously on my left-hand side. Also, is
someone else present? Is the large personage, whom
somehow I cannot face, there? Who is in the shadow?
No answer, no explanation.*

And later that same day:

*V is there, I turn to him, as I think. But in address-
ing him discover, confusingly, that I am not facing
him as I thought – he is standing on my left and I
am at T's feet.* [T was the 'much more important'
figure who entered later in the journey.] *Then T
leaves and I talk to V again. He is utterly delighted
with T's involvement and warns it may change*

*everything. Then we walk along the beach much more
as equals than we have ever been. V tells me he was
asked to guide me. That he is to continue to do so, but
he does not know everything, although he has many
powers. This is a critical point.*

Apparently T is of supreme importance, very considerably more than V, and has the ability to change all factors around the direction of my life.

Then, merging becomes more and more important. On 20 June, I was low that day, and feeling the disparity between my two lives – life on earth and my meditation reality – very strongly:

*With no warning I am pulled into T – it is as if I
merge with him (Much physical shaking accompanies
this.) Then, having been pulled in, I am pulled
upwards into a vast plain of light.*

22 June, Midsummer's Day:

*I tell T I want to merge with him. He urges me to use
his strength for whatever I do – he tells me again how
powerful he is and that his strength is mine.*

It is after this that the figures of Christ and Buddha become regular features. At the same time working with dark forces and a level I think of as the 'Undead' increases. Now, what's happening?

Do these accounts support a notion that I met my guide or guides, and became involved in the affairs of another reality, or another level of reality? Or are they saying something different? Are they wishful thoughts? Or random? Or simply incomprehensible?

First, it's important to understand something of language, culture and metaphor. I saw the beings in the way I did because of my culture and history. If I had been living in sixth-century Tibet, doubtless I would have seen these interchanges in the form of exchanges with deities. In Europe from the Middle Ages onwards there have been reports of sightings of the Virgin Mary and interactions with her. These are rare today.

It does not mean that none of these experiences was 'true', or definitive. But what it means is that they were events that presented in the idiom of the age. Take the process of coming from blindness to sight. In experimental studies, where individuals have been born blind, or lost their sight early on, and later in life their sight is restored, what they see is not immediately self-evident. They don't necessarily recognise what it is they are looking at immediately – they have to learn to make sense of it. In other words, they have to learn what they are seeing (see Gregory and Wallace, page 356). The study of the history of perception has looked closely at this question. One recent work, for example, has concentrated on disease, and the way different ages manifest diseases in different forms. (see *Mad Travellers*, Ian Hacking, page 355)

Then, language and images present their own, particular problems. Much of what I was seeing in meditation was very difficult to put into words. But words are all we have. Extraordinary experiences are usually particularly difficult to describe. Especially if you are describing a domain beyond not simply the everyday, but beyond the emotional and the intellectual too. How to describe the forces of Light? Or dark? Metaphor is obviously the most powerful way, or poetry, or art (see William Blake's work, or that of Hieronymus Bosch).

However, when we attempt to report incidents directly, in the written or spoken word, they may well sound naive, or clichéd. As if Hollywood would have done a better job with special effects. But to take that attitude is to miss the significance behind what the words are describing.

My exchanges with some of the presences I met conveyed first that other relatively but not necessarily altogether independent energies exist. Most significant, though, were my interchanges and eventual merger with T, the most important of the presences I encountered, acknowledged as by far the most powerful by the others.

To begin with, I had great difficulty understanding T and locating him. I could not make sense of, or often even hear clearly, what T was saying. I needed V to interpret for me. Also, I would speak to T and discover that it seemed as if I was not looking at him and talking to him, but talking from the same direction as he was facing. I became aware that when I talked to V, if T was present it was as if I was talking to V from a position at T's feet. Finally, integration with T became my regular aim.

At that point, at last, it became obvious. Despite my deep love for him as a separate entity, I was, and am, T. To put it plainly, the greatest of the other presences I encounter (of course, Buddha and Christ aside) was my greatest self. Which is true for all of us.

Other presences – beings or energies as you prefer – may play 'helper' roles, as guides, comforters or whatever, but they are all much less important than your own power. The greatest force you can come to know, and use, is yourself.

At the same time, reaching or communicating with the greater aspects of myself was very difficult to begin with. Also, it was apparently not necessarily inevitable that it would happen. From the reaction of V, for example, it appeared that it was a cause for great delight that T came to meet me (or I came to meet T!)

Then, there's the fact that I was not immediately able to communicate with this greater self. I had to do so through a lesser figure, V. In other words connection with the reality that the greater self represents was simply a step too far, to begin with. I needed something easier to form a link for me, at first. But the relationship with V was not the end point of my development. The relationship with T – myself – was the real achievement.

All this suggests that though lesser energies may exist, at this time in history the supreme guiding power that we can encounter is the power of our greatest self. It is not a time to aspire to be led by non-material energies, presences or guides – however you see them. Though, of course, all teachers play an important role (see Chapter Thirteen, Teachers and healers), we must not give ourselves over to them – on earth or in any other domain – and expect them to empower us. We are certainly no longer looking for guides to speak through us, or use us as instruments of some greater wisdom. Our aim is to learn to accept power ourselves. To know that greater wisdom in ourselves, and to manifest it.

Dark beings

In my meditation journeys I have met many strange, sometimes horrible or threatening images. Others that have been hugely benevolent, or sometimes quixotic. Many of the less pleasant encounters involve dealing with dark forces in some way. For example:

> *then the ladder grows and I have to climb it. Into the enormous Light. After a few moments two dark shapes, Shadow figures, come forwards. Storming. I try to disregard them, but they stay. It seems as if they are part of the light . . . Then I understand. The dark is essential. The space of the Light and the dark is where I have to work.*

Or a little later, entering the domain of Light, I meet a shadow figure, half man, half panther:

> *it tears strips down me, savages me and I stand impassive. Then, slowly, I begin to fill with Light, from my feet upwards.*

What I learnt above all in these encounters is the importance of neither running away, nor fighting; simply remaining present. Of allowing the dark. Looked at symbolically, they represent the omnipresence of dark psychological forces in all aspects of our lives – both inside ourselves and in the external world, and the need not to run from them.

It is only by allowing the dark force to 'tear strips' from me and 'savage me' that I am filled 'with Light'. In other words, facing the dark – not fighting it, or running away – leads to my being filled with the Light quality.

Darkness within

Psychologically, integration with the dark is a key aspect of our development. We all need to admit and own the darker sides of our natures; however, recognising them is a real problem (see Issues for you to think about, page 199). But, without this process there is no true strength. For example, denying that you are greedy (if you are) gives the greed, an unpleasant or dark force, the power to work unimpeded. If you face it and acknowledge it, the positive forces in your nature will have much more power to deal with your greed. Unacknowledged forces that influence our behaviour are sometimes called 'unconscious drivers'. Unacknowledged dark drivers, like fear or hatred, can be immensely powerful in enabling or encouraging us to take dark actions that we would not normally want to be associated with.

For example, ambition can be a powerful positive motivator and also a very negative self-seeking force. Refusing to acknowledge your ambition, if you are fiercely ambitious, means you can be driven to take dubious actions without acknowledging or perhaps even recognising their unpleasant character. By facing up to and acknowledging your ambition, you increase your ability to resist the pressure to take unacceptable actions to further that ambition. (Given that your intentions are good, of course.)

Dark forces in our personality – fear, anger, hatred, frustration, envy – that are not acknowledged, faced and so integrated, can play havoc in our lives. Some years ago I was consulted by an accomplished medium. He had a large circle of clients, was much in demand and very proficient at his work. However, his inner turmoil had reached a place where he was terrified by his kitchen floor, which was laid out in black and white tiles. Simply standing on a black floor tile filled him with unbearable dread. He felt that the black floor tile symbolised the dark, which he could not face. His inner turmoil was such that he only felt safe if kneeling in a church service where he considered himself 'protected' by the Light.

Clearly, he had failed to integrate the darker aspects of his own personality. It's a process we all have to go through, at some stage. We have to understand that our own natures are not all sweetness and light. That we can be self-seeking, or envious, or dark in any number of ways, some of which are not obvious at all. Feeling inadequate, for example, can make us vulnerable to exaggeration, which can open the way to deception and the path to the dark.

Also, we have to understand that the world contains plenty of dark that we need to be able to, and can, deal with. We teach our children to cross the road – to confront death, to deal with fear, and to go on. Because my medium client had failed to meet it, the dark lurked outside him and, to put it bluntly, terrorised him.

In the same way it is often qualities that we do not acknowledge in ourselves that cause us distress or annoyance when we encounter them in others. When we recognise and acknowledge them in ourselves, we gain power over them and stop being shaken up when confronting them in others.

Darkness outside

The dark presences I met in meditation did not simply represent inner psychological forces. They also represented meeting the dark on the outside, as we all do. But meeting the dark, or dark outer forces, does not have to mean confronting them. It always means acknowledging them, though, facing them and allowing them, without being inwardly overcome.

There are circumstances in which fighting the dark is appropriate, and others where it's important to wait for the right time to enable you to be victorious in dealing with outer darkness. It is rarely necessary to actively collude with the dark.

To put that into everyday language, take a situation in the working world. You are working in a company which you discover is making a product that is harmful to buyers, but concealing the information that makes this clear. You're outraged, you want to expose them. But you do not immediately announce that you are leaving, or go straight to blow the whistle. If you did so, the incriminating evidence might quickly be destroyed, and your own reputation along with it. The company could actually be strengthened. Nor do you undertake a free-lance sabotage project.

But you pause a moment and deliberate on the most effective strategy to obtain the best results for all concerned. You might choose to resign, quietly, without arousing suspicion, and tell your story to a regulatory authority, or even a newspaper with an investigative tradition, underlining the difficulty of finding corroborative evidence. You might decide to wait for a good enough opportunity, which would allow you to photocopy incriminating evidence. Even if it was a long wait. Then you could resign, taking your photocopies to an appropriate authority. Or you might hit on some other strategy.

Most of us do not (fortunately) encounter such cloak-and-dagger situations. But we do meet lesser variants. Constantly. It is vital then to stand up in the face of the dark. But not necessarily to confront it immediately. Which is not the same as colluding with it. Or pretending it does not exist.

Angels

I am deeply grateful to the angel who is a constant companion on my right shoulder. In times of trouble, I turn to him and feel comfort. Does he have white robes, golden hair and wings? Maybe.

I suspect he would look like whatever I wanted 'him' to look like. The fact is that I feel benevolent energy at roughly my right-hand shoulder. If I was born and brought up in India, perhaps I would see a Hindu god instead of an angel.

The benevolent energy that I feel could relate to the spirit of someone who is no longer alive, or to an energy or presence of a different order, not related to a dead person, or some other variation in the energy frequency spectrum. I don't know.

But I know the wonderful, benevolent qualities of angels. That I am glad to have an angel around me (at least one). That I have seen, on occasion, clouds of beautiful angels around clients, particularly clients who had done a great deal of energy or spiritual work. That I don't believe the classic wings and white robe are necessary to the form. And that talking of an angel is talking about an energetic reality. Perhaps one day physics will say something like, 'Oh yes, at frequency xyz we have metaphotonmorphells,' or whatever name they give angels.

Other realities

The domain I found in my meditation was the same

every time I entered it. Of course there were different regions, but it had a basic layout, and that layout did not seem to change. In that sense it was another 'place'. But it seems unnecessary to burden it with a geographical location. To me it had a location in the mind. Obviously.

In the same way, the places I went to, while in my 'other world', were all also mental locations, or would perhaps be better described as states of mind, or even energetic destinations. Remembering always that energy covers a spectrum. What is clear at one end of the spectrum may not be visible at the other end. In the same way as if you blow a dog whistle, a human hears no sound, a dog, whose ears are tuned to a different higher frequency, hears the sound. So, there may be locations that are visible, or accessible, to some individuals, in some states, but not in others.

Some of the places I went to seemed to have marked energetic connections. They inspired precise feelings, and had specific effects. One place, for example, was a place of fire. It burnt my body away, metaphorically. But though my body was consumed, I continued to exist. Then my body was rebuilt, and I was reborn. This particular point was made repeatedly, in many different situations. Emphasising that we are all more than our bodies, and also underlining the normal biological cycle by which the majority of the cells that make up our bodies die and are replaced regularly.

Some of the places I visited seemed not only to be connected with specific energetic experiences, but also through planets, in a way, with astrology. None of the planets had names I recognised, though this, of course, need not necessarily mean that they were different from the planets perceived by astronomers and astrologers today. I am no astrologer, but it suggested I was opening myself to heightened experiences of astrological energies. In later years, working with a close group, I was able to take them to various energetic destinations – again connected with 'planets'.

Then there was the 'Place of the Undead' which I visited on numerous occasions. A place where I believe those who refused to die completely were held in some terrible fate.

This is a metaphor, and a way of expressing a reality. Most simply, it is a point about the need to die, when a situation comes to an end. It is a metaphor for a circumstance we meet regularly. Its message is about the importance of letting go, dying when the time comes. We all know people who continue to pursue a project long after it has stopped being feasible – like hoping or dreaming about a relationship when the other person has clearly chosen to be with someone else. That state is the state of being 'undead'.

My role in the 'Place of the Undead' was to help those who had not died, but had been metamorphosed into ghastly part-human shapes, to die – to let go and pass on.

But the 'Place of the Undead' had another significance. We are more than just our physical bodies. When our physical bodies die, our non-material bodies – our energy – does not just disappear. As science states. Though it may change its form.

My experience supported the idea that our spirit, the shorthand for our non-material essence, moves on to another dimension of reality, after death. Sometimes, though, the spirit is not prepared to do this. Then it becomes trapped in some sort of halfway stage, no longer attached to a physical body, but also not able to move on to a more refined, transformed dimension. This is the 'Place of the Undead'. (I would explain much poltergeist activity, for example, as being associated with this level. But that's another story, and this isn't the time.)

The crystal cave

Another location I visited often was a crystal cave.

> *Then my vision is filled with the sense of crystal. At the other side there is an enormous crystal place – a huge cavern, that seems to grow bigger and bigger . . . Suddenly, I know this is part of me . . . here I have found a core of myself. This crystal place is part of me. I have been here before. A long time ago. I have spent a long time here.*

The crystal cave was usually inhabited by angels – full of benevolence. Its chief quality was its capacity to act as an 'eye' on the world. 'The cave is like an eye, offering special sight on the world.' Again, I suspect this is a metaphor that identified the cave, or 'eye', with the self – 'I' – and, at the same time, represents the third eye, linked to an open heart, which brings the ability to identify with and see into the world. When nothing can be hidden. The cave represents an energetic reality. It is a reflection of a particular state of consciousness and, as such, a real location.

A dimension of reality

My meditation reality was another dimension of reality. The visions I had there relate to other levels of reality or consciousness. In the same way as energy is scientifically recognised as a continuum, different aspects of which bleed into one another, so life and death and beyond are part of a continuum.

In life our physical form is the most obvious to us. Our need now is to allow our awareness to expand, to understand and own the power of the spiritual which brings awareness of other dimensions to reality. After death the situation changes, and our reality becomes a predominantly spiritual one, located in different dimensions.

Life after death

Much evidence from the near-death experience suggests existence after death (see the work of Professor Kenneth Ring, page 355). Some evidence also argues for past lives and a return to earth in another body after death. All I can be sure about is my own experience.

My meditation has brought me into contact with relatives who are no longer alive. The encounters were emotional rather than informative. On one memorable occasion I was supposedly contacted, through a medium, by a relative – who was clearly identified – with a very apposite, if enigmatic, message. Then, I have been sitting with clients when either a message or an image has come to me. This has not happened often, but when it has happened both message and image have been very specific, and were immediately recognised. But that does not mean that I believe in a dimension populated by spirits with the same concerns and interests as they had when they were alive, only perhaps better.

We see death, or life after death, through our own filter. In dealing with others we are always limited by our own bias. We assume what's important to us must be important or obvious to them, especially if they are close to us. (And, of course, we assume it's right, good and for the greater good!)

Similarly, the way we conceptualise another dimension is dictated by our own constraints. We can't imagine the unimaginable – that's why it's unimaginable. We are usually very reluctant to believe what we think can't possibly be true on the basis of our own experience. (The world was definitely, scientifically proven, known to be flat – for hundreds of years. To even suggest it was curved was heresy.) So, if we do take a dimension of life after death to be part of reality, we may model it on our own lives or expectations.

This may not reflect the reality of the situation. At one point I was very close to death. For several months death was inevitable, and coming closer. In that state, my view on life and reality was very particular. My meditation reality and my everyday reality were almost one and the same.

My priorities settled. I had no fear. Acceptance reigned. Those I was close to continued to be just as dear to me, but the love assumed a very detached quality. My senses were hugely heightened – the beauty of the earth was very evident. Striving obviously ceased, while capacity for swift action was accentuated.

In that state, had I been transformed into a spirit, I would not have sent messages back telling Auntie Joan I was well and happy, or advising a loved one that the paper they needed was in the third drawer of the chest in the sitting room. I doubt whether that would have been how I would have considered I could be most helpful to those I had left behind. But I might well have sent my family and friends copious healing, and then done the same for the rest of the world.

On the other hand, it is also possible that, in spirit, out of compassion, I might have recognised that those are just the kind of concerns that most of us living on earth have, and I might respond to them. Until you get there, it's impossible to say.

The existence of spirits after death is difficult to separate from our image of what spirit's concerns or identity would be like. In the cases where I have been with clients and seen images of or heard words supposedly from those no longer alive, I have always felt that the image or words were connected with my client's needs of the dead one, or their relationship with the departed. What transpired was as a result of my client's need, not some spirit's desire. It manifested in the form that my client desired, or understood – not necessarily as a reflection of the spirit's concerns or wishes.

Reincarnation and past lives

I have had several, semi-spontaneous past life regressions. Semi-spontaneous in that I first crashed into a past life experience when trying a breathing technique, aimed at relaxation. The images, and the story they told, were so vivid and extraordinarily relevant to my life that I repeated the experiment several times, always with the same hugely profound and moving result.

Occasionally too, at their insistence, I have worked with others, taking them back into themselves, or time, to see what images came to them. Again, the results have been startling, and very useful to my clients in understanding themselves, and moving on in their lives. But not always. Is this proof of 'past lives'? Or reincarnation?

I found my own past life images very constructive in helping me understand patterns in my own life. But I have never felt the need, or been able, to classify them as 'fact' rather than metaphor.

In the situations where I have helped others find images of their own – not given them images or

identities – they too have often come up with star-
tlingly apposite stories. For example, in *The Pool of
Memory*, I tell the story of Sara, whom I helped find a
level where she saw herself as a medieval man, in a
church, involved in a religious and political intrigue.
As she put it, 'playing one side off against the other'.
In the session I tell her, 'You are caught up in a world
of intrigue. It's a familiar dilemma for you: the inter-
relation of church and state. You're snared in the politics of the situation.' Shortly afterwards she goes on:
'The image of the church vestry is getting sharper, I
can hear rustling – is it coming from the doorway, has
someone parted the curtain? I am afraid, very afraid.'
Then, in her image, she sees the throat cut of the man
whom she is, and he dies.

   Later I learn that the problem facing Sara in the
everyday is as a trustee of a Buddhist organisation,
trying to balance spiritual principles with politics.
The 'past life' images she saw were very constructive
in helping her resolving her problems about what to
do in the present. The exercise of contacting, or constructing, those images was a positive and productive
one. However, that's different to saying they were
'true'.

   Past life experiences, when conceptualised by the
individual concerned, can clearly be useful. Past lives
as allocated by someone else are a very different matter. All too often I hear horror stories from people
who were 'told' by a 'spiritual teacher', or 'guru', or
'alternative therapist', that they had a particular identity or experience in a past life and are now required

to take some specific action – to separate from a partner, to work for the teacher, to encourage the
therapist's work, etc. – to 'repay' a debt or obligation
from a supposed past life.

Obviously I cannot support any of that. In fact, I
strongly advise everyone to avoid any situation where
someone else 'tells' you your 'past lives'. This does not
rule out working on a situation where you envisage
your own notions of other identities. However, most
of the issues that all of us need to deal with can be
dealt with in the present. Either with a practice or a
therapist of your choosing, or simply through life.

Accepting that the past is no more and no less than
an element of the present, just as the future is equally an element of the present, which helps create it,
emphasises exactly how much power we have in the
present. We have the power to change our reactions
to the past, to shape our future.

For some, past life regressions, or past life work,
are attractive, as offering a way of conceptualising
elements of themselves. To others they seem superfluous. The choice is yours – as long as you do not
allow someone else to 'tell' you your past lives! And
you can be certain that when, or if, you need to know
the past, or a concept of the past, it will make itself
known.

The benefits and problems of karma

If reincarnation is reality, as perhaps the majority of
the world believe, a major advantage is support for

the law of karma, which is frequently linked to the notion of rebirth. In Sanskrit the word 'karma' means 'action', but the law of karma is understood as a law of accountability. Basically it states that each individual carries a balance sheet of negative and positive achievements from one life to the next. In other words, you can never get away with anything, and will always, ultimately, be rewarded for a positive action, or punished for a negative one.

It's the ultimate big stick and carrot theory. But it can also be a deterrent from taking power and initiative to change a situation – like growing up in a disadvantaged family – since karma surely will offer a better chance in the next life? Though that may not be an accurate interpretation, it is one that has frequently been applied, in India, for example.

Simple-minded interpretations of the law of karma can also suggest that any misfortune is the sufferer's 'fault'. If you are born with a disability it is a 'punishment' for previous failings; if you live in an area caught up in civil war it's a 'punishment'. All these seem potentially dangerous forms of discrimination, based on a very simple notion of karma.

For example, they ignore the possibility of group karma. The karma of a group may settle on an individual, who as a result suffers particular hardship. (Rather like the psychological concept of scapegoating in families, or groups.) The individual's suffering is not a result of his or her own actions, but those of the groups. Or a group or an individual may face suffering as a result of taking on the role of teacher: to offer an opportunity for the other, or others, to learn, for example, compassion. The story of Jesus could be interpreted in this way. He is supposed to have suffered so others could live. Not as a punishment.

Over-simplified interpretations of karma show an ignorance of the lesson of interconnectedness and depend on a model of the world as a globe inhabited by independent, free-standing individuals, with minimal links between them. The reality suggested by a more complete understanding of energy may be very different.

Rather than puzzling on the law of karma, I emphasise the lesson of the heart chakra. We are always responsible for our actions. Working with the spiritual energy of the heart emphasises our responsibility for the universe, and the interdependence that inspires. Along with the compassion that avoids judging another's circumstances and seeks only to help alleviate them, if possible.

For those who still think they are being rewarded or punished for good or bad behaviour in the past, look at a few examples. Take many of the champagne celebrities flaunted particularly in our tabloid newspapers as enjoying an enviable life. Do you think they are being rewarded for an excellent past? And if so, are they using their rewards appropriately? Or are their lives always enviable? Are the children of a war-torn state being punished for their past bad deeds? Do they deserve their fate? Obviously the answer is no to all those questions.

But the so-called celebs, and the victims of war situations, are facing challenges – often terrible challenges. Their task is no more and no less than the task we all face, to reach the heart and act from the heart. Which is the true fulfilment of our human identity; or the start of it. Many champagne celebrities, whether they are enjoying themselves or not, clearly have some distance to go on that journey. And enjoyment is hugely important. But only if achieved with no harm to another, and at the same time as fulfilling our fundamental blueprint – becoming fully human, embracing our spiritual as well as our material reality. In the words of the song, 'Money can't buy you love.'

Your approach to the other world

It doesn't matter whether you think the other world or worlds and their inhabitants are real, or simply stand for ways of describing your perception of yourself and your interaction with reality. Your mental framework could dictate what you think. For example, take three approaches to my meeting with a wonderful female figure in the other world who epitomised a particular love, fertility and procreation.

A Jungian psychoanalyst might say that I encountered an archetype, part of the universal unconscious as well as my unconscious. A Freudian psychoanalyst might say she was an idealised object that I had created for myself. A Buddhist might describe the figure as the Goddess Tara.

The Jungian might then go on to talk about my self being enriched by a meeting with the collective and creative unconscious. The Freudian might be concerned that a lack in my external life caused me to invest in an idealised object. The Buddhist might instruct me on how to ask Tara for her blessings and to integrate her presence into my being.

They are three very different interpretations of the situation. From my own perspective now, all three are misleading. Simply because each is an interpretation which, taken individually, limits the potential impact of the situation I encountered.

Particularly in the early months of travelling in the other world, it was vital for me to make no interpretations. Not to assume I knew or understood what anything – even the domain itself – represented, or was. In some cases it was only years afterwards that I understood. And there is still material in my diary notes of my journeys that I have not yet turned to. I hope my understanding will continue to evolve. You are in the same position now.

The role of experience

In writing *The Pool of Memory*, I tried to give the reader something of the same experience as I had encountered. I tried not to write down my interpretations of what was happening, and to allow the reader the chance to understand the role of the experience. It was the experience that delivered the lessons, not the mental deductions or instructions. In the same way as no set of instructions will ever teach you to ride a bicycle. They may give you a valuable pointer on how to go about it. But they can never teach you how to do it, as if it were a model aeroplane you were putting together from a kit. Nor does the explanation of some of the skills involved in bicycle riding ever describe the experience of whistling downhill through the early morning on a cycle.

No childcare manual, or story of someone else's childcare escapades, can ever enable you to experience what it is like to have a child. The recounting of the experience does not create the same effect as living through the experience. This is not an easy point to grasp, before you have been there. Especially for those whose brains are highly trained. But no one, however well read, is prepared for what it's like to have children before they experience it for themselves.

A slightly perplexed academic once told me she had read *The Pool of Memory*, and understood that 'my guides' had told me to depend on myself or 'that sort of thing', but she asked, was I taught anything else? She believed I must have been given some information, some lessons, by some superior teachers that could be repeated. This was her model of learning.

She did not understand that the book was an attempt to describe and set down a series of experiences, which were not analysed or understood at the time but which, in themselves, transformed me.

It was the process itself, not any understanding of the process, that effected the changes in me. In fact there were many ways of understanding that experience, and my understanding of the events that made up the experience has deepened over time. Fortunately I had the wisdom not to analyse, interpret, or interfere with what was happening at the time it occurred, but just to allow it. There was no stone tablet handed down to me. No 'god' who explained the nature of the universe. But that model of transformation was very difficult for my academic friend to grasp.

On the other hand I had literally hundreds of letters from people thanking me for my story because it confirmed their own. Many of them then went on to describe deductions and scenarios that I couldn't recognise in any way! But it didn't matter. The fact was that they had been able to identify with the experience of the journey instinctively, because they had had journeys themselves. And to see it as a similar experience, with perhaps similar results to their own. (Of course, the results may not always have been the same, but that's another story.)

Energy and experience

The experience had little to do with brain learning or understanding, and everything to do with opening the heart and energetic functioning.

It helped to alter the range of energetic frequencies I was able to perceive. In doing that it altered my responses and capabilities. Part of the alteration enabled me to see energy in others. It also took me to different locations, and into contact with other presences on another frequency. It changed my perception and my understanding.

Obviously not everyone will be altered in the same way. But everyone is open, ultimately, to their own level of development. And that applies exactly to you. The path I am outlining is an experiential path. It's up to you to take it. And in taking it, don't interpret your experiences in your meditations or contemplations, or you will kill them (and probably misinterpret them at the same time). The act of imposing meaning will undercut the reality you are experiencing.

In just the same way a child's sense of reality is often destroyed by adults who deny the reality the child instinctively knows. Even as adults we are all familiar with situations where you found what you thought was true, though odd, you were talked out of by friends, only to discover at some later point that your original sense was, actually, true. As children most of us believed in magic. Now, as an adult, I feel as if I have been able to rediscover the ways in which it is true. As you can.

Issues for you to think about

1. Focus on your own darkness. That means try to identify and think about aspects of yourself that are destructive – towards yourself or others. There could be strands of you that are envious, ambitious for prominence or power, greedy, self-centred, self-destructive; or strands that otherwise influence you to

behave from a part of you that does not respect the well-being of others, that wants supremacy over them, or wants to be recognised as more than them. Or, there may be a part of you that simply gives way to despair at your own situation, and turns to self-destruction.

They may not all be feelings that you can easily recognise as being directed against others. For example, you may feel weak or vulnerable, but the self-protective impulses which this could inspire might be actions aimed at hurting or harming others. Worse, those others might not even be directly threatening you, but only perceived by you as such. Or they may be posing a threat to your position of power in a hierarchy you have constructed. Many people working in organisations face these sort of clashes during which it requires special effort not to succumb to inner darkness and instead, where it's necessary and possible, join with others to work for the greater good. In other words, where your power is threatened, try to hold on to that power through your allegiance to doing the best you can for the greater good, rather than by attacking others.

Identifying your own darkness is a very difficult task because it is asking you to expose your weaknesses, and consider the way they might affect your dealing with others. We all

like to think of ourselves as kind, decent, hon-
ourable and loving. Usually our intentions
are. But, when it comes to actions, we are all
vulnerable to desire for power, jealousy desire
for revenge and a host of other feelings which
can motivate our actions. Considering yourself carefully, and the responses of others to
you, can begin to reveal those forces, and give
you a chance to disarm that darkness in you.

When it comes to inner darkness, which is
simply despair at your situation in some way,
consider your feelings as an expression of
powerlessness. Why do you feel powerless to
change your situation? How can you take up
your own power? Accept that you have the
ability and obligation to do so. Your life is
your wonderful, extraordinary responsibility.

2. Think how you have dealt with a dangerous
   or threatening situation in the outside world.
   Or, have you been able to deal with darkness
   in the outside in the past? Are you able to do
   so now? Has the manner in which you deal
   with it changed? Are you at peace with those
   changes?

3. Think of a situation in your own life when
   you have been in 'The Place of the Undead'.
   A situation you have held on to long after you
   should have let go of it. Try to identify someone else you know who is stuck in 'The Place
   of the Undead'. Try to decide for yourself the
   difference between hanging on to a situation

that you should let go of, and being persistent in facing a situation that you wish to overcome.

4. Think of someone, or some sector of the population, you can identify as being scapegoated by another individual or group. What do you think about the incidence of scapegoating? Can you see how individuals or groups can sometimes bear the brunt of circumstances not entirely (or at all) of their own making?

Chapter Nine

Spiritual Principles of
Relationships

If you have read this far and followed my suggestions, life may be pretty intense. It might have happened quickly – the culmination of a matter of weeks or months, or, like me, it may have taken you years to get here. You have probably developed a practice, say, t'ai chi. You might well be meditating, an accomplished practitioner, or just starting to experiment with meditation. You will certainly be contemplating, and your head will be swimming with questions. But there is more to it. The following exchange took place at a seminar I was teaching.

Elizabeth is a successful businesswoman, in her late thirties. Dressed in a smart, formal suit, with well-groomed hair and hands, she didn't have to explain to the group that she had reached a prominent corporate position. Which made what she had to say as we paused, an hour and a half later, even more remarkable.

'This, what we're talking about now, is all I want to talk about,' she announced, 'this is all I think about. Of course I'm concerned about my son, but I can't think of anything except this spiritual work – or whatever it is. I'm totally occupied with trying to understand it, or make sense of what's going on, it's almost like being possessed. I play your tapes constantly. I read everything I can that seems relevant. And I don't feel part of the normal world, at all, any more. I have nothing to say at the business functions we have to go to. I can't bear it – it's very difficult for my husband. I look around and think everyone is half alive. I can't join in any of the conversation, it all seems pointless. I feel so isolated, so crazy, but also at some level happy – if that's possible. What's going on? Does it make any sense to you?'

Of course, it made a great deal of sense to me. At times the spiritual journey can seem isolating. But it is actually a prelude to being pulled further into life, to participating more fully, whatever it seems like in its more intense, early moments. I'd heard complaints like Elizabeth's in dozens of different guises. That ache, that isolation, but also the stirring and the compulsion and, somewhere, that irrepressible joy. All very familiar, and necessary, in the beginning.

Ted, sitting next to Elizabeth, spoke before I could. 'Count yourself lucky you've got the husband and the kid already.'

I understood that too. Ted's journey had been particularly intense, and despite his good looks he had difficulty in making and keeping relationships. Like many others. I have seen just how difficult it can be for men and women of all ages at this stage.

Another of the group, Sandy, was not interested in relationships. On a very direct journey, her third eye was engaged, and she was working deeply with her intuitive abilities. 'I don't want to talk to anyone,' she said bluntly, 'it's not worth it. No one else understands.'

'There's no one to talk to,' echoed Laura from across the room. I smiled because I suspected, no, knew, that very soon all that would change.

Relationships in our age are a real area of contention, as barriers and established behaviours of all sorts come tumbling down. On all sides divorce figures and social statistics, politicians' pronouncements (never mind their lives), and the personal columns of most newspapers – from the august *International Herald Tribune*, offering the services of hugely expensive 'personal headhunters', to the pages of almost every local paper all say the same thing. People find it is difficult to make and keep relationships in what seems a new and particularly painful way. The nuclear family is in decline, the notion of family is in turmoil. And so, obviously, are relationships.

The spiritual path can seem, at moments, lonely. Which is paradoxical, because its goal is the heart, and the love that the heart releases. As your understanding and sensitivity develops, so the number of those who seem to share your understanding becomes more restricted. But soon that matters less and less. As your spiritual intelligence develops, it draws you

back into life, insisting that you participate more and
more fully. And connecting you with an ever widening circle.

At the same time, though it's a powerful journey, it
doesn't have to be lonely; the number of people sharing it with you are increasing dramatically, and will
go on doing so. But the journey does offer a very particular approach to relationships. Understanding
exactly what that is helps. But understanding more
about the context in which we relate to one another
comes first.

Interconnectedness

The first, most important relationship for all of us is
our relationship with ourselves. Our material and
spiritual selves. It is at the core of spiritual intelligence because, whilst our material bodies are relatively separate, our spiritual selves are not. As the
heart chakra, whose domain is the world, knows, we
are all linked, and we are all part of the force that
links us. So our relationship to ourselves is in fact
part of our relationship to the whole.

But more follows. The force that links us, the force
of spirituality, is not above us. Or outside us. Or
simply a light inside us. It is both inside us and outside us. If you drew a diagram, it would not be a point
somewhere outside us, or a straight line above or
below us. It would be a line through us – through us
all, and around us. And that line would be like a
thread joining us all together in a great circle. In

short, the force of spirituality is like a process that connects us all. We are all interconnected, joined and held together.

Of course I can't prove that scientifically. But the second intuitive talk I gave in 1997 on relationships made it clear. Whilst the first talk, 'Talk at the Tabernacle', explained the downfall of the hierarchy and the end of the guru, the second talk, 'Relationships', explained how we are all held together. This interconnectedness has massive consequences for our idea of God, or some higher spiritual power, relationships and also intuition.

A new way of seeing God

Of course, another word for the force of spirituality that connects us all is God. But seeing that process as God makes it clear that this is a notion of spirituality that is very different to one in which the ultimate power resides above you, manipulating the strings, perhaps rewarding devotion or good behaviour, punishing the wicked or at least, ultimately anyway, meting out divine justice. This new model says we are all part of the notion of God. Our energy is part of the energy of God.

That is not to say by any means that events depend solely on mankind's actions. We are not, fortunately, capable of controlling the force we know as God. But we are responsible for playing our part in creating the lives we choose and contributing to the life of our planet. Expecting some higher power to take responsibility for you is not enough, or in any way appropriate. Playing your part in working with, forming a part of, and influencing that ultimate power that connects us all is essential.

Interconnectedness and intuition

At the same time, interconnectedness is the mechanism of intuition. Simple observation reinforced this for me.

Lazing on a sofa on a bright Sunday morning, too warm, too contented to move, enjoying the quiet and the clear light of the still winter's day, I saw two birds on the branch of a tree that grew across the road and spread its arms at the height of my windows. Were they pigeons, or doves? I'm no ornithologist. But the sounds they were making could not be mistaken. They spoke – the one to the other – in the language of love. A courtship that is instantly recognisable. Sweet nothings, a give and take, a matching flow of energy between them. And with it, a coming and a going, with all its attendant calls and returns. Fluttering wings interspersed with billing and cooing.

Till finally, a conclusion: one raised his, or her, wings for a longer flight – and was gone. The other hesitated. Mute. Then moved along the branch in the crisp light, swaying slightly. Sorrow, joy, acceptance – or none of those in bird-reality? The winged one left behind waited a moment longer, absorbing the particles of warmth perhaps, then took to the air.

Lying still, capturing the sunbeam that penetrated my window, I felt it all. Felt what? Empathy? Imagination? Or just an anthropomorphic fantasy?

It's hard to know. But what I felt was similar to what I feel when seeing clients as an intuitive. Then, the effect is very much as if I slide into the other. When they or I speak about something sad in their lives, my eyes will sometimes prick with tears in sympathy. It is almost as if I can know exactly what they are feeling. Or have felt. I know their past, I know their experience, their parents, their history. It is as if I know the other from the inside, and yet retain a certain detached quality that allows me to see it, to understand it, but not to be it.

Working as an intuitive is the experience of merging with the force of spirituality that knows all of creation. It is the place where it is possible to see the very best that another is capable of. To really understand the potential, and sacredness, of another's core. To achieve this, it seems I slide on that thread which connects us into the reality of the other, where not only present experiences but the marks of the past and the future are also present. In this way, the thread that connects us all is also the mechanism of intuition.

Interconnectedness and others

Given that the fate of each and every one of us is intimately bound up with the fate of all others, it is impossible to separate yourself from anyone else's actions and fate. It becomes impossible to gain spiritually and psychologically at another's expense. The implications of this for our relations to one another, all the inhabitants of our planet, and the earth itself, are revolutionary.

Take the temptation to say, 'X and Y and I will look out for one another because we went to the same school, and we'll do the dirty on everyone else.' Or, in an environmental context, 'I'll dump this chemical waste a hundred miles away because then it won't affect our town.'

Of course, no one likes to admit to those sort of feelings. We usually offer great rationalisations for behaviour which is in our personal interest, or the interests of our group, at the expense of others. Second chakra behaviour, in fact. But in the light of interconnectedness, and the teachings of the heart chakra, those sentiments are exposed for what they are. They are expressions of our limitations. They take no account of the organising force of the universe.

In the personal, social, domestic, corporate, professional and political, or any other, spheres, inter-connectedness has wide implications. They include dealing with conflict, aid, caring, invention and development, at every level. But first it has important implications when it comes to looking after ourselves, and handling ourselves in relationships.

Respect difference

Sometimes, in relating to others, we allow ourselves –

our lesser instincts – leeway to think that someone else, or another group, is different from us, somehow 'other'. A different colour, different income group, different race – all of those can be triggers to considering other people as less, or more, than we are. And that means that we allow ourselves to believe that they don't feel in the same way as we do, that they are somehow less human, and less worthy of consideration than we are. Or more worthy or more important than we are.

Spiritual intelligence teaches: 'respect difference'. Others may indeed think differently to the way you do, appear to act differently, perhaps even feel differently to the way you do. But the lesson that the organising force of the universe teaches, the knowledge held in the heart, is that in a most fundamental sense, we are all interconnected. We can never disregard, elevate or treat anyone else as 'other'. They are always part of the same whole – the same as us. Not above, or below.

Do no harm

Which is why the basic rule for dealing with others, in all situations, is 'do no harm'. It is also the fundamental law for dealing with yourself. It is never right to stay in, let alone seek out, relationships that do not support your development, or offer you pleasure or interest, let alone harm you. Often, of course, it takes time to see how a situation is harming you. Or you are harming someone else. It is then essential that you take steps to change that.

Of course, we all harm one another, and ourselves, inadvertently. But that's quite different to doing deliberate harm.

Energy of companionship

Relating is also an energetic exchange. When you are with others you are affected by their energy. It's almost impossible not to be. We all know that from the way we react to being with other people. Some people make us feel happy. Others, just by their presence, can make us uncomfortable, or even angry. Sometimes we can't find anyone we are comfortable with. Whether we recognise it or not, we are responding to their energy.

If you are with someone regularly, the situation is greatly emphasised. If you live with another or others, you are all sharing the same 'energy soup' – all the more so if it is a sexual partnership. In an everyday sphere, you sometimes say that couples grow to look like one another. Just as others maintain that pets come to look like their owners. (Or perhaps we choose partners, or pets, who in some way look like us?)

Working as an intuitive, when I saw couples together, sometimes I could see what looked like threads running between them – energy interchanges. It was a practical representation of the way in which they were affecting one another. When exchanging energy with those you are relating to, you will be sharing yourself with them, and sharing how they are too.

Some time ago, Edward, an IT specialist, told me he was going to work with a group whom he saw as particularly tough and greedy. 'But,' he said 'they're very successful, the money is fantastic and I'll be able to do things completely separately, on my own, so I won't have to worry about any dirty tricks.'

It was a measure of what a thoughtful and principled man he is that he acknowledged to himself, and me, that the group was greedy and that he was worried about 'dirty tricks'. I was sad at the thought of him joining with associates whom he saw in that light. The energy of companionship always tells. You can never be separate from those with whom you are associated.

So, I wasn't surprised when a year later, he came to tell me that it had all gone horribly wrong. He had not been paid the money he'd been promised, his work had been stolen, he had resigned and law suits could follow.

It is possible, of course, to change the energy of a group. Because of the dynamics of sharing energy, everyone is affected by the people around them. Of course, whoever is most sensitive will respond the soonest. Edward did not feel he could, nor did he want to, stand up to the pressure of the energy he was encountering. His associates simply responded to him by showing their dark sides increasingly. Had he stayed where he was, it's likely he would have had to become more like those around him – and, laudably, he didn't want to or couldn't do that.

This is exactly what peer group pressure is all

about. And it makes it clear why it is so difficult for all of us, children especially, to deal with the energy of the group. The dynamic is just the same in a one to one relationship, and is particularly important when you begin to change.

Sooner or later your partner, or anyone close to you, will feel that change, and be affected by it. They may react against it, or with it, but they will not be able to remain neutral. It may lead you to the point where the whole relationship changes, or if the other person, or people, cannot adapt to the way you are changing, you may have to think about compromising, or moving away.

Taking responsibility for yourself

While relationships are very important for sharing, they are not a way to escape from your responsibility for yourself. Just as however much you might sometimes want to protect or help or even share something with someone else, it might not be appropriate. There are some things each of us can only do for ourselves.

It was a basic lesson I learnt very early on from my clients. From time to time, a client would ask me to see someone they were close to. I was happy to do so, if the person wanted to see me, and paid out of their own pocket for doing so. Unless of course it was a child, when I dropped the need for them to pay personally, but still firmly maintained that they needed to want to come themselves.

The reason that I insisted any prospective client pay for themselves was to ensure that they really wanted to take part in the process of changing their lives. If they were coming to me just to please a partner, or parent, it was a waste of their time and mine. I found that if someone else paid, a client was much less likely to really make use of their session, and much more likely to simply spend an hour with me, without the outcome necessarily being very important to them. But if they paid my fee themselves, there was a chance they would want to see their money well spent, and would investigate exactly what I was offering.

At the same time, it can be very tempting to want to pass on to others a revelation that you feel has really changed your life. Jodie came to a seminar and nodded vigorously when I explained this point. 'I really wanted to tell everyone when things clicked,' she said. 'I wasn't really sure what I wanted to say, only that things were starting to make sense and it felt so amazing. But of course nobody understood what I was going on about.'

Those of us who are parents know only too well that there is a strict limit on how much we can teach our children from our own experience. They have to have their own experiences to learn from. The poet, John Keats, writing in the early nineteenth century, said, 'Nothing ever becomes real till it is experienced – even a proverb is not a proverb till your life has illustrated it.' It is the same in developing your spiritual intelligence.

It is a journey where each of us must take responsibility for ourselves. You have to learn to take responsibility for your own experiences, and your own learning. You also have to learn to allow others to do their own learning. Often you can share your space with fellow travellers, and you must. For pleasure, companionship, growth and development. But sometimes, it seems as if fate, or chance, has isolated you. Or you need to be alone.

Being alone

For many of us this is a frightening point. Extended families have lost their place, families seem to have lost their way. The number of single heads of households is increasing relentlessly. What might be called 'mating patterns' have changed – dating patterns have certainly changed too. In short, being alone, at all stages of life, is a common and increasing condition.

Sometimes, of course, we are alone by choice. It can be necessary and important. I found myself relatively alone when spiritual reality took over my life. Like Elizabeth at the start of this chapter. Though she (like me) longed for others she could share her spiritual unfolding with, basically she was not unhappy, being relatively alone. Relatively. She is in a marriage, with a child, as Ted pointed out.

Many of us have none of those comforts; or find ourselves at points without a partner, or children, sometimes with few friends or family. But there are ways of dealing with this situation. Time alone can be used very constructively. It can have a purpose, allowing you to re-evaluate your choices, make different ones in the future, change your priorities. Instead of simply being driven by existing commitments, or old fears. But it takes courage.

Your power to look after yourself

One of the features of traditional ways of thinking about spirituality is the comfort of feeling that there is a higher force 'looking after' us, a sort of all-knowing, super-wise parent figure watching over us.

Of course, understanding interconnectedness makes it clear that there is no parent-type figure watching over us. There is no force to be placated or cooperated with. We are part of that force. We are all there is. Which means we have that power, responsibility and ability. We are responsible for taking an active part in creating our reality. We have the power, responsibility and ability to find love and create joy.

Karen's story

Karen felt herself to be completely alone. She came to see me to ask me to 'look' at her and tell her why she was so alone. She wanted me to give her healing, or tell her if there was anything that could be done to help her escape from her misery.

She was in her forties, and pretty. She had never married and worked in an office job, in a responsible position. She was also a talented artist, and liked particularly to draw black and white studies of still-life compositions that were almost photographic. Her isolation hung round her like a heavy cloak.

Looking at her intuitively, it was easy to see the bullying father who had abused her, and her mother who had escaped by dying when Karen was a child. Then her father married again, and her half-brothers, on whom all praise had been heaped, were born. It was easy to understand why she had almost colluded in discounting herself. 'It's as if I don't exist,' she told me; 'no one sees me.' For years her only solace had been the religion she had been brought up in. 'I'm not saying I don't believe it now,' she told me bitterly, 'but I can't go on praying to a God that doesn't seem to care.'

Karen had lost any belief in change. Or, more, her power to effect change. Inwardly she hoped her God would bring her change. Outwardly she was resigned. She didn't feel she had the power to change her situation. She longed for companionship, but no longer felt it was possible, let alone her right. I felt it was important to help her change her perception of her situation in a number of ways – the effects of which might take some time to sink in. And there were some real changes she could make, or try.

First I had to help Karen come to terms with her own power and responsibility for change. She was drowning in a sense of powerlessness. She wanted 'God' to step in and bring her a miracle, or failing that, someone outside, me for example, to give her 'healing' to make her situation better. She needed to take back her own power to effect change.

'Specialness'

Karen also needed to understand the fundamental reality of interconnectedness. Being isolated and alone often leads to a feeling of difference that's almost a sense of 'specialness'. You feel you are quite different to anyone else. In some ways, though this is a very punishing experience, it can also bring a sense of being set apart, being elevated from others, which can be its own reward.

It's crucial when feeling separate and alone to understand how, at a truly fundamental level, one is not. Of course, we are all different. But we are also all linked. Spiritually, energetically, we are linked. Feelings of separateness or specialness are an illusion which lead to isolation. Allowing links with others, building relationships, however small, often depends on recognising the human qualities that we share and making an effort to build bridges to share them.

The perfect other

Of course, the companionship Karen wanted was the perfect other, the dream partner. Finding someone who meets your ideal is rare. The 'perfect other', or the idealized 'soulmate', usually belong to fairy tales, not reality. In reality, the perfect partner is one who will help you grow in ways you can't foretell. Because you can't foretell them, the perfect partner may well be quite unexpected.

Meantime, you need to find someone, or a number of people, with whom you can share different qualities. It may not add up to the dream lover. But it often adds up to a number of different, meaningful relationships. It spells the end of isolation.

It may even lead to a good partnership, based in reality, recognising sameness and difference. Exactly what you need – which you may then recognise as your perfect partnership. Or perhaps it will bring an unexpected union with someone who comes when you aren't looking. It seems quite wrong, but, in time, proves altogether right.

Dealing with patterns

Having been through therapy Karen had considerable insight. She found it amazing that when I 'looked' at her I could tell the pattern of her upbringing so clearly.

'Those patterns never really go away,' I told her, 'but you can learn how to deal with them, and how to emancipate yourself from the effects.'

Acknowledging the past is very important in learning to let go of the behaviour patterns it has taught you. Which is why therapy can sometimes help. It is also why releasing the energetic effects of the past, in meditation or some other way, perhaps a creative way, matters so much.

'I don't meditate,' she told me, 'but I do drawing.' Together we looked at some of her pictures, and I tried, gently, to explain to her how the drawings, fine and precise as they were, reflected her emotions. They were of objects, not people. Each drawing had a static quality – as if the objects were immobilised, frozen in their places. There was no trace of sensual enjoyment or colour. No range of feelings, just a monochrome world of black, white and grey. Each picture was more exact than the last – as if Karen was straining desperately to reproduce reality almost mechanically, without allowing herself any of the human qualities that might be described as 'freedom of expression'.

'It's true,' she said. 'I never feel happy after doing a drawing, I just feel I must go on and do the next one.'

'That's because you're not releasing any emotion, just restating an emotional position,' I explained.

'But even if I do open up,' she countered, 'there's no one around me.'

I hear those words regularly. There is always a person or people around who will supply a little, at least, of what you need. If you will accept it. But what you need rather than what you want: it is an important distinction.

Wants and needs

You want what you think will solve your problems, or satisfy your desires. However, from a wider perspective, your wants may not be in your best interest, or what will help you develop. What you need will probably be different. And you don't necessarily know what you need, to begin with.

But it is certain that there will be one person or even a few people with whom it would be good to spend time, even a small amount of time, during this phase. What you need is human companionship. Other human beings with a variety of talents and abilities. They will always have something to offer you. And while that something may not be what you want, or perhaps what seems enough, it will always be a start. It could be exactly what you need to build a small platform to stand on as you journey into your heart.

Sooner or later, you may find that one of those human beings has actually transformed and become the partner of your dreams. Or is it you that's transformed? But you have to reach out.

Reaching out

Sometimes people tell me that they believe 'the universe' will provide for them, events will simply occur to furnish their needs. Sometimes that is true. Things just work out. But sometimes they don't. Partly, of course, it is luck. Luck plays a part in all our lives. But being able to capitalise on luck, or better still making best use of your circumstances, harmonising with existing forces as well as you can, is crucially important. That means taking up your power and reaching out. Reaching out gives love and intuition the strongest chance to play their parts.

Listening to your intuition

Being prepared to reach out doesn't always mean taking action. Sometimes your intuition will tell you to wait, do nothing for now; sometimes it will urge action. Then you need to know you have the power, and the responsibility, to initiate change. To take a risk. Not to wait for 'the universe' to provide. Equally, you need to listen, and at other times, be able to sit back and let things happen.

Recognising that both those ways can be true is not a contradiction. It is simply an acknowledgement that circumstances vary. What is right at one time may not be correct at another. Your intuition is the best guide as to what to do when. It will be speaking to you. You need to learn to hear it, and to trust it.

'I can't decide if it's my intuition telling me to act, or just my desire to do something,' as one young man agonised to me at a recent seminar.

'If you don't know, there's no way to be sure,' I told him. 'But you can be sure of the effects of constantly doubting yourself. Think of a spoon. Keep on bending it, changing your mind, going backwards and forwards, and the spoon will snap! It's much better to make a decision and follow it than to keep doubting yourself. After all, if you decide your decision was not correct, don't blame your intuition. Just make a new decision, allow your intuition another chance.'

Change for Karen?

I talked all this through with Karen, but she wavered. She was stuck in her pattern. She had given up on possibility, and power. When someone says to me, 'There's no one, absolutely no one,' then I know for sure they're not listening to their heart, or following their truth. They are holding themselves in a vice and not allowing any kind of relationship. Which means they will not grow because they have excluded all others, and are fighting their needs.

I explained to Karen how, because of her past, she would always be susceptible to her pattern. However, her journey in life was constantly challenging her to grow beyond her past. Finally, when she left me, Karen agreed that she would try meditating, or experimenting with the way she used her artistic talent. Some months later, visiting a friend, I was struck by a wonderful sensual painting of a woman, in gorgeous strong colours, that she had hung in her dining room. 'I have just bought it from the artist, a woman called Karen,' she told me, identifying my client. 'Isn't it fabulous, it's so sexy!'

Issues to think about

1. Think of a group you consider to be 'different' from yourself. Then think of as many ways as possible to see how they are human, in exactly the same way as you are.
2. Think of an individual you consider to be

very different from yourself. Consider whether there is any way of bridging that gap. Not of becoming 'best buddies', but of relating to that person in a more positive and constructive way.

3. Think about whether you are jealous of, anxious about or threatened by anyone you consider to be different. It may be hard to acknowledge this.

4. Think of the possibility that someone you consider to be 'different', whom you dislike or disapprove of, is working from a different place to you – perhaps higher, possibly lower. And that you owe them at least your compassion.

5. Think of the ways in which you might be similar to someone whom you think highly of.

6. Think of ways in which you might have similar traits to someone whom you recognise as behaving from the dark or weak sides of themselves.

7. Think about the people you spend time with. Remembering the energy of companionship, are there any you would like to spend more time with? Or less time with?

8. Can you think of a situation where you did deliberate harm to someone else? If so, why? Can you think of a more constructive way to deal with the feelings that motivated you?

9. Can you think of a situation where you did deliberate harm to yourself? If so, why?

Again, can you think of a more constructive way to deal with the feelings that motivated you?

10. Think of a situation where you were helpful to someone for no personal gain. How did that make you feel? And think of an example where you were at the receiving end of someone else's benevolence, again offered for no personal gain.

Part III

How to Live the Ideas

Chapter Ten

Putting Principles into Practice

For some, like me during my spiritual unfolding, or Elizabeth at the start of the last chapter, a pause in the cycle of relationships, or a time when one concentrates only on the most essential relationships, can be vital. It provides the space to go within. If that's the case, don't see it as a punishment.

But for most of us, much of the time, life is a process of coming into contact with others – whether they are casual contacts at the supermarket till, work contacts, friends or lovers. Some people, like Karen, find it difficult to engage in even these relationships. She felt you pulled 'all' or 'nothing' out of the relationship bag, that she had pulled 'nothing' and could not change it! A large part of life is a search for meaningful relationships. Over and over again I hear the complaint, 'I am not meeting the right person, or people.'

Meeting the 'right' others

There is no problem about meeting the 'right' people. Those you meet are right. That means that you always have something to learn from those who cross your path. Whether you need to learn it from being with them, or conversely whether you need to experience the growth involved in learning why you can't or must not be with them. But first you have to recognise 'the point' of the others you meet.

Roddy's experience

Not long ago, I saw a very intelligent, sensitive young man of sixteen. His mother had been a client in years past and she called, asking me to see her son. I explained that I was writing and teaching which left me, sadly, without time to see private clients. However, because it was really difficult to find anyone who could help Roddy, her son, I agreed to see him.

Roddy told me he felt he might be going 'weird', as he put it. He started with one particular incident. Over the last four years Roddy – who had moved schools three times – had repeatedly met another boy, a little older than himself. It seemed that whatever Roddy did, the other boy, Peter, was there, only a little earlier, and now moving on. Finally, they had just met again, and Roddy discovered he was going to be following Peter to the same place of further education. As he said, it 'spooked' him, but there was more to the story than that.

Initially, when they met briefly Roddy felt very intimidated by Peter, who seemed supremely talented and confident. He saw Peter as a sort of demigod, or superhero. In complete contrast he, Roddy, was withdrawn, awkward, a loner and a low achiever. He felt he and Peter had absolutely nothing in common, and suspected the other boy despised him, if he noticed him at all.

But at the same time, every time they met, it was as if the hairs on Roddy's neck stood up. Then recently, just before he met Peter again, Roddy had thought of him, and even dreamt that they would be meeting. When they did meet, Roddy's flesh cringed. He seemed to know Peter was somehow very important to him, and it confused him greatly. (Incidentally, neither boy has any homosexual tendencies.)

Next, Roddy had a conversation with Peter, and to his amazement found it flowed quite easily. All this heightened his sense that Peter was supremely important to him. It was 'really weird', he felt. What was happening, Roddy wanted to know?

Well, it wasn't difficult to see. Roddy is a very sensitive young man. He's part of the younger generation, many of whom are able to tune in to the changes that are happening on earth with much greater ease than most adults. They are experiencing the reality of our perceptual revolution – their intuition is already heightened – but with little to help them understand what they are actually perceiving.

In Roddy's case he was perceiving a subtle reality. Shy, withdrawn and lacking in confidence particularly when he was younger, his own deeper wisdom or intuition had always been trying to make him see Peter as a mirror for himself. Meeting Peter was not accidental or irrelevant. Many of Peter's qualities were, and are, qualities that Roddy possesses himself.

Until now, though, Roddy could not see any similarities between himself and Peter. (I could go further and say that it seemed there was 'unfinished business' between the boys, but I felt no need, and rarely do, to draw on metaphors from past lives.) Now, I suggested to Roddy that they were actually very similar. Almost everything Peter could do, he could too. All the qualities he admired in Peter were his too. That was what his meetings with Peter were trying to tell him. 'Take another look – check out the similarities!'

At the same time Roddy was experiencing precognition – knowing things were going to happen before they actually did so – in a number of areas, which was simply a demonstration of his sensitivity. He was picking up a wide range of information. His problem was to know how to order or classify it.

Roddy is not alone in this. We are all – particularly younger people – experiencing this phenomenon to differing degrees. Our problem is the same as his: recognising what it is that we register. And then, of course, there is the issue of using it wisely.

When it comes to relationships, again Roddy was facing a lesson that applies to us all. We are all prone to idealising other people. We may decide that someone else is really super-capable, or talented, and see ourselves in comparison as not at all capable. Sometimes our assessment of the other person is correct, sometimes it isn't. What is almost always incorrect is our assessment of ourselves in those situations. In Roddy's case, he was helped by circumstances that were actually pointing out his misperception.

At first Roddy felt that meeting Peter was irrelevant – if he could, he tried to avoid him. In fact, as he later recognised, it was vitally important for what Peter had to teach him about his own positive qualities. In Peter he had met the 'right' person.

Susan's experience

It can work the other way. Susan was a massage therapist. A quiet, rather reserved girl, who did not say much. She met Barbara, a psychotherapist, at a conference. Barbara had an acid, quick tongue that fascinated Susan, in a strange way. Susan, who was very sensitive, suspected that part of Barbara, somewhere, might be rather hurt – as she had been herself – which could be, partly, why Barbara was so caustic. As a result, Susan was sympathetic to the other woman. Barbara, in turn, seemed drawn to Susan and began to seek her out, showing off how cruel and sarcastic she could be in biting, funny little asides.

Fortunately Susan quickly realised that in Barbara she had a warning about her own negative tendencies. Barbara was like a mirror for her. The part of Susan that had been hurt perhaps would also have liked to make, or maybe even could have made, those swift, acerbic comments. Susan realised there was a place where she felt inadequate, and resentful of other people. She tried to tell Barbara how she felt, but it seemed to make no impression. Barbara even made fun of her feelings.

The warning was clear. Susan understood the energy of companionship, and knew that if she spent time with Barbara she was in danger of being drawn into a dark spiral. Susan resolved to avoid Barbara and find more positive company. At the same time, the encounter had led her to recognise her own dark side, and by allowing her to choose not to give it power, it had strengthened her spiritual intelligence and the development of her heart. In Barbara she had met the right person to learn from.

Others are a mirror for us. The best mirror we have. We see ourselves most clearly in their qualities and our reaction to them, and their reaction to us.

Seeing too much of yourself in other people

If you feel strongly drawn to someone, look to see what qualities appeal to you about them and whether they are in fact qualities you want, or should be cultivating in yourself. It doesn't mean at all that you cannot, or should not, be relating to the other person. Only that you should be careful that you are not asking them to live out, or share, a reality that you ought to be creating for yourself.

Judy and Tom's reality suffered from that confusion. Tom was a successful graphic designer and Judy an efficient, slightly subdued secretary. They set up home together, but a year later came to see me, perplexed at the fact that though they loved one another, and both longed for a successful relationship, it seemed that however hard they tried, they only made themselves and one another miserable. Of course, there were a number of issues, visible in the tangle of their energies, but none of them was particularly relevant here, except one.

It was clear that Judy was not using her creative talents, while Tom feared he was close to exhausting his. Judy longed to be, if not a designer, then much more creative. But she had great difficulty in admitting her longing, let alone doing something about it. Of course, she was, in part, drawn to Tom because he was in the design world. Which was exactly where she wanted to be, though she was loath to admit it.

After they considered my view of their situation, they decided to make some changes. Judy resigned her job and found another in the advertising world, as an art director's assistant. A lowly start, with quite a drop from her previous level of income and very long working hours. But soon Judy's talent took off, as she started making inroads into graphic design herself.

Meanwhile, Tom found that, with Judy's new hours, he had much more to do on the domestic side of their life, and to his surprise was glad to do it. He had thought he had no talent or taste for it. In fact it had been one of Judy's qualities that had drawn him to her – she excelled at cookery and homemaking. Taking over some of those tasks, Tom experienced a flowering of his creativity and quickly designed a series of paper products that did very well.

Both Tom and Judy were attracted to the other because they each felt the other had qualities they did not. In reality the other had qualities they needed to develop in themselves. Looking at their energy, both were seriously out of balance – in some respects. After readjusting their lives, both became much more capable of achieving an energetic balance, which of course showed just as plainly in their achievements and relationship. As well as in their spiritual progress.

Getting angry

Acting as a mirror, others can sometimes make us very angry. If someone rouses your anger, check whether what's angering you is actually a quality that you share with the person who is making you cross. If you dislike someone, check to see if the quality you dislike is one you fear to find, and would or do dislike, in yourself. If you admire someone, are you admiring something you feel you do not have? Perhaps it is there, and all it needs is to be allowed. If those around you make you feel contemptuous, are you, deep down, contemptuous about yourself?

How you feel about other people always says a great deal about how you feel about yourself.

A good relationship

A good relationship is one that supports you in allowing you to develop to the fullest in making the journey to the heart, to develop the perspective it offers, and to claim your spiritual intelligence. It leads us to explore all the aspects of ourselves. That means recognising the good, the bad, the strong and the damaged in you. It means recognising your connections to all others, not simply a partner or immediate family or interest group. It means accepting your responsibilities in and to the world, an exciting but sometimes daunting prospect.

Others can play a crucial role in supporting you in this process. But that is not the same as suggesting that you should be supported in whatever you do! Real support recognises the aims of your journey. It recognises the values you are trying to reach, and supports you in upholding them. But it can be rare. Often we have a problem understanding what real support in friendships or partnerships means. It does not mean support for anything you choose to do, much less support for your mutual material benefit.

Mutual advantage

The ancient book of Chinese wisdom, the *I Ching*, has many wonderful teachings on friendship. Among them it points out that real friendship is based on sharing common values and a common end that is greater than yourselves. Friendship that is based on mere mutual advantage will collapse as soon as the advantage changes.

So, if you are great friends with, say, a girlfriend in a related organisation, because it is useful for business to be seen with her, and she reciprocates because it suits her business profile too, then you are likely only to be great friends, so-called, for a while. Until, for example, one or other of you needs a change of business image, or sees a better advantage in linking with someone else, or moves to another business.

Or, if you worked in property development, you could become friends with someone working in an estate agency because you might both see it as an excellent 'networking' opportunity. You would have a business link but also interact socially, believing that because you saw one another socially, you were becoming better friends. However, if someone else came along and offered a more profitable business opportunity, it is unlikely that your so-called friendship would count for much. Bluntly, it was always a business arrangement. (Incidentally, as a relationship based on mutual material advantage it would be governed by the second chakra.)

But if the relationship had been based on shared values, heart chakra values, then it would have fared quite differently. You might meet someone and discover that you had both lost friends to prostate cancer. Wanting to share your loss, and love, you decide to start a charity to do holistic medical research in that area. You could have great fun organising charity events, support an excellent cause and share an interest in understanding the relationship between health and illness. That, in turn, could lead to very similar conclusions about the right way to live – authentically and caringly. You would now have a relationship based on very different principles. It would be based on shared, positive values.

As such the relationship would have an altogether different chance of enduring than one based on mutual business advantage – perhaps just a variant on greed. At the same time, the relationship based on shared values could well lead to authentic and sustained business advantage for both of you, because you would be building up a real trust, knowing and understanding one another, sharing the same values. All of which would make an excellent basis for working together. But it wouldn't be the purpose of the relationship.

The same model applies to partnerships of all kinds – marriages as well as friendships. Of course, it doesn't apply in quite the same way to friendships that develop from shared interests – say, golf or gardening. These could become strong, if narrow, bonds. But it's important not to expect too much of them, to enjoy them for what they are.

For a potentially enduring relationship, shared values are essential. And there is another factor. To create a good relationship, you need to take responsibility for yourself and your own growth. When that goes wrong, two dangerous patterns that sometimes occur are 'the prop', and 'the support'.

'The prop'

Energetically, 'the prop' is like a traffic gridlock. Two people are locked in a situation and can't move. Both parties come to a relationship with a mixture of qualities, weaknesses and strengths. But in 'the prop', instead of using the relationship as an area for working on their weaknesses and helping each other to grow straight and strong, they prop one another up. Literally they lean against one another for support, to create a stable situation. They are highly dependent on one another, but also, of course, disempowered. Propped up in this way, it is impossible for either to grow. If the relationship endures, they may well stay frozen and increasingly inwardly limited. Or eventually the prop will slowly slide to the ground, as the relationship crumbles.

Louise's story

Louise came to see me, a warm, highly strung woman with, it seemed, every advantage. Two lovely children, a beautiful home and a high-earning husband whose every word she literally hung on – believing him much cleverer and wiser than herself. Theirs was a stereotype 'prop' relationship.

Her husband 'protected' Louise – from any sort of financial or physical worry. But also from any kind of self-development, or exploration of her own qualities, beyond those needed to keep house for him. In return, she protected him from any need to explore his relationships with his children or any form of self-development. Beyond being a good provider, and 'the wise one', he did not have to worry about extending himself. They lived in a circle of relatively similar friends, in a charmed, if limited reality.

Louise came to me because she felt a lack. Some deep unrest. An ache she could not name. Her overwhelming desire was to further her spiritual connection which she hoped would also deal with that ache. I thought she was right. It seemed clear that it was time to work on widening her perception and move to open her heart. But it soon became clear that there was another dynamic at work.

Louise responded beautifully and enthusiastically to our sessions, developing her meditation and opening to new areas of thought, understanding and perception for herself. But her husband quickly found subtle ways to undermine her development, even to make it difficult for her to visit me. He did not want her to change. He was afraid of change.

Remember the energy of companionship? You are energetically linked to your partner, and in this case the partner was resisting change. His highly stressed way of life was based on his adoring compliant wife staying just that way. For years she had been his support system, enabling him to do the things he did, and he had 'taken care' of her presumed weaknesses. Now, she wanted to explore and develop her own strength. In other words she felt it time to alter 'the prop', and he was afraid, and consequently using all his considerable strength to block any change.

Their dialogue is still continuing. But especially because they both have good intentions, I suspect they will work out a new way of growing beyond 'the prop' and developing themselves as well as this relationship. Both will have to change.

'The support'

The trap demonstrated by 'the support' is rather different. In 'the support', one party, usually the so-called weaker, supports the other, the so-called stronger, in whatever he or she wishes or does. So, a friend who took the role of 'support' might support all your actions, irrespective of whether or not he or she really believed them to be correct. Which, of course, would mean that you would be without reliable feedback and liable to have anything or everything you said or did endorsed. A flattering situation perhaps, but not a healthy one. Energetically, it's likely that your friend would be feeding off you, causing you to become gradually weaker and weaker.

Alexander's experience

Alexander was in quite a state when he came to see me. He'd been born lucky! His father, a prosperous industrialist, had gone into politics in later life and achieved considerable success. Alexander had grown up surrounded by wealth and influential circumstances. In his early twenties he had had some success in the film world, but nothing much had happened subsequently. With his wealth and connections he lived well. At the same time he was generous, and anxious to do good too.

Despite several relationships, he had not married (yet?), but had developed a number of friendships that were very important to him. However, many of his friends relied heavily on his patronage. A word from Alexander could be very helpful in fixing a contract. An invitation to an intimate dinner at Alexander's could mean meeting the right contact, or even an invitation to spend time at his country house.

As a result, most of his friends were very slow to contradict Alexander. Most simply agreed with any opinion he held, or course of action he proposed. Anyone who opposed Alexander was immediately dismissed by his loyal friends. From the outside it seemed as if he could not put a foot wrong, so supportive were his friends.

Eager for love and attention, he welcomed their support which is what he thought it was. But as time wore on, Alexander became more and more unsure of his own judgement, and erratic in his reality where everything seemed to rotate around him. Though of course he could not see that that was what was happening. He became less and less connected to the values he claimed he was supporting, until it was hard for him to know what doing good was.

In short, he was a true victim of 'the support'. He needed a great deal of courage and determination to break away from the world that surrounded him. The process is ongoing. We see examples of the same situation all around us – in our professional, personal and social worlds.

Changing needs

As you develop spiritually and intuitively, your needs in relationships and your perception of relationships change. Self-gratification becomes less important, the simple need to 'do no harm' becomes more important. It's essential, though, that joy remains a constant, high on the list.

At the same time, we all face the need for change and movement in our relationships. That does not necessarily mean parting. All relationships face ups and downs. If you have made a mature choice in a friend or partner, dealing with the challenges relationships invariably bring us is a powerful – perhaps the most powerful – route to all aspects of self-development and a deeper, truer joy. But sometimes, sadly or gladly, you grow beyond – literally, out of a relationship, in the same way as you grow out of your clothes, in childhood, or wear them out. There is a point where your understanding and perception change, and what once fitted no longer does. And the compromises necessary to accommodate your enlarged perception to another's view of reality are sometimes no longer possible. It brings a new set of problems.

Dealing with change in partnerships

Politicians regularly pontificate about 'family values'. All too often, if we were really honest with ourselves, many of us would admit to secretly longing for things to be more stable. Change in our time is frighteningly fast. If you consider that the last century opened with the aeroplane and closed with the internet, it is not surprising that family structures have been similarly revolutionised. And it's hard to tell where they will end.

The morality of change

Worst of all for some of us, relativism rules. Society no longer seems clear about what is acceptable and what's not. It's as if enough people say something is acceptable, then it is. Ultimately, if enough people – or vociferous enough people – said that sex with children was OK, perhaps even that would become accept-able? Morality and ethics are not popular subjects – let alone widely taught in schools. Too many groups shun any formal teaching in this area as an invasion of personal choice. But most of us want to behave well, and to observe a moral code. The problem is, what? Especially when it comes to relationships.

We see frightening, disturbing or radical changes in our societies, but no longer know what is the desir-able or 'correct' pattern for relationships. Looking at one index of change, in the year 2000 (and for the previous four years) Britain has outstripped America in violence against persons, sexual offences, property crime and robbery, when these are measured as offences per 1,000,000 people. American sociologist Charles Murray, Bradley Fellow at the American Enterprise Institute, is reported as attributing this fact to the growth of an underclass, whom he sees as the product of an upbringing where many 'children have not been socialised to the norms of self-control, concern for others and the concept that actions have consequences. One of the leading reasons is that large numbers of British children have not been raised by two mature married adults.'*

Others, of course, see differently. Whatever the cause of social unrest, by far the majority consider a lifelong partnership the ideal relationship for themselves and to bring up children. However, it doesn't happen to everyone. And few are surprised at not attaining that ideal. Most young people still hold that as their dream, and if it fails to materialise they are very disappointed. Moral standards don't seem to have a place. Chaos and turmoil may seem inevitable in these circumstances. But there are other ways, constructive ways. Once they are understood, we may even come to welcome the opportunities that change offers, or at least to make the most of it.

First, it is impossible, and altogether undesirable, to put the clock back. Energetically we have moved on. The vibrations that the universe is facing are faster and faster, finer and finer. We have an unparalleled opportunity to embrace the whole of our nature – to realise our spiritual selves.

Changes in relationships are like growth points. They are points at which we are challenged to make

---

* *Sunday Times*, 13 February 2000.

the same mistakes again, or to free ourselves of the patterns that have governed our behaviour up to that point. Change actually offers the chance to widen your perception, and function on a higher level.

It also offers endless opportunities to be distracted in dozens of different ways, and to miss the point of this age and stage. Never before has history offered a challenge of this order. Never before has there been a chance for so many to see it.

Of course, spending a lifetime with one person, growing together, sharing your individual development, is a glorious prospect. And an ideal situation in which to bring up children. But it does not always happen.

The person you chose as a partner three or thirteen years ago (or even three months ago), planning to face the future together, may no longer be seeing the same future as you. Perhaps you are not even looking in the same direction any more, let alone making out the same road. You may feel that your relationship (this stage of it, anyway) is drawing to a close. It could be that your self-development is proceeding at a different rate to your partner's, and the gap cannot be bridged. Or it could simply be that as you find out more about yourselves, you realise or suspect or fear that your needs and desires in life are not compatible. There is no one rule to determine your action at this point. There are several.

Personal responsibility

The process of developing spiritually is closely linked

to the process of taking responsibility for yourself in every aspect. Reaching towards spirituality means not blaming others, or a cruel fate, or seeing it as someone else's job to change your situation, or deal with a situation you can see. But accepting that it is your responsibility. And being careful not to harm others. Remember, especially when you approach change, that we are all energetically linked and fundamentally interconnected.

Personal gain

In handling change there can be no real personal gain at another's expense. A notion which the cult of the self that flourished in the 1980s and 1990s would not have understood. The cult of self's mantra was 'me, me, me'. It put you, yourself, your needs, your desires, your achievements, above all others. It forgot completely that 'No man is an Island':

> *No man is an Island, entire of it self; every man is a piece of the Continent, a part of the main; if a clod be washed away by the sea, Europe is the less, as well as if a promontory were, as well as if a manor of thy friends, or of thine own were; any man's death diminishes me, because I am involved in Mankind; and therefore never send to know for whom the bell tolls; it tolls for thee.*
>
> John Donne

It believed personal advance was all. The 'other', or

others, didn't enter the picture, apart from as fodder for your self-satisfaction. The assumption that gain was possible at another's expense didn't even merit a second thought. It was later linked with 'networking', a notion that purported to have some higher purpose, but often (though, significantly, not always) was simply a way of trying to achieve personal advantage – power or material gain – through connections.

All that, of course, led directly to the moral relativism we so often live with today. Most of us are as keen as ever – maybe more so – to 'do the right thing'. But we need to understand what that is.

Honouring the circumstances you've created

When it comes to change in relationships, in deciding – or accepting another's decision – to move on, you are responsible above all for the circumstances created by your coming together. First and foremost, if there are children, they continue to be your joint responsibility, for ever. Likewise you never completely lose a connection with, and so some form of responsibility for, your children's other parent. At the very least because the well-being of that parent is important to your children's well-being.

So, if one parent has given up work in the outside world to keep home, then both parents need to address the issue of helping that person to become self-sufficient. Or be supported, as necessary. And it could go on a long time. It's no use to argue, 'But it gives a former partner a real chance to be such a drain on a new relationship,' or 'What about second (or third) families?' The answer is very simple.

What came before can never be wiped out. What came before will always be an integral part of you. All aspects of it need not play an active part in your present or future, but you must always honour it and observe all the proprieties connected with it, before moving on to develop new areas. That means a second family's claims on your money, time or attention are not superior to your first family's claims.

To think that what is over is over, and you can wash your hands of it, is to fail to understand the basis of spirituality. We are all connected. We are all connected for ever. Honouring the spirit in you is to honour the earthly circumstances you have created – and that means all the earthly circumstances. Not just those your friends can see, or you feel like concentrating on at the moment. The past has huge power over the present.

James's story

James came to see me to talk about spiritual development. As I listened to this thoughtful man, with his excellent record of charitable work, it soon became clear that he could concentrate on nothing except his catalogue of the failures, in his eyes, of his ex-wife, the mother of his two daughters. He even accused her of being 'mad'. (A common accusation flung at anyone whose behaviour we do not understand, or make enough effort to do so.)

He wanted to punish her – or 'make her see reality', as he put it. Clearly, circumstances between the parents were very strained. However, it seemed James's income would allow him to supplement his ex-wife's earnings and look after the daughters comfortably. This he refused to do.

He believed he loved his daughters very much but was determined to make life as difficult as possible for their mother. When I tried to explain that he could not separate his daughters' well-being from their mother's, he exploded with rage. In his mind they were quite separate – as if he could punish one, and the others, standing by, watching, would not be affected. He could not see that he was transgressing the basic principle, 'do no harm', let alone failing to understand interconnectedness. And his good record of charity work, as well as his professional achievement, allowed him to justify himself. At that point.

However, I hope that in time James's spiritual development will continue once more. I suspect that one day, perhaps when his daughters are grown up and can put their experience to him, he will see matters differently.

Of course, I have heard variants of this story from many others, men and women. And their children, whose suffering their parents sometimes do not see; or if one parent does, they cannot protect the children from the other who does not.

Angie's story

Angie's story was rather different. Angie came to see me at a crossroads in her late forties. She had done a great deal of spiritual and energy work. And she wanted to go further. Her development was impressive, she was easily able to connect with her spiritual reality. But there seemed to be a block she could not overcome. She wondered if her relationship was the problem, or her work, or something else. A darkness hovered in her semi-conscious – some sense she could never quite conquer. She had seen a number of alternative therapists who had suggested various remedies – from homeopathy to dance. I saw differently.

Angie had had a baby, a son, in her late teens. That baby had been adopted, and there had been no further contact. Angie had gone on to marry and have a family in comfortable circumstances. Her husband knew the facts and, supposedly, the issue had been resolved. But when we discussed it, Angie admitted she still missed her first-born. Deep down she had never been able to stop worrying about the well-being of the baby she gave up as a teenager. As we talked, she resolved to try to find her son.

She followed all the appropriate channels. Eventually she had news that her son had been located. But he had told social workers he did not want contact with his birth mother. However, the social worker was able to reassure Angie that he was in excellent circumstances and very well.

When the news came through Angie knew without

my saying it that she could lay the matter to rest now. She had fulfilled her obligations – she had honoured the spiritual law that she knew she needed to honour. She would always feel some pain. However, in making sure that her son was well, in offering herself, she had finally met her obligations to him. The next time I saw her she had started a new career, her life was revitalised and, best of all, the shadow she had felt for so long had lifted.

Wiping out the past?

It is impossible to wipe out the past. Many parents think they will avoid the mistakes that they believe their parents made in bringing them up. In practice this is rarely true – they make the same mistakes, or fresh mistakes in trying to avoid the old mistakes.

The way you deal with your children strongly influences the way they will deal with their children. From an energy point of view, the energy you grow up with is the energy you are most familiar with, and are often most comfortable with. Even if it is very uncomfortable. In a sense you are 'comfortable' being uncomfortable. Children are likely to recreate the energetic situations they grow up with.

At the same time, because they share your energy, your problems will be your children's too. Or, where parents separate, the children will experience the circumstances of both parents, particularly the one they live with. Which means that, growing to physical and spiritual maturity, you will have to confront the issues confronted by your parents and family collectively. In esoteric concepts this is expressed as facing your family's karma. We all bear the imprint of our own energy, and that of our family.

As Rita's story shows.

Rita's story

Rita had been adopted at birth and as a young woman, she had a son on her own – much to her adoptive parents' distress, who wanted little to do with mother and son. The boy's childhood was not happy. Wrestling with her difficulties, Rita tried to find her natural mother. She traced her, but though the woman was prepared to see Rita, she could not offer the help, love and support Rita needed. Rita became less and less able to deal with her own and her son's problems. Eventually, the boy was institutionalised. He is now fighting to recover. I lost trace of Rita.

Changing family patterns

From looking at family patterns, it is clear that issues are played out through families, and through generations within families. They do not occur in isolation. Many psychological studies bear this out. The energy logistics simply support the same truth. As you begin to work more on your own development, resolving issues and purifying your energy, you will be emancipating yourself from your inherited issues. Developing your spirituality should lead to greater resolution of your family issues, and that may make you much more comfortable, in a true sense, with your family. Though you may no longer be like them!

Equally, your progress will affect your children, because they will share it. In that way change, if well handled, can have positive consequences, not only for you but for future generations too.

Looking after our families, and extended families, or reconstituted families, is a basic part of attaining a spiritual maturity that recognises the interconnectedness that the heart teaches, and our responsibility and involvement in the well-being of the greater whole.

The new family

Legislators haven't yet worked out how to deal with changing patterns in relationships. Newspapers print lurid stories of the rich and famous or poor and powerless. But ordinary people may be beginning to understand how to handle the changing face of the family.

Last Christmas I watched Marie, a second wife and mother, invite her husband's first wife, along with her children, to spend Christmas all together. Potentially difficult? Not really. It was a generous, kind and wise act which showed maturity and love. A real demonstration of concern for the well-being of all. Marie's spirituality went beyond an interest in books, or a limited idea of personal gain. She cared deeply about all those in her life. Her step-children and her own children's chances of dealing with reality will only be enhanced. Of course, there could be tensions, but the gains for all concerned will outweigh any disadvantages.

Our future will be composed of reconstituted families and other family groupings. Recently a newspaper reported on a case where a child was being looked after by the mother's first mother-in-law, while the parents were at work. The mother's first marriage had ended, but her link to her mother-in-law from that marriage had not. And now the older woman looked after the child of the second marriage, with whom she had no blood tie. But who perhaps was half sibling to her other grandchild or grandchildren.

It was an excellent example of ordinary people dealing with new family relations, in advance of legislators who have consistently had little positive to offer. Of course it will not deal with the problems of those utterly disempowered socially, financially and psychologically. But it points the way towards a society based on human values, heart values, of love and kindness. It recognises the truth of interconnectedness. It points towards spiritual intelligence that knows our responsibility and involvement in the well-being of the greater whole. And it is certainly not limited to the rich, or the clever, who may have to follow the example of the rest of society in creating a more secure future for all of us, and our children.

When a relationship without children ends

Of course, relationships that result in children, though particularly important, are only one of the many sorts we have to deal with. But all relationships, especially those that touch us deeply, are important.

The rules are exactly the same – do no harm. Honour your responsibilities. But there is a difference. In ending a short-term relationship you have, in fact, made a statement that you do not want the connection to continue, or to continue in a particular way. Given that both parties are adults, and adults aiming to be responsible for themselves, you are not beholden to the other person. Your responsibilities are very different to what they would be in a situation that resulted in children or perhaps involved joint finances.

It is possible to separate and move on to a future that does not include the person you are separating from. Sometimes it is even important to be able to make a clean break to be able to continue your development. Which is usually the purpose of your move.

When someone says to me, I'm good friends with all my exes, I can sometimes be suspicious. I am glad to hear there is no enmity. Parting with respect intact is important, if possible. But I wonder why the relationships ended. All relationships face difficult patches. It's important to stick through those that simply indicate the struggle of development, rather than to discard them. If you are such good friends it can mean you have not developed. Was it a question of change just for diversity? Or 'change to stay the same'? If it was a change to allow real development, it is likely that you will need at least a spell where you are not 'good friends'.

On the other hand, one of the joys of developing spiritual intelligence is the knowledge that sooner or later, it will come to most of us. Which means that from time to time you will have the pleasure of meeting someone from your past, from whom you parted because your development was going in different directions, and find you have come together again. Change is ongoing.

Many close relationships?

If you lived in a small native tribe, perhaps most of the tribe would be your friends and relatives. Our society is rather different. Inevitably as your spiritual intelligence develops and your heart opens, the numbers of those you can be intimate with will become fewer and fewer. Paradoxically, you will probably find that you are able to relate comfortably to a larger number of those you meet than you were before. You will be able to be generous, to appreciate the human qualities of others in an open-hearted way. With luck you will not be annoyed, intimidated or hurt, nearly so quickly. But it won't necessarily make you want, or be able, to be particularly close to a large number of those you meet.

The circle of those with whom you can really open

your full self, will be those who have enough under-standing of the journey you are making. As that journey progresses, that group becomes smaller. But the connections you make are all the more special. That will be your compensation.

Forgiveness

Relationships are perhaps the greatest source of pain and pleasure for us all. They teach many lessons. One that isn't often mentioned is forgiveness. To be blunt, none of us expresses our highest capacity at all times. Even if we are trying to do just that. Bias or emotion may make us – perhaps unintentionally, unfortunately perhaps sometimes even intentionally – hurt those around us.

Being human means being fallible. It means learning from our mistakes. So, we all need from time to time to ask forgiveness of others – whether it is in words or simply in our hearts. We need to be forgiven. But if we need to be forgiven, so does everyone else.

If you need to be forgiven, and you want to be forgiven, how can you deny forgiveness to anyone else? In the words of the old prayer, 'Forgive us our trespasses, as we forgive them who trespass against us.' It isn't some God who needs to do the forgiving – it is you.

Punishment by law is different. If circumstances have been created that deserve punishment under the laws of the land, that is another matter which needs to take its course; along with forgiveness. Forgiveness is always in our gift. Give it.

Exercises for you to think about

1. Find one new activity to share with at least one other person. And practise it regularly. It could be an e-mail exchange with a new correspondent. You could join a class – yoga or dancing or pottery – whatever you like. Or take up a sport. Or whatever else catches your fancy that you can share.

2. Find one new activity that gives you pleasure on your own. And practise it regularly. It could be swimming, drawing, cookery, a card game, an early morning walk. Or something quite different.

3. Allow yourself to let go of one person or activity that no longer adds to your life. But be sure that is not a person or matter for which you have responsibility. Remember that as you grow and develop, your tastes and needs change. Make sure, from time to time, that you are not holding on to people or activities through sheer habit alone.

4. List the top three – only three – issues concerning relationships for which you want to be forgiven and make time to hold each one separately to your heart. Express your remorse and ask for forgiveness. Wait until you feel a response that tells you you have forgiven yourself. Don't be surprised if it takes days, even weeks, to forgive yourself. As you release issues, you can add others, if you want to.

5. Forgive someone else for an action or attitude that hurt you. Try to understand where their action or attitude could have come from. Send love from your heart to that person – even if you could not, or would not want to, express those feelings to her or him if you met in person.

6. Think how you could contribute to the well-being and joy of those in your immediate circle. Consider if you are doing the most you could.

7. Think how you could contribute to the well-being and joy of your fellows in the world. Are you doing all you could to contribute?

8. Think about the priority you give your own joy and well-being. Are you easily able to harmonise your needs with the needs of those around you? If not, do you accept the need to compromise? In compromising, do you look after yourself well enough? Do you allow your needs to be supreme sometimes? And do you allow the needs of others to outweigh your own sometimes?

9. Aim for balance. Make space every week to be on your own. Notice how long you are able to be on your own, comfortably. Are perhaps the pressures of your life such that you can hardly snatch a moment alone? Does life allow you far too much time on your own? Whatever your situation, try to limit your thoughts to the present, and enjoy that

present. So, if you are alone don't despair of a future made up of aloneness. Make every effort to enjoy the present. If you are overwhelmed by the needs of others, don't despair of a future that offers you no space for yourself. Check whether those needs of others that press so tightly on you really do have to be fulfilled. Or do they have to be fulfilled by you? Or do they have to be attended to immediately? If not, let go of them. If they really are essential, make your best effort to find something to enjoy in whatever the present offers. Without prejudging the future, which will be different.

Chapter Eleven

Truth and Illusion

The ache that brings many people to me has various faces. Of course, it is the longing to be whole. But other needs and desires show themselves too. The desire for companionship is one. The deep desire to know 'what's true' is another.

The longing for certainty

Deep down, where many of us long for certainty, we want to know what's true and what's not. 'I don't know what to do' – these are words I often hear. And they are not said because the speaker doesn't have enough information to base a decision on. Often there's too much conflicting information and experience. As well, probably, as not enough certainty about what's wanted.

You might begin to wonder about a truth that seemed certain last year, or even last month. Today, it might not seem quite so true. And because you've made 'mistakes' before, you're worried. You don't want to fall for an illusion again. You might even feel you've been misled, in the past, with dire consequences.

You wonder, are you are seeing things as they truly are? Or as you want them to be? Or as you fear they are? You might blame yourself. You could feel you are naive, too trusting, short-sighted, or just confused.

If you have that experience repeatedly, especially over a short period of time, it can be very demoralising. You start to doubt yourself. Seriously. It becomes hard to trust any perception, if you suspect it is going to be overthrown at the next corner. But that's a needless and destructive reaction to what is in fact a very positive experience which is crucial to your growth.

Childhood

We take it for granted that growing up means change, developing new ideas, leaving old concepts behind. The early nineteenth-century poet Thomas Hood wrote:

> *I remember, I remember*
> *The fir trees dark and high;*
> *I used to think their slender tops*
> *Were close against the sky:*
> *It was a childish ignorance,*
> *But now 'tis little joy*
> *To know I'm farther off from Heav'n*
> *Than when I was a boy.*
>
> *'I remember . . .'*

We take it for granted that we 'outgrow' ideas we hold in childhood. As we grow older we come to know better. So, when, as adults, we 'get it wrong', when what we have accepted and believed to be true transpires not to be, it is very unsettling. The relationship you were passionate about last year has crumbled this year. Was it an illusion – did you miss the truth? The friend you really liked and now go out of your way to avoid. Again, did you simply not see the truth? The belief that you held in the company you work for that simply doesn't seem to be justified now – was it an illusion?

What is going on? Is it simply our naivety or lack of knowledge or experience that leads us to mistake the truth? The need to find an answer can lead to psychotherapy, cynicism, or a wary retreat. It can lead to an unwillingness to take any risks, in case they turn out to be illusions. Or to the stout embrace of 'something you can definitely depend on' to protect you from the deceptions of reality. (Whether or not it will in the long run is another question, of course.)

As well as the problem caused by finding that something you believed was true is not, sometimes there is another effect that's equally unsettling – though we recognise it much less frequently. We find that something we knew in childhood, but later learnt to reject when we 'knew' better, was, after all, actually true. It could be no more than a memory, or a sensation, or a fleeting perception. A reality that wasn't even acknowledged, or if it was, that was overlaid by experience. It returns – and you feel it's true.

In just the same way as a first impression, often brushed aside by more carefully observed so-called facts, returns to confront your deductions of a person or situation. And it's proved true. What's happening?

The emperor's new clothes

Children often see the truth when adults don't. There's nothing to distract them. Remember the story of the emperor's new clothes, where it was only one little boy who could see, or would say, 'But the emperor isn't wearing any clothes!'

None of the adults dared admit they could not see the Emperor's supposed new clothes. They had been hoodwinked by the rogue tailor's claim that the fabrics were invisible to everyone who was unfit for the office he held, or who was extraordinarily simple in character. So what the adults said they saw was constrained by the belief that anyone who was worthy would be able to see the emperor's fine clothes, by the desire not to offend, by the fear of admitting they couldn't see anything, and probably by a host of other feelings as well.

It's the same for all of us. Plus the need to make a living, and the need to fit in with our peers. And the lessons that experience teaches about what happens to those who are different from the rest.

Experience and attitude

We see the world through the filter of our experience,

and our energy. In a sense the two are the same because our experiences register on our energy.

It's common sense to recognise that an accountant, trained in understanding figures and doing calculations, will probably assess the contents of a shopping basket first of all on price, later taking into account other factors. A nutritionist would be interested in the nutritional content of the same basket of food. An advertising executive might be interested in what proportion of goods in the basket had been the subject of television advertising in the previous week. An environmentalist might look to see which products were environmentally friendly and which were not.

They would all be true and valid responses – authentic to those who were making them. They would also all lead to different descriptions of the contents of the basket. But if you chose any one as the definitive, absolute, overall truth you would be wrong. Each approach would be the result of education and experience.

Attitude and circumstances play a similar role. A refugee with no means of support would look on a basket of shopping very differently from a multi-millionnaire, who never even purchased groceries. Likewise the shopping basket would arouse very different feelings in an anorexic and in a cook preparing for a dinner party. Each one would describe what they saw very differently.

In finding truth, it's important to remember that there are many different truths about a given situation. Many of our approaches are learnt. The results of our education, or experience, or circumstances. They reflect what we have been taught, what we need or what we want. Or think we need, want or have been taught.

All those are different to the intuitive's truth, which is also the innocent's truth. It is what you saw but hardly registered when you were a child. It is still available to us all. When we understand enough about it.

Energy and truth

In energetic terms, the reason the little boy saw the truth about the Emperor's clothes, and children often do, is that their chakras are much clearer than adults. There's nothing obstructing them. There is often a purity and simplicity about children that we all recognise. But, of course, life, the example of adults and the education we choose for our children change that.

First impressions

First impressions can be the fleeting register of a response, untrammelled by all the other, conflicting desires and lessons that life teaches us. Working as an intuitive, it is important to hold on to first impressions, and to detachment. To allow a reality to register that has not been taught, and that is detached from your needs or desires. As well as coming from an open heart. As they often do with children. Then and only then are your intuitions for another – or yourself – likely to be true.

Of course, if you work as an intuitive, expressing those truths is another matter. Often we do not hear a truth we are not prepared to hear, or don't want to hear, or are not yet ready to know. Just as adults often can't hear children. Though many of us ask for 'the truth', sometimes we don't want to or can't deal with what comes back to us. Which is an excellent reason for working to develop your own spiritual intelligence.

Truth and development

As your spiritual intelligence develops, your perception expands and your energy clarifies, your grasp of truth will change. According to Nobel prize-winner, physicist Richard Feynman, a scientist bent on progress 'tries to prove himself wrong as quickly as possible'*. Being able to see new truths is a measure of your development – not of having 'got it wrong' in the beginning!

Expanding your understanding will always mean that your truth will change. If you believe yourself to be and see yourself as an ant, interacting only with other ants in your anthill – then you only have an ant's attitude to the world. A wristwatch means nothing to you. You don't recognise its shape, or function, or any-

---

* My thanks to Richard Wardle for giving me Richard Feynman's book *The Meaning of It All*.

thing else about it – much less understand the concept of time that it measures. A wristwatch has no truth for an ant. But if you come to see yourself as a human being with human purpose and capacities, then your attitude towards a wristwatch will be very different.

Stuck?

If your views stay the same – if you don't change your ideas about people, relationships or events – it can be an indicator that you are unable to develop and grow. Think carefully about your attitude towards change – are you afraid to let go of truths that no longer work for you?

Chakras and truth

Most of us recognise the need for a balanced approach to truth. We try to steer ourselves to some mid-point, to have an unbiased view. In describing the chakra meditation, I emphasised the need to find the mid-point, to find balance, and to follow your meditation from that central place. It is possible to think of your relation to truth in a diagrammatic form.

Your truth is a line through the centre of each chakra. If your chakras are aligned and balanced, that line will be exactly through the centre of you. Your truths will be consistent and you will be in balance. If, however, the chakras are each slightly out of balance, the lines will not join to make a straight line.

So, for example, if your base chakra is heavily weighted on the right-hand side, it could mean that practical issues connected with home and stability are very important to you. Too important. Your view of truth would emphasise the importance of practicalities in those areas. So, for example, you would believe it essential that the place you lived in was very solidly constructed. That might seem much more important to you than that the location had a pleasing feel about it. And that belief would influence your approach to the world, and what you considered true and important.

However, you might then come to adjust your beliefs. To see that a solid structure and a congenial location were both equally important. Diagrammatically that would change the shape of your chakra, and also move the location of the line that went through the middle. In other words, your viewpoint would change. Truth, as you saw it, would change. Welcome that change.

Forgiveness, again

Letting go of old truths can be painful, and can lead to considerable upheaval, for you and for others. If this is so – and it is at many points for all of us – learn to forgive yourself. As long as your actions are carried out with the best possible intentions, then it is only right to forgive yourself for the inevitable pain that life causes. But at the same time remember that just as you need to be forgiven, so others need to be forgiven. You cannot deny to another the forgiveness that you recognise you need. This is the essence of compassion.

Fundamental truths

In the midst of change, and given the inevitability of change, some truths stay the same. They're very simple. Because they are very simple, it seems they must be easy to follow. Don't be deluded.

1. Do no harm.
2. Honour interconnectedness.
3. Accept responsibility for yourself, your actions, the situations they create and their effect on others.
4. Respect difference.
5. Understand that things change.

Do no harm. No one likes to think they do harm. But we all do harm to someone or something simply by walking on the earth. But that is quite different to intentional, deliberate harm. Deliberate harm sets out to hurt someone else, by a cutting word perhaps, as much as a blow. It is always a manifestation of our lowest impulses, hurt, envy, inadequacy, as much as ignorance or desire to do harm. But the justifications can be endless. The fact is simple – do no harm.

Honour interconnectedness. This means truly making the concept a reality for you. Understanding that we are all linked, that there can be no real gain – no psychological or spiritual gain – at another's expense. It means looking after the well-being of all, starting with those close to us. It does not, of course, mean overlooking your own needs so that you can take care of someone else! It means finding the pleasure in sharing your surplus.

Accepting responsibility for yourself and the situations you create: this seems obvious. But the mind and the emotions create curious effects. Being unwilling to accept that a certain set of circumstances is the result of your actions, even in part, can lead you to manufacture the most elaborate justifications. Often with huge mental barricades. All to make it absolutely 'clear' that your justifications are 'true'.

If you need, emotionally, to believe in your actions, whatever their consequences, your mind will help you. In an extreme case take the behaviour of some of the doctors who took part in perpetrating the Holocaust. They needed to believe their actions were justified. To support this they engaged in complex so-called genetic experiments, measuring, cataloguing, observing. In reality they were simply torturing their victims, in the name of scientific reseach. Mental justifications to avoid the implications of their actions. Less horrendous examples bombard us in the everyday. The mind constructs a truth of its own.

Respecting difference shows that you understand interconnectedness and honour both the material and the spiritual realities of others.

In understanding that things change, you recognise that situations, and your perceptions of situations, develop. In the same way as it would be ridiculous to hold you to the tastes you held as a thirteen-year-old, so you may come to see so-called facts differently as your development deepens. As always, balancing our mental and emotional needs and desires to allow a deeper truth, the product of our spiritual intelligence, can be difficult.

The mind's perception of truth

Of course, our society puts a great deal of emphasis on the functions of the mental body. We believe in brain power. We are taught to perceive our world through the medium of our brains. We educate for mental achievement. It's supposed to be detached, scientific and 'real'. In practice, with our brain in a dominant position, it is impossible to realise our human potential, or to know truth, or to develop our spiritual intelligence.

The brain can deduce how to make a nuclear bomb. But is much less clear about outlining when or how or if it should be used. Genetic manipulation offers unthought-of possibilities for reproduction and interference in our natural world, but again, we hesitate to say how or if those possibilities should be exploited. Proponents argue that what can be achieved by our scientific advances should be 'for the benefit of mankind'. Opponents find it difficult to halt the progress of 'knowledge', in pursuit of scientific truth.

For many, putting mind truths in perspective can be very difficult.

Peter's experience

Peter, a man approaching forty, came to see me some time ago. A successful academic publisher, he was highly educated and very intelligent indeed. He came in desperation really. He was quick to point out that I probably had little to offer him, but he had heard I was clever! (I took that as a compliment.)

Peter saw his problem as relationships. He was unable to have a successful or sustained relationship. 'I get it wrong every time,' he said. 'Of course, I'd like to have a relationship. I feel it is right and appropriate to share concerns and develop mutually. I know all those things, and I would like to be able to do them. But I have come to the end of yet another relationship, and frankly I don't know what to do. I've had so many. Every time I think I have assessed the situation correctly, I have been involved with intelligent, attractive women, of the right sort of age and background, but every time it's proved to be an illusion. I've just decided that I'm no judge of women – I don't know what's true – and I'll never be able to have a long-term relationship.'

Peter had been in therapy, which he felt had been very helpful, but had reached the point where he said, 'I'm much cleverer than my therapist, and I feel I've probably learnt as much as I can.'

Whatever the truth of Peter's story, one thing was clear. His mental body was hugely developed and his emotional body hardly touched. He agreed he had had a very formal upbringing with distant, unemotional parents, and no siblings. Peter simply did not know how to listen to his feelings, let alone his heart. His reduced view of truth might work when considering an academic publication – but it certainly didn't work when it came to relationships.

'Have you ever considered dating someone who is quite a bit younger than yourself ?' I asked. 'I'm not necessarily suggesting a permanent relationship, or that you should mislead anyone, but perhaps that you might enjoy going out with someone quite a bit younger than yourself.'

'Why's that?' he asked, looking rather hopeful for the first time.

I explained how emotionally he was not educated. In going out with women who seemed to be his peers, he was meeting partners who were close to his mental level, but much more emotionally developed than he was. Spending time with someone younger might make it easier for him to communicate and develop emotionally. He made a few objections and we talked about other factors that related to his problems, but he left me visibly cheered, saying he was going to think about what I had said.

When next I saw him, Peter was deeply involved with a girl more than fifteen years younger than himself. He was, he said, in love. Academic publishing had taken a back seat, as well as other intellectual and spiritual interests.

Six months later he came to see me again. He had decided his relationship with his young lover was true love and they were getting married. At last he felt he had touched something that was really true and enduring. However, yet another six months later, he came to tell me his young wife had left him because, she said, he was 'too old'. Although he was very sad, he was also relieved. Emotionally, he had developed enormously.

He did not think he had been 'deceived', nor did he doubt the truth of what he'd felt before. He explained to me how he'd enjoyed the time with his young partner, but towards the end, had come to feel that it was limited. Intellectually, spiritually, they did not share the same tastes and, he admitted, he had even begun to feel a little emotionally staid in comparison with her! Now, in looking forward, he wanted a companion whose mental and emotional age was closer to his own, with whom he could enjoy interests and share experiences more equally.

It wasn't, he said, that he'd been wrong, just that things had changed. And it did not seem to worry him any more. In that place I feel he is far more likely to establish a real partnership – with shared truths.

Overemphasising the emotional

Sometimes it is your emotional needs that dominate your perception of truth. Anna came to see me distraught at her lover's behaviour. A warm, very musical woman, she was deeply involved in her spiritual path. She believed her partner, with whom she shared a love of music, held similar values. She needed to believe that because she was deeply dependent on the relationship.

However, time and time again she had found evidence that he was cheating on her. Each time she accepted his apologies – she needed to believe them. Then she made an excuse for her partner, reaffirmed the basic commitments that they apparently agreed on – to do no harm, and to pursue a way of life in harmony with the universe. All would go well, until, again, she found evidence of fresh infidelity.

It was clear that Anna was making her decisions with her emotional body. She seemed unable to engage her mental process. Her brain would quickly have told her that, whatever he said, her partner's behaviour did not bear it out – it was not true. She needed to listen with the power of her mental body too. Unfortunately, her emotional needs were so strongly in control that she was unable to hear anything else.

I looked at her energy and explained where some of the major blockages lay in her past. Her father had been repeatedly unfaithful to her mother, a woman who owned little of her power. The family had never admitted this to be a problem. In time her mother had suffered a mental breakdown, which made her even more dependent, while her father had continued his affairs. This was the truth that Anna had not been able to acknowledge, and consequently the area in which she was now blocked.

Her task – as it is in all cases – was first to acknowledge the blockages, feel their impact and then work to release them. She had to look at why she had not registered, or listened to, the truths of the past. Probably because of fear of dealing with the pain that listening to that evidence would have brought.

Once Anna began to allow her brain – her mental body – to play its part, her notion of truth became much firmer. At the same time she made huge strides in developing her spiritual intelligence, with the good base of the marriage of her mental and emotional bodies, and her firm grasp of the fundamental truths.

Spiritual truth

Spiritual truth is, of course, spiritual intelligence's understanding of truth. It holds the five fundamental truths. Do no harm. Honour interconnectedness. Accept responsibility for yourself, your actions and their effects. Respect difference. And understand that things change. At the same time, it balances mental and emotional truths. In doing that, of course, it introduces its own very broadly based morality. It gives you a framework that makes it clear what is firm and unchanging – the fundamental truths – and what can, and sometimes must, change. It reassures you that it is acceptable, in fact important, to allow many of the other truths you hold to change, because it is impossible to grow unless you do change. It takes away the fear of illusion.

Some exercises for you to think about

1. Think of a truth you held because you wanted it to be true.
2. Think of a truth you held because someone else, perhaps a parent, told you it was true.
3. Think of a truth you held last year and are not so sure about this year. Can you see reasons to welcome that change? Can you see the positive consequences of your truth changing?
4. Can you think of how the change in your understanding might have hurt anyone else? Could they have seen you as deliberately doing harm by the change in your truth? Try to put yourself in their shoes.
5. Think of a truth that someone close to you held last year and then seemed to change. Think how that made you feel. If you felt resentment, or anger, should you in fact have forgiven them? And can you do so now?
6. Can you think of a friend who does not understand or share your spiritual path? Can you accept that they do not hold the same or similar truths to you at the moment? Can you see that their truths, or yours, might change in the future? If or when their truth changes – for example, if they come

closer to your truth – will you be able to forgive any past distance, and just be glad to welcome a new closeness?

7. Can you think of a friend who might feel that you had, inexplicably perhaps, turned your back and walked away from them? Try to understand their attitude and pain.

8. Can you think of an example where you deliberately set out to do harm, to hurt someone else? Acknowledge the incident, put it to right in any way you can and forgive yourself.

9. Think of an incident where another did you harm. Forgive them. That doesn't mean place yourself in the same position where you can be hurt again, but forgive the harm, and at the same time, try to put yourself out of harm's way.

10. Think about your life. Think of all those you feel have done you harm. Perhaps the harm was deliberate, perhaps it was the result of their shortcomings, perhaps it was the result of their ignorance. Forgive them. Move on.

11. Begin to pay more attention to your first impressions. When approaching a new situation, try, consciously, to 'catch' your first impression and stick with it. If you can, simply accept it. If it is too difficult to do that, turn it over in your mind until you think you understand it. If you feel you have

to choose to take another course of action, write down your first impression so that you can check out the ways in which it might have been correct, at a later date.

12. Pay attention to the truths that those around you hold. See if you can understand why the people you know might hold the beliefs they do. This is not an excuse to be cynical – unless you are looking largely at politicians! But it is an opportunity to try to stand in the shoes of others, and broaden your understanding of the world, by trying to see it through their eyes.

Chapter Twelve

In Search of Balance

Issues such as feminism, post-feminism, the problems of transsexuals, the future of marriage, homosexual marriage, the role of homosexuals in the armed forces, the age of consent, date rape, sexual relations in the armed forces, sex in the workplace, marriage contracts, women in the workplace, the role of fathers – all these issues occupy TV time and the pages of our newspapers daily. The list of concerns that relate to gender and sexual preference is a very long one. Above all else it shows that what we think of as normal, right or true differs greatly.

No one (or few people) prefaces a statement by saying, 'I'm wildly out of balance but I believe . . .' Most people say, or think, 'I am trying to be balanced, and as a result I think . . .' Also, most people are able to pinpoint attitudes or behaviour in others who they feel are seriously out of balance. This behaviour could range from conditions that are mentally certifiable to criminally deviant. But between those extremes there is a huge area where most of us try to find a balance. So much of our development depends on finding and maintaining balance, at the same time as allowing our perspective to widen and our understanding to change.

No area is potentially more bewildering, more difficult to find your balance in, than the whole arena relating to gender and sexual preference. Which is why it's important to remember a few basics.

The basics

We are all a complex mixture of male and female. We are governed by our outer form, and the variety of factors that make up our inner needs and drives. The development of our spiritual intelligence demands that we develop our understanding and human potential as far as we can. That includes the expression of our sexual qualities – which has nothing to do with having a sexual partner, or partners, but everything to do with honouring the expression of both the male and the female aspects of our nature in the everyday. And, most importantly, achieving a balance between them.

Male versus female

Energetically, we are facing two relatively new factors that are having an effect on the way we deal with the male and female in ourselves and in our society.

The first is the breakdown of the hierarchy. Of course, this has been happening for some time. It is resulting in a reorganisation of the order of society, both the material and the spiritual. In spiritual terms, as in material terms, we are working to come to terms with a new order which, instead of imposing a hierarchy on us, asks each and every one of us to connect individually with our inner power, or spiritual reality, and with one another as spiritual beings.

Second, the vibrations reaching us today, which are partly responsible for the breakdown of the hierarchy, are increasingly 'feminine'. That does not mean they apply increasingly to women, or make us all subservient to femaleness. Or make female qualities more important than male ones. Instead they bring certain female qualities back into our consciousness, rebalancing it. Those qualities apply just as much to men as to women.

The first millennium after the birth of Christ can be described as female in its qualities with its predominant acknowledgement of the role of mystery and the unknown in the universe.* Procreation and the forces of the universe were equally mysterious and a source of wonder. The second millennium was male in the way it gave increasing power to the male quality of scientific thought or analysis in understanding, penetrating and conquering the mysteries of the first age. It gave man a new ability to act, and take control of his world, based on his knowledge. At the same time it was also an era when the hierarchy that made women subservient to men was firmly in place.

---

* I first heard this theory expressed by Satish Kumar, Director of the Schumaker Centre, Devon, UK.

The age before us urges the reintroduction of the female. Not to take over from the male, but instead to unite with it. To achieve a new wholeness as we bring together both sides of our nature, the male and the female. The acceptance, affinity with and understanding of the mystery the female brings, with the action and control of the male. A parallel to the spiritual and the material.

One problem we face, though, is how exactly to recognise these two aspects of our nature – apart from cultural conditioning – and how to act appropriately on them. The male approach and the female approach are very different. Each has its own power.

Understanding male power

Both men and women must deal with the issue of how to use male power appropriately. What is appropriate male power is a real problem for many. Men and women have told me of different solutions. Adam, for example, joined a men's group that met regularly to perform secret rituals – which he could not reveal. Many men whom I see admit to fearing women's female power, and as a result find relationships very painful. Usually they inflict as well as receive significant amounts of pain. All because of misunderstanding.

Male power lies in the ability to act. To initiate. Feeling the ability to do something, and being able to take action. Or being able to make the deliberate choice not to act. The feeling of being powerless, unable to act with no control over the environment, is the most debilitating of experiences. It seriously undermines male power.

In today's world taking action can be hard. Scope for decision making may be limited, fear of consequences may be great. But exercising our male power means feeling able to take control of a situation by taking action to master an aspect of our environment or ourselves.

Understanding female power

Female power on the other hand means concentrating on sensitivity, receiving and holding impressions coming from the environment, or from ourselves. And it's an enlarged environment – one that is moving towards the inclusion of qualities previously unseen and unheard. So, it is the sensitivity to be able to recognise and appreciate the qualities of the expanded world, without needing to take action. Or immediate action.

Female power understands and appreciates, without needing to act. At the same time what it appreciates and understands is much wider than the impressions that register on the male scale. All of which gives female power the opportunity for a very different understanding from the male analysis, which is oriented towards taking action and producing an effect.

Of course, it is really important to understand that the expressions 'male' and 'female' do not equate with

'men' and 'women'. We all have male and female qualities. Our task is to unite them. Uniting female power,
with its wider register and understanding, with male
power and its ability to act, is the route to a higher
form of action, and ultimately – as consciousness of
the new universe filters through – the expression of
spiritual intelligence. It is an ongoing task.

Getting the balance right

As our understanding develops we consciously
participate in the process of adjusting our balance.
Recognising and cultivating the influences of the
male and the female is a constant challenge. Each of
us, in our own lives, faces the need to create this
union of the male and the female, honouring the dictates of our outer form, and also our inner make-up.
We all look to develop our male mental analytical
characteristics along with the ability to act, and at the
same time honour our female intuitive, receptive
qualities and the ability to see and be at one with the
marvels and mysteries of the world. Each incident is
a fresh opportunity.

One man's solution

At a seminar on this subject recently a man
approached me with a small machine. Dressed in a
business suit, white shirt and tie, he was clearly an
office worker. He had introduced himself as John.
John explained that he realised he was deprived, as

a result of his environment, of a full spectrum of light and colour. He told me how he felt this as a deficiency, which his partner, who stayed at home to look after their children, did not have to contend with.

Of course colour and light are important in both energy and emotional terms (see Chapter Four). I was impressed that John saw the link. He went on to show me the device he was carrying and explained that it irradiated water, or any food put under it, to allow the water or food to carry the full spectrum of light. John wanted to know if I felt this would solve his deficiency.

I told him I couldn't say whether or not the machine would be effective. But what I could say was that there was a much simpler solution to his problem. And it was freely available. Fresh air, and colour.

I explained that as John wanted, and needed, to expose himself to a wider range of the energy spectrum, this was easily done by going out of doors. By simply making sure that he spent some time every day, more perhaps at the weekend, in the open air. Then, the particular needs he sensed in himself could be addressed by allowing himself access to colour. But not from some machine. Why not, in his free time, allow himself to wear the colours he felt he wanted contact with?

From his face it was clear that it was difficult for him to think about the idea of 'wanting' colours. He could understand needing a full spectrum of light, but

he found it a little more difficult to understand needing particular colours. However, with a little thought
he agreed that there were times he longed to wear a
blue shirt, or would even have liked to wear a red
shirt – if he'd had one. I urged him to allow himself
those freedoms of choice in his private life. To think
about the colours around him and to consciously
choose colours he felt like seeing. Even if, for example, it meant going to buy some new tableware with
his wife in colours he felt a need for. Or painting a
wall a particular shade because he wanted to see that
colour – rather than simply leaving the choice to his
wife, or a decorator.

I explained how he was reacting to the female
vibrations and trying to accommodate them by considering a very male technique. A machine. But in
fact he could deal with the same needs by traditional
female means, and reap their benefits. This would be
a small but significant way to work with his own
balance.

The male need to embrace male power

George was a charming man. Very gentle, in some
ways, perceptive, and spiritually oriented. It was
clear that he was closely linked to his female power.
He came to me complaining of tiredness. He worked
as an alternative therapist and wanted to find a way
of increasing his energy.

It was soon clear that his problems centred on his
male power. Using his intuitive sympathetic qualities,

he was able to help his individual clients greatly, but he had few outlets for his male side.

I suggested he think about finding a practical business outlet for his talents, perhaps as well as what he was doing, or instead of it. But it was important for him to establish an arena in which he had more scope for action, based not on using his receptive qualities with one individual, but on his understanding and skill in dealing with a practical situation. Of course, his intuition and female qualities would be of great help in whatever he did, but it seemed he was relying on them too much, at the moment.

Over time George researched and started a small business selling nutritional supplements, about which he accumulated a great deal of knowledge. Not surprisingly, with his intuitive touch, the business flourished, and he soon gave up seeing individual clients, as he needed all of his by now greatly increased energy to deal with his orders! His male and female powers were in much better balance.

One woman's way

Facing the issue of female power, a highly professional female client, who spent a great deal of time in a corporate situation handling male power, explained to me how she was planning to join a party to worship a female goddess as a way of harmonising with the female energy of the time. Her well-meaning endeavour made me smile. I explained that of course if she wanted to join the party and engage in the ritual she was welcome to do so. Rituals have their own wisdom and power. Though there is need for caution when they link with superstition, which may build on fear, to take away your power for independent action – rather than increasing your scope.

However, I explained, appreciating or harmonising with female energy did not require worshipping a female goddess. Cooking a nice meal – appreciating all the skills involved, the atmosphere created, the response of others if you are cooking for them – rather than buying a take-out or pre-prepared TV dinner, was a good way of achieving the same effect. But there are any number of others too. Arranging a vase of flowers is one of my favourites for allowing the female and bringing the vibrations of beauty and nature into my everyday environment.

Power and balance

Balancing the male and the female within us is a vital part of finding truth and developing spiritual intelligence. The challenge of the age is to bring together the male and the female in a balanced union, as never before. It is up to each of us to find out exactly where the balance lies. At all times, of course, honouring our external form, as well as our inner composition. However, developing one side of our nature cannot be done at the expense of the other. The more male power you have and use, the more important it is for you to develop your female power. And vice versa.

Some exercises for you to think about

1. Think of a problem you have faced recently. Try to work out what would be the solution of male power to that problem, and how an analysis from the perspective of female power might differ and suggest a slightly or very different solution.

   For example, you are dealing with a junior colleague who has made a mistake. Male power, eager to correct the situation straight away and ensure that it is not repeated, might take a strict attitude towards the junior, demanding the immediate correction of the circumstance and warning of dire consequences if it is repeated. Female power would be more interested in understanding the reasons for the mistake.

   Both approaches could lead to unbalanced consequences if taken to an extreme. Male power's approach could set this situation to rights but have done nothing, except arouse fear, to ensure that it didn't happen again. Female power might have investigated all the causes but done little to make sure the junior concerned would be vigilant against making the same mistake, or would take responsibility for the situation. Needless to say, male power's approach could have come from a woman just as easily as from a man, and vice versa.

Now think of a situation you faced and how you dealt with it – are you happy with the fusion of the male and the female you achieved?

2. Think of one situation where you needed to quickly sum up a situation and act. How difficult did you find it? If you found it hard, can you see that as a reflection of your difficulties in mobilising male power when you need to?

3. Think of one situation where you took action too quickly, or took an action you later felt to be limited. Can you see ways in which that might reflect you imposing a limit on your female power? Or being unwilling or unable to give the female sufficient power?

4. Think of the people around you. Can you see one example of someone who is dominated by the need to hold on to male power? And someone who is unable to understand and use female power? Look for an example of someone you feel balances both appropriately. Spiritual intelligence needs both qualities.

Chapter Thirteen

Power to the People

My inner teachers were very fierce with me. 'No books – and no going to other people. You have to learn to know what you know.' It could have been an uphill battle. Fortunately I was desperate enough to at least suspend disbelief, and cooperate with the process. Had I not been so desperate I might have gone on doing what I had done for so many years. Rely on my brain, and look for authorities.

Authority figures

We are all predisposed to defer to authority figures. From infancy – when we have no choice – onwards. Later, on the path to spiritual intelligence, teachers and healers play a crucial role. But unfortunately, it is all too easy for us to see them as the authority figures we grew up with. Even understanding that the role of the guru is over does not free us from the inclination to think that teachers and healers are somehow superior and so should be deferred to.

Sometimes, in our search for someone superior who knows more than we do, we can be dazzled by the mantle of a so-called celebrity – a 'fashionable' teacher or healer. Or one who promises instant gratification in one way or another. The sheer number of teachers and healers available also presents a problem. There is a great temptation to fall into what's sometimes called 'spiritual shopping'. Never really following through with one course of ideas because another, that promises better or quicker results, appears.

They are all the temptations of our age where ideas multiply quickly, methods and markets proliferate. Problems we have to face because it is foolish, or worse, to ignore the role and input of teachers and healers. My inner world was my best teacher, in helping me to reclaim the knowledge I already had. And a crucial healer, helping me to become whole physically and spiritually. But input from the outside played an important part too.

However powerful the inner teacher, most of us – rightly – look for someone to share our journey, or teach us along the way. Which presents the problem. Whom to go to? Whom to trust? And we face the same problem when looking for help in healing our bodies, or working with our energy.

Teachers and healers

There's a smorgasbord of teachers and healers available. But they are far from the only sources of help. In reality, it's not only so-called teachers and healers who have the potential to help us. Almost everyone we meet has the potential to teach us. Not necessarily what they intend, or claim, or would want to pass on. But we have the opportunity to learn in every interaction. Equally we become teachers in every exchange. Again, we are not necessarily teaching what we intend to pass on, but in some way we are conveying something to someone else. Which, if they 'hear' it, will help them to grow in their understanding or energy.

In just the same way, every circumstance in our world has something to say to us. Right down to a glance at the sky which shows a cloud drifting by. You could see it as a symbol of the way that clouds in our own lives pass. Or it could point to the seemingly arbitrary shape that clouds in life take on. Or it could be showing the relation of clouds to other internal weather conditions – or a host of other notions. You will know which are true. Or explore each possibility.

Some lessons life teaches – we learn as we pass along our way. Sometimes we discover, perhaps to our surprise, though we should not be surprised, that others have used us as teachers. At still other times, we feel the need to look for particular teachers. Or perhaps we may need to look for healers. In those circumstances, my journey taught me the guidelines for choosing.

You know best

Your own knowledge comes first. No one knows you better than yourself. Your connection to spiritual reality is your own. No one can or should orchestrate the development of your spiritual intelligence, or try to put it in place for you. The age of the guru is dead. There is no one who will take you to the Light. But what a teacher may be able to do, if you are lucky, is to spark the process in you. Help you widen your perception. Help you to see, understand and feel a wider reality.

In the same way your body is your own. You are responsible for the well-being of your body in many ways. If you need help you will be responsible for the help you choose. Though ultimately, of course, you have to put yourself in the hands of the healer you choose. But you retain the right to change that choice too. Remember though, with physical healing, just as with spiritual growth, no one can do it for you. The ultimate responsibility is yours. And sometimes healing does not mean making the physical body whole, or perfect again, but accepting the gift of an expanded spiritual intelligence instead.

Your choice

There are many people who claim to be able to heal or teach you – in some form or another. In finding a teacher or a healer, your choice is always best. Because someone was very helpful to your friend, or a teacher has been very highly recommended, it does not mean that they will be any use to you.

Love

There is only one way to choose. Love. Can you feel

love for the teacher and what he or she is saying? Can you feel their love for you? That does not mean a personal, intimate one-to-one love. But spiritual love. The love that connects you to the widest reality and shows you the best in yourself and all others. The love that brings a sense of wonder, awe, humility and devotion too.

It may well defy all logic. There may be no good reason for loving a particular teacher, for example. Energetically, of course, it will mean that there is a connection. That, in some way, you feel very comfortable, or more, with the other person's energy. In that case, follow the promptings of your heart – which is following your intuition.

That love is appropriate, in its way, for those you go to as healers, as well as teachers. You are entrusting them with your body – the physical expression of your existence. For example, to be very down to earth, if you are able to love your dentist, to respect his divine potential, to see the best in him and to allow him the best opportunity to help you, it will help to ensure that the help you receive from him is the best he can offer. Of course, I am not saying he will know that is exactly what you are doing! But I am saying he or she will sense your attitude, and respond to it. And if you try that approach, and can't sense any response – then you will know that you have to find another dentist!

Don't be a doormat

Loving your teacher or healer does not mean being a

doormat, though. It is your responsibility at all times to keep your intelligence. Is the teacher or healer respecting your wisdom and your intelligence?

James came to me puzzled by a relationship with a teacher whose workshops he had been following for a year or so. He told me how impressed he was by the man's wisdom, and explained how he thought the teacher had come to know him quite well. 'I'm a bit of a loudmouth,' he said, smiling, 'and I sometimes speak without thinking.' The problem, James said, was that the teacher repeatedly humiliated him. 'Seems like every time I ask a question, he makes fun of me. I don't understand it.'

I asked James whether he thought the teacher respected him. Was he perhaps trying to show James his own qualities – show him how he was, as he admitted, a bit of a loudmouth, and help him change those aspects of himself? Or was he simply poking fun at him? Giving the others a chance to laugh at James's expense? James was not sure. I suggested he think about that question. It held the answer to his problem – was he being respected? Was the teacher entitled to his love? Did he feel the teacher's love?

Behaving from a higher wisdom?

Sometimes, if you are lucky, the teacher's wisdom will be at a higher level than your own. That does not mean you have to accept their behaviour blindly. In a recent case in the USA a woman went to a well-known Buddhist teacher, much troubled after the death of her father. She claimed the teacher started an affair with her, saying that it was for her benefit and for the benefit of her recently deceased father. Where the truth lay is difficult to say as the case was settled out of court, but it's a familiar story – I have heard it several times. One client came to ask me about an episode where she had had sex with a teacher and was trying to work out what 'the teaching' was! Need and gratification, I suggested – but was it mutual?

Understanding a higher wisdom

However, there are genuine cases where it is difficult to understand the place the teacher is speaking from. I have had experiences where clients have disagreed with what I was saying, only to come back some time later, even years later, to thank me and say they had finally understood what I had said. If you can, and it does not disrespect you, be careful about dismissing what a teacher is saying. If it does not make sense to you, simply put it to one side.

Only human

In accepting your power and responsibility as a human being for choosing a teacher or a healer, remember that the person you choose is human too. Being human means being fallible. The teacher you choose will be learning – just like you. Though the lessons may be at a different level to those you are working on – above or below! Never believe anyone who says they are not learning themselves, or tries to present a front of infallibility. All teachers and healers are fallible. Being human means they have to be. If you are looking for an infallible teacher, you are looking for a guru to place above yourself. You are making yourself powerless and childlike – not furthering your spiritual intelligence. You want clear evidence of your teacher's love, integrity, wisdom, knowledge and experience. Not pretensions to infallibility.

The same applies to a healer. Look for a high degree of knowledge and skill. You cannot expect the sublime, though. It is not good enough for a surgeon to tell you that he did his best at setting your broken leg but as he's never done it before, it's not very good! On the other hand a surgeon might have to tell you that, operating on your rare tumour, she or he has not been one hundred per cent successful, though he or she has done their best. Understand: healers are learning.

Your part

Equally you cannot expect to be healed by a hands-on healer of a condition where lifestyle has played a part, without addressing your lifestyle as well. And do not submit to a programme of treatment unless you understand what it aims to do and the basic mechanism. Don't, for example, take an unknown substance just because someone else tells you it will 'be good for you'. Ask what it is, and enough about it to convince you that you want to try it. Hold on to your power. But don't ignore your intuition.

There is always the chance that you will want to follow a teacher or a healer, though there don't seem to be good reasons for doing so. In that case never ignore your intuition. You will be responding to an energetic force, and a different sort of information. Rest assured that if your choice turns out to be wrong, you have the power to change it, to learn from the experience, and to make a new choice.

Any allegiance?

Allegiance, or even devotion, to a teacher or healer can seem a foreign quality, especially when you are guarding your own power and ability to choose and to change your choice. But when you are secure enough in your own power, and you trust your intuition sufficiently, it can be a way of extracting the most from your circumstances.

Building up trust and a full health record with a doctor who has known you for a number of years, and has helped you well, is important. It can be a much surer bet than constantly looking for someone with new knowledge. Even if the newcomer promises the earth (usually without even examining you). Spending time with one teacher can pay real dividends. And teach you the rewards that come with the old virtues of perseverance and patience.

There will always be cases where you outgrow the teacher – or the healer. But if you are lucky enough, you will find someone whose work you can follow for years, perhaps. When you feel you are working with someone who has real knowledge and experience, the benefits you gain from that connection may well grow over time. The deeper you study with that person the greater the dividends.

Being taken advantage of will not be a problem at that stage because you will know the teacher respects your individual power, just as you respect the teacher's power and position. You will also be able to understand and accept the teacher as a human being, at the same time as respecting the position of someone who is teaching you. The more powerful you are, the more you will respect and understand the teacher's position.

Of course, it does not mean that you may not continue to find input from a variety of sources useful. But it does mean that you are ready to explore the benefits of working in depth with one particular person. Of continuity, rather than nibbling at the smorgasbord. It also means that you are ready to give up the expectation of and search for instant enlightenment – whatever that means – to work on developing true spiritual intelligence.

Teaching and healing others

You may sometimes be tempted to pass on your wisdom to others. To play the part of teacher, or healer, deliberately. Don't. Unless you are asked. Not only is it inappropriate on your part, but the other person is not ready to hear what you want to say, until they ask. Which they may not. And don't let anyone impose on you. Power in teaching and healing is always open to abuse. Expect to be respected, and respect others.

Your all-important example

Lastly, remember the power of advertising. Throughout life, in all areas, you teach by example. Just as others teach you by example. The simple example of your behaviour has the power to influence those who observe you. Just as the example of others has the power to influence you. Which is why it is so distressing for most of us when our leadership display debased values in their behaviour. At the same time it is a reminder of the enormous power we all hold to contribute to the positive character of our world simply by holding to the highest standards we can in our own actions. And if you ever need inspiration, examples of the real heart values and goodwill of our fellows are all around us.

Ideas to think about

1. Remember your childhood. How did you regard your teachers? Do you have a memory of a good teaching situation? Can you remember a teacher who behaved in a destructive way towards any pupil or pupils? Do you remember a teacher you loved? What effect do you think your childhood experiences have

had on your attitude towards teachers as an adult?

2. Think of a situation in your adult life where someone else has been a teacher to you. How do you feel about that person? Have you been concerned about their welfare in return? Have you considered how you may be able to offer to them, as they have offered to you?

3. Think of a situation where you have tried to teach another. Has it worked? Can you see that teaching is more effective when it is asked for, rather than when it is pushed at you, or at someone else?

4. Can you think of a situation where someone has thanked you for your input where you did not intend any specific input?

5. How do you feel when you go to see a doctor or healer? Are you inclined to accept whatever is said to you? Do you give yourself the right to question what you are told? Have you ever asked for a second opinion?

6. Do you accept that you have some responsibility for your health? Have you ever tried to cure a condition by changing your diet or lifestyle?

7. Do you feel powerful enough to approach and benefit from a teacher? Can you trust your intuition sufficiently to choose a teacher who is right for you – who will help you know and understand your spirituality –

not necessarily one whom your friend finds fantastic?

8. Are you still looking for 'instant enlightenment', a quick change that will instantly transform your life with relatively little effort on your part?

9. Can you find joy in learning?

Chapter Fourteen

Power Tools?

Y ou are working well now. You are becoming more confident in your own spiritual connection. You understand your own energy better. Your heart is more open. Your intuition is stronger. In other words, you're developing your spiritual intelligence. But, of course, you are keen for all the help you can get, and also to explore your growing spiritual confidence. What about astrology, you wonder – could that offer even more guidance? Or tarot cards – would it be helpful to learn to do the tarot now? Or to go to someone to read the cards for you? Or is there some other tool you could put to work?

I wondered the same things at the start of my journey. I even asked my inner world. When my guidance told me my job was to learn what I already knew, I asked, innocently and ignorantly, whether that had anything to do with the tarot or astrology. Was I to learn them? To my surprise, the answer I received was rather cool: 'You can if you want to but your job is to learn inside to outside processes – not outside to inside processes.' I didn't understand what that meant, then. I do now.

Outside to inside

An outside to inside process is one where you learn a set of skills and use them to interpret your inner world. So, for example, the *I Ching* is a very ancient outside to inside process. By throwing coins, or sticks, you build up a picture that corresponds to your inner world. Usually you ask a question to begin with. Say, what are my chances of having a baby in the coming year? According to the hexagram – the picture made by the coins or sticks you throw – the *I Ching* would give you an answer. Of course, the answers are difficult to decipher, and are open to different interpretations.

The tarot is similar. It is a pack of cards that has been used over the centuries to tell fortunes. Each card has a different meaning, and the placement of cards in different spreads will give different answers to your questions. There are many different approaches to reading the tarot.

When you throw the *I Ching*, or read the tarot cards yourself, you are creating an outside image to represent your inner reality. In that sense it is an outside to inside process. In a slightly different sense, using someone else to read the cards or interpret the *I Ching* is very much an outside to inside process.

In this situation it includes all the complicating factors related to someone else's role and interpretation.

Anyone who tells your fortune from your palm, or simply uses their intuition in giving you a reading, is essentially doing the same thing – though perhaps with fewer props. They are looking at you as an outsider, and interpreting you to yourself.

Inside to outside processes

Inside to outside processes are much more mysterious. Since they come from inside, no one else can 'do' them for you. Dreams are a common inside to outside process. A dream comes from your inner world and often, when you listen to your dreams, you find they are speaking to you.

At the start of my meditation journey I dreamt repeatedly of finding new space. In one case it was a semi-industrial building which offered wonderful living space that somehow no one else could recognise. In another case it was a home, where I realised a false wall concealed a huge space which, if I took possession of it, would transform my living conditions. Both were excellent metaphors for expanding my spiritual consciousness and so my reality.

These dreams brought information from the inside to the outside. It was my interior speaking to me – telling me a reality and a future that my conscious mind was not recognising. Meditation and contemplation can also allow uncensored images or information from the interior to come into your mind. In other words, allow what you know to surface. Often, you then have to interpret it. Intuition does exactly the same. As your intuition strengthens it helps you to know what is there but not immediately visible, in your own life and in the world around you.

Which way?

The difference between inside to outside processes and those that come from the outside to the inside is that the first category definitely give you more power. They do not make you reliant on anyone or anything else. Instead, they build up your trust in your own abilities and power. And they support your intuition. The more you turn within, the more attention you give to the messages from your interior, the easier they become to read. Processes that come from the outside to the inside may have few, if any, of those qualities, though they can have uses.

Prediction

When you go to someone else to predict or perhaps to interpret your future, you are placing power in their hands. You are making them into an authority figure. Most predictions are interpretations. 'It will rain tomorrow,' is the weatherman's interpretation of the facts to make a prediction. Looking at a glass of water, 'The glass is half full,' is one person's interpretation of the facts. Another could easily say, 'The glass is half empty.' In the same way, anyone making a prediction for you is interpreting the information they perceive.

Different levels of energetic development will also mean that different people will have different perspectives. In other words, one person may see five factors around a situation, another will see ten factors. Or they will see different factors according to which chakra or what circumstances are foremost in their consciousness.

In going to someone else to predict your future, the hope is implicit that they will use that power in an impartial way. There could also be a hope – if you think about it – that, as they are an authority figure, their consciousness will be above yours. In other words, when you put yourself in their hands, you trust that their prediction and interpretation will be detached from their own needs and limitations. And that in making their interpretations – because almost all predictions are interpretations – they will be guided by a perspective that is at least as developed, if not more developed, than your own. But that, sadly, is often a misguided hope.

The person you are talking to may be influenced by any one of a number of factors. For example, sympathy for you and the desire to make you feel better. The need and desire to please you, especially if it will lead to repeat business. Their own bias. For example, their beliefs about the nature of the universe. Or their emotional beliefs, needs or limitations based on their personal experience. They may even be driven from a lower chakra than the one foremost in your own development, which again would bias and limit their interpretation.

Many years ago, looking for someone who knew 'better' than me, I was recommended to see a medium with a strong following. When I arrived, the lady concerned, who was probably from a relatively secluded background in rural England, with little formal education, had a problem with my name. In reply to her questions, I explained my first name came from the Old Testament, and my second name was a relatively common Jewish surname. It was clear that she had not come into contact with many (any?) clients from an obvious Jewish background.

She began to tell me about myself. Surprise, surprise, one of her first 'predictions' was that I would be going to 'the land of the Hebrews', which was 'where I belonged'. In the many years that have followed I have not done so, nor do I feel it is where I 'belong'. But the direction of her bias was clear.

Self-fulfilling prophecies

Had I believed what this medium told me, I might well have looked for an opportunity to go to 'the land of the Hebrews'. If I looked hard enough I expect I could have found or manufactured such an opportunity. But to do so would not have been following some fate. It would have been a trip I made happen. In itself there is no harm in that. But believing predictions brings the unfortunate tendency to make them come true. And, of course, that has the dramatic effect of taking away your power to act.

Several years ago I saw an attractive, intelligent woman in her late thirties who explained to me that she had no hope of finding a partner. Partnership, she explained, was not for her; instead she was building up her career. When I questioned her belief, she told me that a powerful fortune-teller had told her not to waste her time looking for a partner, as she would never find one, but she could achieve career success. Consequently, in the years that followed, she had turned away from a personal life and concentrated on work.

I could not believe what I was hearing. It was a most destructive example of a self-fulfilling prophecy. I told her the prediction was nonsense, and that I hoped, sooner or later, to hear news of a happy relationship in her life. The next I heard, a long-standing friendship became a romance which has lasted for several years now.

Losing your power

It's not only what you are 'told' that can be dangerous, but what is suggested too. For example, if a tarot reader warns you that a woman from an earth sign is working behind your back and you should be very wary of dealings with this woman, you might think it is a 'helpful' piece of information. But who is this woman? Asking round, you find a few of your friends and colleagues belong to earth signs (about a quarter of the population do). Which one is working behind your back? Which one to beware of?

Before you know it you are overtaken by suspicion and anxiety. You may put your relationships in real jeopardy and you will certainly feel very worried. You will have given your power away – and probably be contemplating going to your tarot reader again to find out more about this 'earth sign woman'.

If you do, you may find that next time the cards and your reader say the problem comes from an earth sign woman and an air sign man – which only complicates the picture, but now there is the promise of financial success if you take a risk around the middle of the year . . . You will put a great deal of energy into working out who could be the relevant people, and watching and wondering about this risk you have to take. So much so that you miss a real opportunity – because it comes in the spring and does not involve much of a risk! In short your power is reduced, not increased.

But could it be true?

Of course, all of that says as much about how you use the information, as it says about the information. The information may be biased, or limited by the source it comes from. You may respond to it with anxiety, obedience, relief, trust or any of a number of reactions that could affect how you use the information. But could it ever be true?

The Greek tradition is famous for the use of oracles – the oracle of Delphi, for example. In all dealings with the oracle, two factors played an important part. The exact question that was asked. And the ambiguity of the answer. The same is true today. There are different approaches with different predictive methods that are worth considering.

The I Ching

The *I Ching*, the ancient Chinese oracle, is a book made up of a series of verses. You choose from them by throwing coins or sticks. But it does not simply tell you the future. It is much more complex.

In using the *I Ching* I find the best approach is to phrase the question in the form, 'What should my attitude be towards . . .' And then ask about the situation that is causing you concern.

The answer you receive will not tell you what will happen. But it will offer a perspective on your situation. However, it could well be difficult to understand. You might be able to see a number of ways to interpret it. If you consult any of the many books available that offer interpretations of *I Ching* readings, you will find several answers! Which, of course, reflect the authors' different biases. While this could be confusing, it can also open your mind to considering a range of new possibilities. Approaches you might not have thought of. In this way it can give you more power, without telling you what to do.

Whilst the answers of the book may make you think about how you act, it is worth remembering that the answers also come from a particular philosophy. That philosophy is based on certain ideas. You may agree with the recommendations and the social assumptions behind them, when it comes to, for example, how to behave as a stranger in a foreign situation – with deference and respect to the customs of others. But you may not agree with the recommendations of how to act as a wife towards a husband – with deference – or the assumptions behind those notions.

If you remember that the book's answers are simply one way of approaching a situation, and it's an approach that displays the preconceptions behind the wisdom of the *I Ching*, it can be helpful in adding to your power. In the same way there are a number of other tools, from board games to books of wisdom. The same strictures apply to them all. They all reflect the mindset of their authors. And they can all be counter-productive, or even dangerous if used as guides to tell you what to do, rather than as a means of widening your perception and so giving you more power in choosing your own actions.

The tarot

The tarot is perhaps aimed more specifically at predicting the future. Many books have been written on the meaning of the cards, and the significance of the way they appear. I find that in laying the cards down for myself, I can often 'make' them reflect my mood. If I am in a difficult position and feeling anxious, I can 'produce' dark cards that reflect my worries. If I am feeling optimistic and hopeful, I can draw cards that reinforce that feeling. In other words, the tarot can become a self-fulfilling prophecy. But the experience of learning this from practice is useful. It helps understand the importance of your input and your own power in constructing your reality.

At the same time, curious to understand as much as possible about the process, I have also worked with the tarot both for myself and for friends – not clients. I have been surprised at the accuracy. Future events do sometimes occur on the cards. Particularly if I am looking at them for someone else. But what I see could also, of course, reflect my training in detachment, which is the way in which I have learnt to use my intuition – consciously detaching myself as far as possible from my own issues when working with others.

However, in deciding whether or not to use the cards yourself, the problem remains: how to know whether what you will see is potentially a self-fulfilling prophecy or a helpful insight? It is a very difficult problem, and the consequences of getting it wrong are much worse than any benefits of getting it right.

The same applies to a reading from someone else. First, though, there is the problem of the other person's bias. Then there's the question, is it right or wrong? Sometimes, allowing for bias, much of what you are told is correct, sometimes nothing is correct, and often it's somewhere in the middle. But how much of what you are told is 'true' and what is not?

Believing what you are told can produce anxiety, suspicion, optimism, a sense of security, despair, or even encourage you to do things you might pause before doing but believe are 'ordained'. Or it can encourage you to ignore situations and opportunities you would gain from. In short – relying on someone else to interpret the tarot cards for you, or tell your fortune in some way, can actually rob you of power. The actions you choose as a result of a reading will be based on your response to what you have been told – whatever its status. Your actions will not be based on your own understanding and intuition about a situation.

The benefits of limited use

There is one way, though, that someone else's predictive input can help – if you use it carefully – and that's for emotional support. Many of us experience times of emotional stress or isolation, when there is a sense that there is no one to turn to, or problems become overwhelming. A benevolent tarot card reader, or psychic counsellor of some sort, can be a help at those times. If they are benevolent, they can help you hold on to the knowledge that there is a brighter future, and encourage you to feel better about your ability to realise it. Provided you remember the limitations of what you are hearing!

It is no substitute for developing your own spiritual intelligence and sense of connection, and certainly no substitute for the power of your own intuition. But you may, on occasion, feel the need to turn to someone else for temporary support on your journey. We all need other people. As long as you remember that the aim of your journey is to build up your own power and ability to face the world and the circumstances you encounter, you can use every experience you choose for your own benefit.

Astrology

Astrology often comes up at this point. Given that we all need help and guidance from time to time, and if you have an understanding that astrology is important, or even suspect that it might be, this can lead you to turn to it for illumination. Again, like all tools, astrology can be helpful if used correctly, and destructive if used incorrectly.

Astrology is not a map of how your life will be. It does not tell you what you can or can't do, or what will or will not happen to you. A birth chart is a map of the forces in the sky at the time of your birth. In Jung's words in *The Secret of the Golden Flower*, 'Whatever is born or done this moment, has the qualities of this moment in time.' The ancient wisdom, or traditional esoteric teaching, teaches the same idea in the notion 'as above, so below'. And new developments in physics are beginning to suggest that there may indeed be a correspondence between different levels of the universe.

Each planet in an astrological chart has different characteristics and rules certain areas of your life, according to where it is placed. The placement of the planets at your birth is like a psychological map of your nature – it indicates your strengths and weaknesses, areas where you have issues to overcome and areas where you have particular strengths.

Of course, like all metaphors it is open to interpretation and any analysis of your birth chart will reflect the thinking and development of the person making the analysis for you.

The chart does not, however, lay down the limits of your development. For example, it does not say that because your Mercury is poorly aspected, and Mercury represents communication, you will be poor at communication. Instead it indicates that communication is an area where you will have to work to develop your power. It may even, depending on the way you interpret the planets aspecting your Mercury, describe ways in which communication could be challenging, suggesting how to overcome those challenges. Your job is to overcome the problems showed by the chart – not to accept them as limiting 'facts'!

As for predicting the future, astrology is a very unreliable predictor. Some years ago, I conducted an altogether unscientific, or unrepresentative, experiment of my own. I asked a professional astrologer to draw up a chart of my future for the coming year. (A little difficult because I don't have my birth time.) His findings were interesting, but at the end of the year, I decided they really were not at all conclusive one way or the other.

So, I picked half a dozen dates from the previous five years where really important events had happened in my life. Without telling him what the events were, I asked for an interpretation of the astrological forces at those times. This time the report was very disappointing. Only in one case was the prediction close to my experience. And in another, possible. The rest were miles from the mark.

Had the astrologer known my experiences, perhaps he could have matched his interpretation of the planetary activity to the events rather better. Of course, our levels of understanding were probably different – again the problem of interpretation – and that could have partly accounted for the disappointing results.

But it underlined for me that what happens in our lives is not the product of what happens in the sky, but rather of how we use the circumstances at our disposal. In other words, our own power.

Your aspects at a given time may be marvellous, but unless you use them, some fate will not inevitably drop the result you hope for, or some wonderful event, in your lap. Of course, helpful or easy astrological aspects at a given time may make it easier to achieve your aims, or encourage helpful circumstances – but they will not ensure your success. Using your own power and intuition will do that. In the same way astrology will not prevent you from being successful – though at a difficult time it may be a little harder for you to achieve your aims.

Many people find the study of astrology very helpful in understanding the forces of the universe better, and guiding them in using their own power. It's worth remembering, though, that even with a birth chart there is always the issue of interpretation. As one of my favourite professional astrologers said to me, looking at my birth chart, 'I can't make anything out from this, it's completely opaque.'

Some exercises for you think about

1. Read a little of the original *I Ching* (translated by Richard Wilhelm). Have a look in a bookshop at a couple of modern interpretations of the *I Ching*. Can you see how very different they are?

2. Look for a serious book, or books, on the tarot cards. Establish for yourself that there are many different ways of interpreting the cards. Some books will tell you, for example, that it matters whether the cards appear upside down or the right way up. Others will insist this is not important. Most will have a slightly different slant on what the cards 'mean'.

3. Half full or half empty? Think about the way your own mindset influences how you perceive events.

4. Try the ink blot test with a friend. Make a row of ink blots on a piece of paper. With a friend, without conferring, write down what you see in the blots. What shapes or configurations do they suggest to you? Then swop

your perceptions. You are likely to have come up with very different ideas, in other words interpretations, in at least some cases. What does this tell you about the way different people interpret metaphors?

5. If you are interested, try to interpret your own birth chart. It is not difficult to do with the help of astrology textbooks. First, though, you need a chart. It is a great help to have a computer program, or a professional service – draw one up. Then check out what the placements mean. If possible look at more than one book's views on the planets. Try to include the work of Robert Hand, who is particularly insightful (see page 356). Compare your findings with your own experiences. Does your experience match any of what the chart suggests? If or where your own experience is different to the find-ings suggested by the chart, ask a friend if they are aware of the qualities the chart sug-gests in you. If there does not seem to be a match, stick with your own perceptions and intuition. The purpose of the chart is to help you, not to label you.

6. Consider that Indian astrology is very differ-ent from Western astrology. House place-ments, for example, are different – you may be one sign in the Western system and another in the Indian system, and the whole manner of looking at the chart is different,

from its layout to the cycles it deals with. Bearing that in mind, do you think one system or the other is 'wrong'? Can you see that both could be useful metaphors? But at the end of the day, power lies with you.

Chapter Fifteen

When the Fire Goes Out

I t is the moment we all dread. You feel you can't go on. You feel all power has deserted you. You feel you don't know anything. You feel you can't depend on anything. You don't understand. Your meditation doesn't work – or you've never had any luck with a regular practice. The complexities of energy are beyond you, developing your spirituality is beyond you.

This is the dark night of the soul. Scott Fitzgerald said, 'In a real dark night of the soul it is always three o'clock in the morning.' And so it is.

For everyone there comes a moment – it might be a very private moment – when you feel the fire has gone out, and you are facing the dark. You can't go on, or you feel there is no point in going on. When you know and recognise this point in yourself, and you know how to deal with it, this is a most exciting place – you are on the brink of a breakthrough. It is part of a pattern.

The natural world

We belong to nature. Every lesson you need to learn

is contained in the earth or the flora or fauna of the universe. We live to the same patterns as the natural world. One of the most basic is the seasons.

Spring is easy. It is the first stirring of your energy. When you wake to the potential of transformation. Like a plant scattered with buds that hold the promise of a future, you begin to stretch out in the weak, new sun.

Summer is glorious. Provided you receive enough water to feed you, you take your energy from the earth and the heat of the sun, and you grow. There seems almost no limit on your growth. But better not to grow too fast or your growth will be unsupported and spindly. You risk being toppled over by your own weight, or being dragged down by even a light breeze.

In other words, you risk becoming too full of yourself – overconfident. Or of your new development being overturned by some passing influence – a person or an event, which you really should be able to withstand. As the summer proceeds you show your colours, and are likely to experience a wonderful flowering.

All too soon the season begins to move on, though. At first the change brings new gifts – autumn's harvest – which distract you from the coming of the winter. But winter's tread is certain.

Metaphorically, the temperature begins to drop. And continues falling. It is dark outside, perhaps inside too. This is your low point. Where you cannot go on any further. When you suspect it may all have been in vain. All your growth appears to be dying around you. You are unsupported. Nothing makes any sense any more; all you see is the bleak world around you in the growing cold. The dark enfolds, perhaps confronts you. Now is the time to die back.

The plants that survive winter, particularly when they have been pruned appropriately, are the stronger for it. Often no outward signs of life will show on the withered remains of what was a glorious display in summer. It is nature's wisdom. Winter allows the dormant plant to strengthen. To conserve energy for new, strong growth. To consolidate the gains of the summer. To prepare for the next glorious year. Better a cold, true winter than a mild season which encourages straggly, early spring growth, bringing with it the remnants of last year, and an increased chance of disease.

For you, the experience of descending to what might seem like a dark, cold wilderness allows the mystery of life to re-form, deep in your subconscious. As you believe increasingly in the power of spirituality, and begin to know the strength of the union of the spiritual and the material, your spiritual intelligence urges you to welcome the dark days. To allow the feeling of collapse, to allow the 'dark night of the soul'. To welcome it. Because of the rebirth that will inevitably follow.

Repeating winter

In human life, though, winter is not simply an annual event. It happens time and time again. As each cycle is completed, it means leaving a stage behind. Each step forward means the death of the old, and perhaps a significant encounter with the dark to allow new light to be born. The process has been compared to the coils of a spring. As you complete each cycle, which will involve passing through 'winter', you move on to the next. Each time completing the same shape but constantly moving upwards – if that is your choice.

Of course, it means that your ability to grow is directly proportional to your ability to let go of the past, and embrace the future. The down places, the times where it seems there is nothing further you can do, are the points at which you are letting go of the past. Which might often mean accepting the dark and, metaphorically, allowing death while a deeper process – beyond your conscious control – takes over. You have only to hold on to the certainty of spring and the next cycle.

My experience

In my meditation journey I experienced this point over and over again. Each time was like a mini death. At the very start of my encounters with the Light, I discover that travelling into the Light, I meet dark forces. And by not resisting, simply submitting, I am strengthened. The first time the dark comes in the shape of panthers. Partly because I feel I have no other option I stand still, while they savage me, tearing great strips off me. Finally, when I am decimated, my body begins to fill with Light and I am able to pass on.

Later, in the same position, I see myself as a glass or crystal container.

Then I see the dark force close around the glass. It grabs hold of the container. The glass breaks where the force closes around it, but the pieces do not fall away, nor are the contents spilled. The dark recedes, only to come again. Meanwhile, the glass has re-formed. This time it is stronger. It only cracks, it doesn't break. Again and again the same attempt is repeated, but the glass seems to become stronger and stronger, until it is absolutely unbreakable.

Sometimes, on the journey, confronting a situation when I felt I could go on no further, I faced death. Submitting to the circumstances without needing to understand them, I was reborn with a glorious new strength.

For example, I had many encounters with a snake, which represented an aspect of my developing energy. On one occasion I entered my meditation world feeling very low. Despite my extraordinary spiritual experiences I was very aware of problems in my practical life.

Up to that point it had seemed as if the snake, which I was afraid of initially, was a benevolent force. In my journal I record:

Suddenly the snake darts forward and bites my heart,

*she eats and eats, leaving the cavity empty. What is
going on? I collapse on to my back. Another death. I
am not going to resist. What is the snake – good or
evil? Triumphantly she stretches herself out over my
body. I have given up. Gleefully she urinates and
defecates in me. Surely I am not expected to put up
with this? I jump up and rush down to the sea, to
wash. I don't understand, and cry with incompre-
hension.*

*Then the force with me urges, 'Relax, do nothing
except the jobs it is your duty to do. Stop searching so
frantically.' I sit more peacefully. In my peace the
Light comes down to me. I wonder if this is death, of
a kind. Then, the light fades to a single beam and I
hear a voice. It tells me that the beam will always
stay with me.*

Through simply submitting to the incomprehensible, allowing myself not to know, and in a sense to
give up, I attracted a permanent beam of Light – a joy
to me.

In another experience, again I am working with the
snake – my energy. Dramatic changes are taking
place. New growth, in the form of two flower bushes
that have sprouted from the base of my neck, are
threatening to take me over. Instead of panicking, and
trying to resist this change, I simply allow it. My
diary records:

*They rise and rise, they are taking my body over. Is
this death? V [my companion at the time] says it is*

*time to put my body in the earth. There is no emotion.
My head must go in too. The earth opens to accept
me. Now in the place where I was sitting there are
only two beautiful bushes, live, growing, and covered
with buds. I cannot find my consciousness under the
earth. I am no more. There was no struggle. The
plants are beautiful. Soon the buds will open – they
do. Inside each is a tiny image of me as the Golden
One [an identity in meditation]. The whole picture is
extraordinary.*

    *A faint vibration begins to grow in the air. As if
responding to the sound, the tiny figures at the hearts
of the flowers seem to join together into the image of
me and grow. I grow and grow, towering in the air. I
become a huge giant, overshadowing V. He smiles.
'That is your strength, be careful how you use it. Now
come back.' Slowly I reduce to normal size, till I am
sitting beside him again, perhaps just a little smaller
than before. There is radiant white light all around
me.*

That episode shows how when change begins, it
threatens to overtake my entire consciousness, even
my life. But rather than resist or be afraid at the
prospect of being blotted out, or see the change as
damaging, I simply submit. I die. Metaphorically. I
allow my body to be put in the earth – I lose all individual consciousness. Instead, the new growth – the
growth that led to my death – takes on a vigorous life.
From this life – the two flower-covered bushes – I am
reborn in a new, beautiful and hugely powerful state.

A much more powerful state than I was in before. So powerful that it is like being a giant, and I am warned to use this power carefully. In response to the warning I immediately return to my previous size, concealing this new power, even perhaps becoming a little smaller – a little humbler – than before.

Of course, at the time, I did not understand that this was what the metaphors of my journey were teaching me. But I did not need to understand, only to experience. In the same way, when you reach a low point, or when life threatens to overtake you with incomprehensible new circumstances, you must submit. The process is like death. Or winter in the cycle of the seasons. But from that death you will emerge with new strength, able to realise more of your potential. The fact that you can't see how you will emerge, or even if you could emerge, is often part of the fear and misery that makes you feel trapped in a despairing state when there appear to be no positive options in front of you.

Giving up attempts to control or turn around events at this point requires great faith. It may be no more than simply giving up an attempt to control a relationship that seems to have lost all direction. It could be giving up a search that does not seem to be bringing what you are looking for. It could be letting go of an enterprise that seems unable to move forward. Giving up allows you to harmonise with the greater forces of the universe.

It is not the same as discarding your past. It does not say that all that has been will never be again. Or

I have done with that and will only accept something altogether new.

It says, I do not have the power or the intuition to move events forward. Therefore I give up. I wait for the greater forces of the universe to direct the situation. I accept what comes to me. I try to lay my emotions to rest and allow the future to take form, when it is ready.

That may mean that the situation you were desperately fighting to hold on to will come back to you in a new, stronger form. Or a different form. Or you will gain new resources to apply to your life. Or, perhaps, events will develop in a completely different direction.

It is not an 'off with the old and on with the new' response, but a wisdom that urges that the wisest use of your power may be to accept winter, secure in the knowledge that a glorious spring will follow.

Your enemies

In this endeavour you have two enemies, stronger than all others. Doubt. And fear. They will try to undermine your response to events.

Fear

Fear may make you want to run away. To do anything to escape the horrors it produces. Or it could paralyse you, locked in the embrace of terror. If you are attacked by fear, the first step is to name the fear to reduce its power. Accurate naming is the first step to gaining power over a situation, or entity. What is named begins to be known. What can be seen can be dealt with. It is only the unknown that can be all-powerful. Left to its own devices, imagination will run riot and create a vista or scenarios beyond any control. Sadists through the ages have worked on the mind's ability to imagine and build up terrors.

If you are faced with fear when your inner fire seems to go out, name the fear, precisely. That will be the first step in gaining control of your reactions. Naming your fear will always help you in choosing how to respond to it. Which, if it is winter you face, may be by simply allowing it, secure in the knowledge that it will change.

Doubt

Doubt is your other great enemy. Doubt is a particularly insidious form of negativity. It is rather like the serpent in the story of Adam and Eve. It doesn't seem very serious or powerful to begin with. But if you listen to it, it overwhelms your entire reality. Doubt undermines your belief in your own power, and in the possibility of a positive outcome.

You know the outcome will be positive because you have the power to adapt to circumstances in such a way as to take greatest advantage of them. At the same time, circumstances, like seasons, inevitably change. Doubt makes you question this. Doubt whispers that you do not have power, and nothing will ever change. If you listen to it, it is a self-fulfilling prophecy.

Doubt is different from the wisdom and power that inclines you sometimes to suspend disbelief. To neither accept nor reject a situation or proposition until you are more certain. Suspending disbelief has its own certainty – the certainty that, in time, you will know, and at that point be able to take action. Doubt merely paralyses.

Children's perception

Children's perceptions in most situations can be remarkably clear. Those who write for children face this fact. From time to time a writer emerges who captures the hearts and minds of a generation by the accuracy with which they reflect the child's deeper knowledge of the world. Or even some of the deeper principles of the universe. Today, J. K. Rowling, with *Harry Potter*, has written a story that touches a deep chord in a huge audience of children. And their parents. Whether it was intended or not, many (though not all) of the principles illustrated in the stories are absolutely correct. For example, Harry Potter shows you how to deal with fear.

Harry Potter's experience

Harry Potter is a small boy who, unknown to himself (to start with), is a wizard. His parents are killed when he is a baby by a very powerful wizard who has gone over to the dark. The occupants of Harry's magic world are terrified of the dark wizard. They call him, 'You-know-who'.

Harry, innocent of the fear that cannot name the dark one — though he killed Harry's parents — simply calls him by his name, Voldemort. By doing so, he impresses and terrifies those around him. Except the revered headmaster of the school for wizards, which Harry attends. Dumbledore, the headmaster, simply tells Harry he is right to use the wizard's real name. He explains it is important to call things by their proper names. Because fear of using a name increases the fear of the thing itself.

Harry Potter and the Prisoner of Azkaban, which is the magic world's prison, deals with the power of doubt and despair. Prisoners in Azkaban are not held in by walls, but by prison guards of a particular sort. The guards are called dementors. They feed on their victims' positive feelings, leaving them prey to their own doubt, despair and negativity. If the dementors feed on their prey for long enough, they reduce them to something like themselves. Creatures devoid of all positive feelings, memory, hope. According to Harry Potter's informant in the story, non-magic people are very aware of dementors too, only they don't see them.

Dementors sound very much like the forces of doubt. When the flame goes out, recognise the situation for what it is. Don't give way to fear or doubt. Allow winter to be. Let the old forms that need to die pass away. Wait to welcome the new.

Exercises for you to think about

1. Think of the last time you felt your fire go out – did you fight the feeling? Did you put up a battle against what was going on? Write down the history of events so that you have a record – try to be as honest as possible.

2. Next time you are in a similar situation go for a walk, or a swim, play a game, go dancing, anything – but let it be. Don't try to influence what happens. Later, compare it with your record of your past. Remember, a record written a while after an incident will be different to a record written at the time, but you should still be able to see significant differences in the effect of the two strategies on how you felt. You may also be able to see real differences in the outcomes.

3. Think of a character in literature who faced a misfortune and accepted their new circumstances. How did they deal with it? Of course, children's books often offer very clear examples. Take Katy in Susan Coolidge's *What Katy Did*. Katy injures her back in a fall from a swing and, being a very active girl, desperately fights her new condition cooped up in bed all day. Things go from bad to worse. Finally, through the example of a much respected and loved adult, Katy stops fighting her predicament. She does her best to accept her circumstances. Miraculously,

she changes beyond all recognition, her situation is the key to real personal growth, and in the best tradition, she recovers her ability to walk too.

4. Think of someone in your life who suffers from doubt. Can you identify an instance where you saw the negative effects of doubt in inhibiting their actions? What were your conclusions? Can you think of a parallel instance in your own life, and how you could have handled it differently?

5. Think of something that arouses fear in you. Analyse exactly why that fear can grip you. Is it, honestly, realistic? There is a good chance that it is not – it is a 'worst case scenario'. For example, you are afraid of being hit by a car as you cross the road. Statistically, that is an unrealistic fear. By allowing it to hold you, you are deflecting energy away from the all-important task of constructing the best outcome. That you cross the road safely. Letting yourself succumb to fear and anxiety will actually increase the chance that your concentration will waver, and an accident occur. In that way you are letting the fear rob you of power.

If you believe the fear is realistic, name it properly – assess its characteristics. Then turn your power to preventing the fear from becoming a reality. For example, you fear 'illness'. Actually, your mother died of breast cancer, therefore your chances of susceptibility to the disease may be greater than average. Instead of worrying about it, name the problem. Then, take all the positive steps you can to prevent it – for example, take proper medical advice, consider your diet. And emotional factors. Then concentrate on creating joy and satisfaction in your life. Stand in the face of the fear, and allow it to pass over you.

6. Think of the things you like about winter. Think of how to handle bad weather appropriately. First and foremost – be prepared, it comes regularly! Think about the winters of your personal life. How have you coped with them?

7. Think about spring. Remember how difficult it is to predict whether spring will be early, late, wet, dry or something else. Think about the springs you have encountered in your personal life. Resolve to fully enjoy the next spring, recognising that it will pass, but will come again.

8. Consider which season you like the best. Can you see a parallel between your choice and the conditions of your life? For example, if you like autumn best, it could indicate that you like a situation that is relatively temperate and very fruitful. Because autumn is a time when the heat of the sun has receded and the harvest is coming in. On the other

hand, if you preferred spring, it could be because you most enjoy the time at the start of ideas or projects, you like the sense of budding possibility. Try to find aspects in all the seasons that you can enjoy.

Chapter Sixteen

The Phoenix Rises

Inevitably, the blossom that signifies spring will come. You know it is no more than a turn of the wheel that brings spring. You have trust. You trust that the circumstances of the outside world will move on.

Trust

This trust in the cyclical nature of events, and the inevitability of spring, is one form of trust. At the same time you have come to know more of your own power. You are learning to trust in yourself. You can survive without the protection of someone else. You recognise that you have your own power.

In the children's stories of Harry Potter, Harry had to learn a charm to conjure up an image of his own positivity to protect him. The image, which the story calls a Patronus, personifies Harry's hope and happiness, and it protects him from any dementor (the magic world's prison guards). To conjure up his Patronus, Harry has to say 'expecto Patronus'. In other words, if Harry's expectations are positive, he is protected from the powers of doubt and despair.

It is absolutely the correct strategy. But you don't need a charm. In fact it could be counter-productive if it encouraged you to depend on, say, a special chant to make you feel protected, and then why not a special crystal to have the same effect and so on, until your power rested in all those outside objects, and not in your own self! Which is exactly what Harry's Patronus is – his own positive powers. Hope, trust, joy.

Your power

All you need is to remember your own power to act. And to act from the highest place you can. You will always be aiming to act from the perspective of the heart chakra, understanding interconnectedness and knowing that your remit is the world, not your own interest group. Knowing that you are acting from your widest possible perceptions and intentions will greatly strengthen your resolve in your actions. In other words, it will help you to really believe in the goodness and appropriateness of what you are doing, and so add to your power.

The cycle of the seasons

At the same time, understanding the cycle of the seasons in our lives gives an added perspective on events. Spring will always follow winter. The cycle of the seasons is never-ending. Success in each season is different. And attainable. Spring is a time for beginnings. To put plants, ideas or projects into the earth. Only the earliest species flower, some still need protection. Success in spring is very different from success in autumn. Autumn's success will depend on harvesting crops, harvesting the fruit of your ideas or projects. If you tried to do that in spring you would fail – there would be nothing to harvest. In spring success will be in planting, in starting out. Winter's success is in dying back. Not in trying to push ahead when outside or inside conditions are adverse.

Sometimes, because summer is so enjoyable, you may be tempted to hold on to it. The outside world is sunny and pleasing – the responses you receive are positive and warming. Everything is in bloom, or smiling at you. But it is not possible to hold that state if growth is your aim. It leads you into the position of adjusting your behaviour to elicit the smiles or warmth of others.

Whilst the approval of others is important, it is essential to hold on to your own truths, even when others don't smile on them. Or when they change their attitude to you. Like the turning of the seasons, sooner or later, conditions you meet on the outside will change. In every sphere of our lives a cycle is inevitable – personal, professional, financial, psychological, emotional, spiritual. A season can last an hour, a year or more. The change of the seasons, and your ability to make the best of each season, is the pathway to growth. Meanwhile, hold on to your authenticity, to the dictates of your spiritual intelligence.

Avoiding attachment

Knowing the inevitability of change helps to guard against a possible pitfall. Attachment. Attachment urges you to try to hold on to a person, a place, an idea or a situation. A lover, or a home, or a job you have outgrown, or something else that no longer suits. The laws of nature say it is not possible. Those experiences that belong to you – with which you resonate energetically – where you share moral and ethical values, not simply material interests, they will stay with you. Others will leave you, or try to, as part of the inevitable flow of the universe. Let them go.

Your life is a journey towards clarity, integrity and authenticity. All the old words that uphold the values of your heart and your spiritual intelligence, which clearly is not some bauble you magically 'acquire' if you repeat enough affirmations. Have courage, follow your journey.

Finding the courage you need

Becoming the best that you can, following your heart, holding to integrity and authenticity, needs courage. Following your heart, integrity and authenticity means that embracing principles will be an integral part of encompassing spiritual reality. And that needs courage.

In all spheres. You will be tempted to deviate by doubt, peers who follow a different path, supposed material interests and a host of other diversions. It is only by following the best in yourself that you will reach the best in others.

Deep down, there is a voice in each of us that knows. It tells us where to go, it leads us in the next direction. Or tells us to stop, not to go any further. And that is the voice you must listen for and have the courage to follow. Because, at the end of the day, it's the only voice that can really speak to you. My voice, any other voice you will happen to hear – and there are many who would teach you along the way – has nothing special to say to you, except as a route that will help you to learn the voice within yourself. It is when your heart is most open that you will hear your own voice most clearly. Have the courage to follow it. And not just in the future.

The part that time plays

Most of us love speculating about the future – you can plan to be very courageous, in the future. What will happen and what won't? Or sometimes it's the past that draws, just as we go over events again and again, rewriting history, wondering what it meant. How it could have been interpreted, what the implications are? Dreaming of the best outcome.

Actually, all we have is the present. The only opportunity for producing the best that you can is in your hands, this instant. Life is not something you think about doing next week, or regret having done last night. Life is what you do with the extraordinary potential in your hands at this precise instant.

I remember the moment I faced death, as I stood ankle-high in freezing cold water under a fierce sun, on a beach, in my birthplace, South Africa. I had just been told that without the appropriate operation, which would leave me partly deaf, probably disfigured too, I would die, at any moment. Certainly soon – maybe within weeks. I had come down to the beach, to think, to be. The sun was blazing hot. Behind me was an ancient mountain, great rocks tumbling into the water. The cold, strong moving Atlantic ocean stretched out in front of me, a lazy tanker chugging across the horizon. It was beautiful.

My dilemma fell into perspective. The moment was all. The future was unknown, it would be like nothing I had ever known before. I could not plan for it. I felt a deep calmness. The gifts of the present came rushing over me. The wonder of the icy water, the wide sky. I loved life. It was glorious. The very moment, which was all I could count on.

In all our lives there is sometimes real anxiety about the future, regret or nostalgia for the past – especially where relationships are concerned. Holding spiritual reality offers the opportunity to extend your awareness in the present, rather than dwell on the past or the future. The message is: understand and use to full advantage the opportunities offered by the present. Which is surprisingly difficult sometimes, as you wait, hope and pray for a future that will solve your problems. Or ruminate over a past that could or might have been otherwise. Savour, taste, swallow it, let life feed you. Use the full power of each moment. Now is all you have.

But there is no purpose to now, there is no purpose to your journey, your spiritual intelligence will never show its promise, without joy.

The problems of our lives can be so overwhelming, pushing us insistently one way, holding us frozen in another, that joy can seem almost irrelevant. A mere frivolity to be attended to when other, more important matters are in place. But it's not.

Joy

Joy is at the core of life. That is, physical life and spiritual life. It is an integral part of all reality. If the force of the creative is a great band running through and around us all, then joy is a glimmer found at every level, from the densest physical reality to the finest billowing spiritual clouds.

Often, though, there is even a question about what joy is. We live in a world of superlatives. Is joy having more and more? Power? Love? Possessions? Or is joy not needing anything? Does five seconds of happiness count as joy, or does it need to go on for a day, or a year? Does it matter what comes afterwards?

My own journey has known what could be described as great pain. One client read the story of my unfolding in *The Pool of Memory* and came to me, angrily, accusingly, asking, 'How could this happen, why did you have to suffer so much pain – how can it be right?' He shook his head. He was terrified by the potential harshness of physical reality, and very attached to his material comforts; especially having grown up in a wealthy family. He suffered from a particular sense of powerlessness. His money, his possessions and almost superstitious beliefs were his protection. He had not grasped the joy that all aspects of the life spectrum had offered me. And has to offer to us all.

My client understood the joy of a new car, a great professional success (that brought lots of money, of course), a new love affair. He needed pleasure – big time, and continuous – to make him feel good! Not the everyday. He did not see others – apart from as potential sexual partners, business partners, threats, aides, employees or authority figures. Not surprisingly, he suffered mood swings and depression.

He did not recognise the need to notice and savour the steady stream of lesser but – in a way that is not purchased by money or fame – far more powerful joys that fill our lives and emphasise their meaning. His senses had been blunted by our material world, and the fear that so often drives it.

The joys of the heart chakra are very different. There is great joy in knowing your link to all others and honouring it. Helping others. Sharing. Joining together with them to create the well-being of all. Communicating. Experiencing the extraordinary joys of life on earth. From the sublime, which must include expressing love to another and receiving the same, to the everyday and the pleasure of a clean floor, a meal well cooked, a shelf hung, a bicycle ride. In feeling part of the universe and enjoying it.

At the same time there are the deep joys of seeing each aspect of our physical world for what it is – a gift. The wondrous reality of the physical , with a new delight at almost every turn – if you look. From the tiny plant that has fought for the gift of life in a crack that seemed to hold no opportunity at all for growth, to the Grand Canyon. Out of your back window. On the way to work. The joy of appreciating, protecting and contributing to our environment. In short, the joys of people, place and the human condition that fill all our lives.

What he also did not know, and should be forgiven for not understanding, is that at the far reaches of reality, where the extremes of joy lie side by side with all the other extremes, one quality blends into another as each loses its specialness and joins a place simply of heightened awareness. Resting in the arms of creation. Which brings bliss of its own.

For all of us, though, in the everyday, we overlook joy at our peril. I sympathise with the social worker burnt out by his job. But only up to a point. I take a very firm view that he must look after his own welfare – his spiritual and material well-being – to enable him to do the work. Much as I appreciate his excellent intentions and self-sacrifice. Or the school teacher bent double by the problems of her work. Ideals cannot be achieved by becoming a victim of your own circumstances. Exactly the same applies to the lawyer working a hundred hours a week to make headway in a cut-throat position. Material success is not enough, or all-important.

We are all responsible for looking after our well-being. That means allowing joy in our lives. We all need pleasure. Which doesn't mean pain is to be avoided. On the contrary. Life is pain and pleasure, both of which are essential to growth. William Blake put it prosaically, and exactly:

> *Man was made for joy and woe*
> *And when this we rightly know*
> *Thro' the world we safely go*
> *Joy and woe are woven fine*
> *A clothing for the soul divine.*
> *'Auguries of Innocence'*

The phoenix

And so the cycle repeats itself. From joy to pain, and back again. From winter to spring. The clearer your energy, the easier the transitions. The more developed your understanding, the richer your path. The wider your perception, the deeper the development of your spiritual intelligence and intuition. Then you will be like the phoenix, the mythical creature worshipped in ancient Egypt. The only individual of its kind, it burnt itself at the end of each cycle, to rise rejuvenated, reborn from its own ashes. You are facing the opportunity to be reborn, rejuvenated on a new plane in your life. A plane that far exceeds your previous understanding and brings you all the benefits and responsibilities of the spiritual and the material. The whole world is in your hands. Now. With joy.

Where Do I Go from Here?

Michal Levin holds regular series of seminars and talks based on *Spiritual Intelligence* and other aspects of her work. Courses are also held by leaders she has worked with and trained over time. Cassette tapes of Michal's talks are also available. Full details are available on request from the address below. Please contact:

'HOME'
PO Box 20120
London W10 4WR
UK

Telephone: (44) 01654 761 262

E-mail: info@michallevin.com

Or see Michal's website at:
http://www.michallevin.com

Further Reading

General

Advances: The Journal of Mind–Body Health, Linda G. Russell and Gary E. Schwartz, Fall, 1996.

Anatomy of the Spirit, Caroline Myss, Harmony Books, 1996.

The Dancing Wu Li Masters, Gary Zukav, Rider, 1991.

Dogs That Know When Their Owners Are Coming Home, Rupert Sheldrake, Arrow Books, Random House, 1999.

Heading Towards Omega, Professor Kenneth Ring, William Morrow, 1985.

The Heart's Code, Dr Paul Pearsall, Thorsons/ Broadway Books, 1998.

I Ching, Richard Wilhelm (Editor) et al, Arkana, 1997.

Lessons from the Light, Professor Kenneth Ring, Moment Point Press, 1999.

Mad Travellers, Ian Hacking, Free Association Books, 1999.

Many Lives Many Masters, Brian Weiss MD, Piatkus Books, 1994.

The Meaning of It All, Richard Feynman, Penguin, 1999.

Mind–Body Medicine, Dr Alan Watkins (ed.), Churchill Livingstone, 1997.

On the Trail of Merlin, Deike Rich and Ean Begg, Aquarius, 1991.

The Pool of Memory: the autobiography of an unwilling intuitive, Michal Levin, Gill & Macmillan, 1998.

The Principles of Shamanism, Leo Rutherford, Thorsons, 1996.

'Recovery from Early Blindness: a case study', Richard Layton Gregory and Jean G. Wallace, *Psychology Society Monograph*, 2, 1963.

Reviving Ophelia, Mary Piper PhD, Ballantine Books, 1994.

The Second Brain, Michael D. Gershon, Harperperennial Library, 1999.

You Can Heal Your Life, Louise Hay, Eden Grove Editions, 1988.

Astrology

Planets in Transit, Robert Hand, Whitford Press, 1976.

Star Signs, Linda Goodman, Macmillan, 1987.

True as the Stars Above: adventures in modern astrology, Neil Spencer, Gollancz, 2000.

Psychology

Aspects of the Feminine, C. G. Jung, Routledge & Kegan Paul, 1982.

The Secret of the Golden Flower, Richard Wilhelm and C. G. Jung, Arkana, 1992.

Biography
Sky Dancer, Keith Dowman, Arkana, 1989.
There is a River: the story of Edgar Cayce, Thomas Sugrue, A.R.E. Press, 1989.

Novels
All The Pretty Horses, Cormac McCarthy, Picador, 1993.
A Far Off Place, Laurens van der Post, Harcourt Brace, 1978.
River Sutra, Gita Mehta, Minerva, 1994.
The Road from Coorain, Jill Ker Conway, Vintage, 1992.
A Story like the Wind, Laurens van der Post, Harcourt Brace, 1988.

Poetry
Complete Works, William Blake, Penguin, 1978.

Children's books
Harry Potter and the Philosopher's Stone, J. K. Rowling, Bloomsbury, 1997.
Harry Potter and the Prisoner of Azkaban, J. K. Rowling, Bloomsbury, 1998.
Huckleberry Finn, Mark Twain, Penguin, 1970.
Narnia Stories, C. S. Lewis, HarperCollins.
The Secret Garden, Frances Hodgson Burnett, Penguin, 1995.
What Katy Did, Susan Coolidge, Penguin, 1997.

P 250

58
55
40
68
71
74-5
80 PRACTICE
116 BASE CHAKRA
164 contomplation
204 what I lizabeth thinks
211